The Flight from Authority

REVISIONS

A Series of Books on Ethics

General Editors:
Stanley Hauerwas and Alasdair MacIntyre

We are too often in our contemporary ethical debates and disagreements the prisoners of an unrecognized moral history. The fragmentation of a complex past —Jewish, Catholic, Aristotelian, Puritan, Humanist and more—has left us as the warring heirs of an inadequate inheritance. So our disagreements are all too easily framed as a series of encounters between abstract and unreal stereotypes in which a rootless liberalism is counterposed to a reactionary conservatism. In this situation the dominant modes of recent ethical writing, whether philosophical or theological, are often unhelpful. They encourage us to lapse once more either into unhistorical abstractions or the unargued dogmatism surrounding discussion of concrete moral issues. This series marks an attempt to recover what is viable in the traditions of which we ought to be the heirs without ignoring what it was that made those traditions vulnerable to modernity.

The Flight from Authority

Religion, Morality, and the Quest for Autonomy

JEFFREY STOUT

UNIVERSITY OF NOTRE DAME PRESS
NOTRE DAME   LONDON

Library of Congress Cataloging in Publication Data

Stout, Jeffrey.
  The flight from authority.

  (Revisions ; v. 1)
  Includes bibliographical references and index.
  1. Ethics. 2. Knowledge, Theory of. 3. Religion
—Philosophy. 4. Authority. I. Title. II. Title:
Religion, morality, and the quest for autonomy.
III. Series: Revisions (University of Notre Dame
Press) ; v. 1.
BJ1012.S85   170'.42   81-2340
ISBN 0-268-00954-6   AACR2

Manufactured in the United States of America

TO SALLY, SUZANNAH, AND NOAH

Contents

. . .[T]ruly to escape Hegel involves an exact appreciation of the price we have to pay to detach ourselves from him. It assumes that we are aware of the extent to which Hegel, insidiously perhaps, is close to us; it implies a knowledge, in that which permits us to think against Hegel, of that which remains Hegelian. We have to determine the extent to which our anti-Hegelianism is possibly one of his tricks directed against us, at the end of which he stands, motionless, waiting for us.

Michel Foucault

Preface

This book emerges out of the frustrations I encountered, first as an undergraduate at Brown University and later as a graduate student and teacher at Princeton, in trying to understand the status of morality in modern life and thought. My reading in philosophy and theology brought me back, again and again, to something called the "autonomy of morals." Not only did most modern writers — theologians included — seem to agree that morality is logically independent from both theoretical reason and theology, but even those who expressed dissent seemed content to treat the issue as a matter to be resolved by the relatively straightforward techniques of conceptual analysis. Hegel's critique of Kant made me doubtful on both counts. But I left Brown unable to put my Hegelian suspicions and my modest analytic training together.

I spent much of my time as a graduate student scrutinizing assumptions built into the vocabulary analytic philosophers used when they framed their theses about the autonomy of morals, though I did spend enough of it making sweepingly Hegelian comments about the importance of historical perspective to keep my instructors alternating between bemusement and dismay. It pleased me to discover that much had already been done, by those working (however uneasily) within the analytic tradition itself, to make these assumptions visible and place them in question. My dissertation used the work of W. V. Quine, Wilfrid Sellars, and their followers as a means toward the end of dissolving the problem of morality's relation to religion as it had been posed in analytic philosophy. I suggested in closing that moral philosophers and philosophers of religion would do well to follow the lead of colleagues in the philosophy of science by recasting their problems in historical terms.

It soon became clear to me that this "dissolution," whatever it merits, had failed to take its own advice, that despite the neo-Hegelian moral proposed in my conclusion I had treated the analytic debate over autonomy as resulting from nothing more than a philosopher's mistake. This realization led to a new question. Against what background would modern preoccupation with the autonomy of morals have to be placed to be rendered intelligible as a historical phenomenon? The present book is the fruit of my attempts to answer this question. It is of necessity a book in which more topics are introduced than could possibly receive complete attention. No one could hope to tell the stories of foundationalist philosophy, secularization, and analytic ethics between the covers of a single volume without leaving much of importance unsaid. Many readers may find my speculations on these topics premature or wrongheaded. But I do hope to show that the "autonomy of morals" will remain at best only superficially understood so long as these stories are not woven together as strands in a single historical narrative.

So while I set out to write about morality and its putative independence from religion — a fact which explains the appearance of the book in this series — I found that much would have to be said about matters bearing little obvious relevance to ethics. Indeed, readers will find little mention of ethics until Part III. My own reasons for being interested aside, this is manifestly a book in which epistemology, religious thought, and moral philosophy are given equal billing. If the three sections at first appear as independent essays on their respective topics, it should eventually become clear that I have actually told the same story from various points of view — each time adding new complexities, at every stage presupposing what has gone before.

The result, taken as a whole, is a schematic history of modern thought. I have portrayed this history as taking its point of departure in the early seventeenth century's crisis of authority, which I view in turn against the background of Reformation polemics and the religious wars. The word "crisis," as I use it here, is a term of historiographical art, to be understood in the sense explicated artfully by Theodore K. Rabb (*The Struggle for Stability in Early Modern Europe*, New York Oxford University Press, 1975). By "crisis" I mean a relatively brief period preceded by malaise and followed by dramatic resolution of some sort. In contrast, I do not use the word "authority" as a term of art. This book contains no positive theory of what authority is or once was. In using the term, I mean simply to repeat (or to translate) the language of early modern Europe, treating the term, in effect, as an artifact to be studied with the tools of the historian. If I have a theory to offer, it is not a theory of authority *per se* but rather a theory about the cultural and linguistic status of this artifact at various points in modern history. Needless to say, I have not tried to write a complete history of "authority," let alone of modern philosophy, theism, and morality. My interest in old concepts and controversies dwells in implications for contemporary thought and practice.

If this book is a philosophical meditation on themes in modern history, it is also, in no small measure, a meditation on the motivations behind, and the merits of, historicist orientation in philosophy. As such, it often takes the form of a running dialogue with the philosophers who have in recent years influenced me most: Ian Hacking, Thomas Kuhn, Alasdair MacIntyre, Richard Rorty, and, though perhaps less noticeably, Michel Foucault and Hans-Georg Gadamer. Students of religion will recognize my debts to Hans Frei and Stanley Hauerwas. The extent of these influences far exceeds my ability to offer specific acknowledgments in the text or the notes, but I trust that those with the eyes to see will have little trouble finding the more important dependencies and differences.

I have been extraordinarily fortunate to have Stanley Hauerwas, James Langford, and Alasdair MacIntyre as editors. Their encouragement and criticism were invaluable to me as I wrote and rewrote the various chapters. Malcolm Diamond, Ian Hacking, Van Harvey, Mike Michalson, Victor Preller, Paul Ramsey, and Richard Rorty were all kind enough to comment expertly on drafts of one or more chapters. My teachers, students, and colleagues have contributed far more than I could ever specify. Lorraine Fuhrmann, Pat Halliday, and Jonathan Piper helped me greatly with the mechanics of preparing the manuscript for submission. To all of these people I am deeply grateful. This book is, in many respects, a community effort.

I also wish to thank Princeton University and the American Council of Learned Societies for funding the year's leave of absence that made the timely completion of the book possible, as well as Christ's College for gracious hospitality during the part of that leave my family and I spent in Cambridge.

Of the material published here, only portions of chapter 10 have appeared before. One section was first published in *Religious Studies* 16/2 (1980) by Cambridge University Press; the other in *Religious Studies Review* 6/4 (1980) by the Council on the Study of Religion, Wilfrid Laurier University, Waterloo, Ontario. I give thanks to H. D. Lewis and Harold Remus as editors of these journals and to the respective publishers for permission to use the material in somewhat different form here.

Introduction

Here is Wittgenstein, discussing discourse:

> Our language can be seen as an ancient city: a maze of little
> streets and squares, of old and new houses with additions from
> various periods; and this surrounded by a multitude of new
> boroughs with straight regular streets and uniform houses.

This passage comes from section 18 of the *Philosophical Investigations*, [1] just after an intriguing reference to "the symbol-
ism of chemistry and the notation of the infinitesimal calculus"
as "the suburbs of our language." We might also include among
the suburbs of our language the austere architecture of modern
thought: the straight regular streets of utilitarian and Kantian
ethics; the uniform houses of foundationalist philosophy; the
new boroughs in which sanctuaries of worship, if they appear at
all, are indistinguishable from the buildings around them.
From these suburbs, the old part of the ancient city — which
used to be at the center of things, marked off by monuments
of authority and replete with sacred spaces — is barely visible.
It seems an isolated district, one from which relatively few of
us can take our bearings and in which relatively few of our decisions on matters of public importance are taken.

We can appreciate the motives of those who built what we
now have, of those who sought a new life beyond the shadow of
authority. The ancient monuments had begun to crumble.
Sacred spaces had become scenes of fragmentation and occa-
sions for conflict. Better to begin again from scratch in circumstances of one's own choosing. And yet we are not very happy
where we are. We have lost our center. That was the price of
our autonomy. Our attitude toward ancient monuments and
sacred spaces wavers between an iconoclasm that long ago lost
its point and a romanticism that could never be more than

1

nostalgia. We even sense that our ancestors' attempt to rebuild everything anew was determined not only by the negativity of conscious rebellion but also by the unconscious use of traditional materials. They did not so much begin again from scratch as plunder the ruins for stone and lumber. Our autonomy is itself more dependent, and therefore less thorough, than we had thought.

The present book might well be termed an exercise in conceptual archaeology.[2] I propose to undertake an archaeological dig in the part of town that, thanks to erosion and reconstruction, opened the way to all those straight regular streets and uniform houses. I shall open a site in the vicinity of terms like *knowledge* and *authority, certainty* and *probability, mystery* and *paradox, God* and *good.* These terms are like old houses with additions from various periods. The paths that now connect them differ from the paths that once did. The story in which this difference comes to light sheds light also on the genesis of modern thought and on the intellectual predicament in which we find ourselves. That, at any rate, is the hope to which this book owes its existence and on which its successful completion depends.

The book falls into three parts. Each part considers a debate in contemporary philosophy — the theory of knowledge, philosophy of religion, and moral philosophy, respectively — and aims to disclose, by means of historical excavation, the conceptual formations in which the debate took on its familiar contours and texture. The point is to expose a substructure of dialectical pitfalls and blind alleys, and thus to promote the freedom that comes from knowing the necessities of our situation. Whatever freedom we have, in thought as in action, is limited by the historical conditions in which we exercise it. We can, however, free ourselves from delusions of one important kind by subjecting the conditions of thought to historical scrutiny, by discovering how our thought is situated. The conceptual dimension of circumstance is neither as timeless as most philosophers assume nor as innocent of social reality as historians of ideas sometimes imply. Nowhere do these truths come more clearly into view than in the history of "authority," a history we shall be returning to again and again, if often by indirect routes.

The unifying historical theme is this: that modern thought was born in a crisis of authority, took shape in flight from authority, and aspired from the start to autonomy from all traditional influence whatsoever; that the quest for autonomy was also an attempt to deny the historical reality of having been influenced by tradition; and that this quest therefore could not but fail. But there is more to the story than this.

In the first place, it can hardly be denied that modern thought did succeed in demoting authority, even if it failed to transcend history. I shall try to disentangle the success from the failure, the better to understand each. The failure is the story of those, like Descartes and Kant, who sought to philosophize from the "perspective of eternity" of foundationalist epistemology or transcendental method. The success is the story of those, like the Huguenots of the sixteenth century and the Jansenists of the seventeenth, who contributed to the creation of discursive practices in which appeals to authority played no essential role. The unintended consequence of this success, which was rooted in the simultaneously social and intellectual strife of Worms, Trent, and the religious wars, was the secularization of public discourse — the language of lawyers, scientists, politicians, and historians. How this process of secularization altered the relationship between theism and culture, and gave rise to the differentiation of morality as a relatively autonomous cultural domain, will be a central concern in these chapters.

In the second place, any book that, by virtue of its historical orientation, opposes the tradition of Descartes and Kant owes its audience some account of how it intends to avoid the perils of historicism. This too I shall try to provide. The problem of historicism is how to overcome the Enlightenment's antihistorical overcoming of traditional authority without falling into either the bad faith of Hegelian metaphysics or the inconsistencies and possibly pernicious implications of conceptual relativism (the claim that all rational appraisal is relative to independent conceptual schemes). Unpleasant alternatives have made allegiance to the tradition of Descartes and Kant seem mandatory. So I intend not only to exemplify a kind of historicism but also to strive for a formulation that sidesteps standard objections. I use the term "historicism" advisedly, fully aware of assorted unwanted associations. The most significant of these I will try to disown as the argument proceeds. A more satisfying statement of my relation to the tradition descending from Hegel will have to await the final chapter. For now we may rest content with the vague notion that historicism consists in a predilection, an affirmation, and a denial. Its predilection is to view all thought as historically conditioned. The affirmation follows: if all thought is historically conditioned, historical insight must be essential to self-understanding. The denial pertains to orthodox philosophy: if the tradition of Descartes and Kant is largely an attempt to transcend history by purifying thought of historical contingency, this traditional quest must surely fail to account for its own history. To view modern thought historically is to oppose an antihistorical urge.

Contemporary historicism must be distinguished from its nineteenth-century ancestors. In its most defensible form, it does not imply or presuppose conceptual relativism. Nor does it require anything like Hegelian metaphysics to hold the relativists at bay. Nor, for that matter, does the position I take bear any significant resemblance to the one Karl Popper attacked with such zeal in *The Poverty of Historicism*.[3] My historicism does not pretend to explain the past and predict the future in a single stroke. What it shares with its ancestors is primarily a criticism of the philosophical tradition's quest for a perspective outside of or more fundamental than historically conditioned thought. Earlier versions of historicism failed not because this criticism missed the mark but rather because they drew too heavily upon the vocabulary invented by, and tailored to the purposes of, their opponents.

Historicism says to traditional philosophy what we are all inclined to say to adolescents from time to time: you are going through a phase. The analogy accounts both for the style of explanation historicists give and the kind of reaction they typically call forth. Orthodox philosophers sense condescension in historicist criticism — an air of superiority, a reductive intent, a failure of seriousness. But historicists are largely talking to themselves, disarming the voice of temptation by giving it a context and thereby coming to grips with their own past. Historicism needs to find the right tone of voice. We need not imply any disrespect when we assign the great their moments in the dialectic. Such is the plot of any family romance. To be assigned a moment in the dialectic is a fate any good historicist both expects and welcomes in humble spirit. Viewed from up close, the spectacle of philosophers trying to *aufheben* each other's distinctions can look like the scene of some primal crime. Still, provided we pay ample attention to preserving each other's nobler parts, it is the closest thing we have to progress in philosophy. By historicist lights, the claim to have achieved "the perspective of eternity" is itself the height of condescension. If so, then historicism is rightly understood as a flight from condescension in favor of modest claims and unrarefied air.

Can historicism account for itself? Might not historicism itself be but a passing phase? I see no harm in answering "yes" to both questions. Someday there will probably be little point in calling oneself a historicist. That will be when transcendental and foundationalist philosophies no longer seem worth opposing, when the chorus of that particular congregation of temptations has been stilled. By then we shall have new problems to worry about and new names to call ourselves and each other.

We are indeed unlikely to outgrow the need for historical understanding, for the stories that help us locate ourselves meaningfully and realistically as human agents in space and time. But that is not because, as some historicists have been tempted to say, historical understanding is foundational to understanding as such. Understanding neither has nor requires foundations. We need historical understanding because we are finite beings, shaped by history and capable of shaping it. An unhistorical understanding of ourselves would simply leave too much out of account. Historicism does not propose a new foundation. It resists a reduction. It is hard to imagine *dispensing* with historical understanding without dispensing with understanding altogether. Why? Because it is hard to imagine assessing a theory of *anything* without giving the theory itself a context of problems and choices and predecessors and competitors — without, in other words, situating the theory historically.[4]

Part I attempts to situate contemporary epistemology historically. Its point of departure is the debate over foundationalism as a theory of knowledge. How can knowledge be justified? Foundationalism answers that the chain of reasons which would constitute a justification cannot be circular without begging the question of justification itself. Justification must therefore consist in a linear regress of reasons. What stops the regress short of infinity? If nothing does, then no justification could ever be complete. If there are justified beliefs, the regress must end in a foundation of beliefs that require no additional reasons for their justification. Such foundational beliefs would be, as it were, immediately justified. A foundationalist holds at least this.

Whether a foundationalist must hold more than this to get any hold on our attention is a good question. It is now widely agreed that most characterizations of immediately justified beliefs — for example, that they are immediately given, or self-justifying, or incorrigible, or indubitable — are open to devastating objections. But do these objections, taken jointly, dispose of foundationalism itself? William Alston, for one, thinks not. I hope to show that the question of what foundationalism is (or was) generates merely verbal disagreement unless interpreted as a historical question about an actual tradition of thought: the circumstances of its birth, the dialectical aims of its founding fathers, and its subsequent fate in debate. My conclusion will be that the era of foundationalist epistemology, the era in which epistemology was the basic concern of philosophy, is now as a matter of historical fact over. The position called minimal foundationalism has lost its connection with the purposes that gave Cartesian philosophy, as a human project, its point.

In the course of defending this conclusion, I shall place the father of modern philosophy, Descartes, at a particular point in the history of the vocabulary of cognitive appraisal. His foundationalism was, in the first instance, a response to the disintegration of the epistemic vocabulary at his disposal. Terms closely connected with "knowledge" (*scientia*), such as "certainty" and "demonstration," had come under increasing suspicion during the period from Ockham to the revival of ancient skeptical writings in the sixteenth century. Another cluster of terms, including "opinion," "probability," and "authority," had been severely eroded by the forces of Reformation and Counter-Reformation throughout the sixteenth century. Together these two clusters of terms exhausted Descartes's vocabulary of cognitive appraisal. Their disintegration entailed an epistemological crisis of the first order. His response was to eschew any term essentially connected with "authority" as hopelessly beyond repair. He pinned his hopes instead on a reconstruction of "knowledge" in which everything we know would be demonstrated with absolute certainty and thereby fortified against skeptical objections. In rejecting authority Descartes tried to make received opinion and conceptual inheritance inessential to thought. He sought, as Michael Oakeshott put it so memorably, "to live each day as if it were his first." He also unconsciously carried on the tradition of Plato and Augustine, from which he drew the crucial metaphors he never subjected to methodical doubt. This tradition became, in Descartes's hands, the tradition that would rather not be a *tradition* at all.

We must also place Descartes's project *before* the emergence of what Ian Hacking has called the new probability. 'Probable' opinions were, for Descartes as for Aquinas, opinions approved by authority. They did not possess authority by virtue of statistical frequencies or what we would deem strictly evidential relations. The only evidential relations available were demonstrative and conferred, not probability, but certainty of truth. Our notion of probability, as distinguished from certainty only by degrees of credibility, was lacking. I shall argue that the emergence of the new probability, a decade or so after Descartes's death, had extraordinarily important consequences for modern thought. One of these, to which I shall return in a moment, was the secularization of a significant domain of discourse. Another, more germane to the fate of foundationalism than to the fate of theism, was the resolution of the epistemological crisis to which Descartes's foundationalism responded. By severing the ancient connection between probability and authority, the inventors of the new probability cast doubt on Descartes's willingness (in Gilson's phrase) to eliminate the probable. It then became more plausible to argue, as antifoundationalists from Blaise Pascal to Frederick Will have, that Descartes merely repeated the skeptic's mistake and aided the skeptic's cause when he insisted on the absolute certainty of *scientia*. For now there were evidential relations less stringent than perfect demonstration to fall back on in the battle with skepticism. The skeptic's doubts seem as unjustified as Descartes's response.

Unfortunately, just as skepticism receded as a major cultural concern, Descartes's technical understanding of *ideas* as objects of mental vision became the common coin of late seventeenth- and early eighteenth-century philosophy. That is, as the prephilosophical problem to which Descartes responded dissolved and the crisis of traditional authority was resolved by the forces of secularization, the subjectivity of Cartesian ideas gave rise to new forms of skepticism with which philosophers have been preoccupied almost to the present day. The battle against these forms of skepticism has largely been a kind of poetic struggle with the metaphors Descartes inherited from the Platonic-Augustinian tradition he unwittingly sustained and transformed — especially, the image of knowledge as vision. So in attempting to explain the demise of foundationalism, I shall not only have to place Descartes before the emergence of the new probability but also must at least describe the poetic devices philosophers have used in recent years to undo the power of his imagery. This I will do with the help of Harold Bloom's theory of poetic influence. Historicism will itself appear here as a poetic struggle with the influence of a tradition, in particular the influence of the Cartesian quest for autonomy from history.

Do we, then, have any knowledge? The answer depends, of course, on what we take knowledge to be and, most interestingly, on what standards of justification we mean to apply in posing the question. Our temptation is to search out an essence by analyzing the term. But the rival analyses seem only to beg the question. Conceptual archaeology shows that our term "knowledge" is indeed like an old house with additions from various periods. Our use of the term has more than enough complexity to encourage conflicting intuitions and rival analyses. It owes something to Cartesian *scientia* and something to the new probability. It is too eclectic to *have* an essence. Even if it did have an essence, this would not tell us which standards to apply in appraising beliefs. If we identify knowledge with *scientia*, it may well turn out that knowledge is in rather short supply. But this would show only that knowledge, thus identified, presupposes standards of judgment too stringent to matter. What matters is that we *can* apply the standards implicit in the new probability and that these standards, correctly applied, give no reason for despair. It seems silly to call ourselves skeptics if all we mean is that *scientia* is empty or nearly so. What it means to call oneself a skeptic has changed drastically since Descartes first put pen to paper. In the absence of both Cartesian metaphors and a nostalgia for *scientia*, epistemology lacks a skeptical dragon to slay. Foundationalism loses its *raison d'être*. Minimal foundationalism diminishes in interest.

Parts II and III will take this conclusion for granted, and aim to show what cultural criticism might look like in the wake of the concerns that defined the era of epistemology. If foundational or transcendental standing is finally judged impossible, what should be said about such cultural domains as religion and morality becomes once again an open question. Must we, for example, abandon empiricism's traditionally negative conclusions on theism as we enter the age of Wittgenstein, Quine, and Kuhn? How can we approach morality and its putative independence from both theoretical reason and theology if Kantian assumptions can no longer be taken as given? Can we avoid the unpalatable extremes of Hegelian metaphysics and conceptual relativism without falling back on the distinctions of unhistorical philosophy after all? Is responsible criticism of culture even possible once those distinctions have been left behind?

These will be the central questions of the second two-thirds of this book. Part II will begin by raising the general question about the possibility of responsible criticism, moving immediately to the criticism of theism as a specific case. Here I shall try to show that the Enlightenment's criticisms of theism are strengthened rather than weakened when reformulated in a nonfoundationalist idiom. I will argue that it was the secularized discourse of the new probability more than the empiricist version of foundationalism that caused trouble for theism. When probability consisted in approval by authority, even the most paradoxical belief would count as highly probable, provided only that it found support in the testimony of the right persons and books. It could then be viewed, not as a potential obstacle to assent, but as a mystery whose incomprehensibility might even enhance the power of religious experience. Sheer paradox invites the intellect to rise up and demand an explanation. Mystery compels the intellect to bow down in humility.

But when the connection between probability and authority was broken in the mid-seventeenth century the pronouncements of authority no longer seemed inherently probable. A large collection of dogmas, some utterly mysterious and some relatively straightforward, came to seem improbable. Mysteries became mere paradoxes. Many historical claims simply became questionable — hypotheses to be tested in light of all available evidence. The doubts thus engendered were not the doubts of the radical skeptic, for whom all (or almost all) beliefs fare poorly when subjected to the excessive demands of ultimate justification. These were doubts of a limited and nuanced sort. The problem for theism was not failure to achieve absolute certainty, like Hume's problems with knowledge of other minds or inductive scientific theory, but rather that theism could not supply what the nascent natural sciences plainly could: namely, good reason for believing its central claims to be more *probable* than competing alternatives.

The attempt to reformulate theism by reducing its paradoxical content and establishing its remaining claims as probable hypotheses is known as Deism. But Deism had trouble distinguishing itself from orthodoxy on the one side and atheism on the other. To remain religiously interesting, it would have to retain at least some of the content of traditional theism. Yet this constraint clearly conflicted with the aim of high probability. To heighten probability was to lower religious satisfaction. Deism, it seemed to many readers of Hume's *Dialogues,* was destined to become a terminological variant of atheism.

How then to reformulate theism? If theism was not to become Deism, it would have to distinguish itself from the systems of more or less probable hypotheses brought before the court of theoretical reason. Hence Kant's consignment of religion to the realm of pure *practical* reason and Schleiermacher's stress on the *feeling* of piety. These alternatives to Deism, however, threatened to reduce the content, and therefore the interest, of theism as much as Deism had. They did, nevertheless, win wide acceptance as theoretical expressions of and justifications for a post-traditional, differentiated culture. The price of saving theism was to isolate it from the theoretical life of the culture and to confine its impact for the most part to private, as opposed to public, existence.

Hegel sought to avoid this outcome, first by toying with the idea of Christianity as a folk religion and later by embracing the hard paradoxes of Christian faith as the prephilosophical formulations of the highest truths given proper form only in his own philosophy of spirit. But several things undermined this attempt. One was the difficulty Hegel's followers had understanding his reformulations of the paradoxes. Another was the fragmentation, in the 1830s and '40s, of the social reality presupposed by Hegel's system. Still another was the recurring problem of modern theism: the project of recasting the "essence" of theism in a modern philosophical idiom once again seemed indistinguishable from transcending theism altogether. Hegel's most insightful followers illustrate the dilemma well. They either turned the remnants of Hegelian philosophy against theism or, like Kierkegaard, accepted Christian religion while proclaiming it irreducibly paradoxical. The upshot of this development was Barth's insistence that theology could not be apologetics. The greatest theologian of the twentieth century argued forcefully that the dialogue between theism and secular culture could not continue as a *debate*. On what terms it can continue, if it continues in a culturally significant way at all, remains unclear.

It is hard to resist the conclusion, after recounting the details of this story (as I shall in Part II), that theism is not entirely healthy as an intellectual stance in our cultural setting. That is to say, theism seems to have fared rather poorly in its attempts to justify itself in terms of post-seventeenth-century standards of judgment. There are, of course, various ways to respond to this conclusion, even if it is correct. One can, first of all and most obviously, simply reject theism as unjustified. Or one can, alternatively, become Kierkegaardian, maintaining one's theism in spite (or because) of its improbabilities and paradoxes, viewing the latter as the cross faith must bear in modern times.

One can also, however, argue as follows. If the standards of judgment now commonly used to cast doubt on theism differ from those once used successfully to defend it, this only shows that rational appraisal is itself inherently relative to one or another conceptual scheme. What we lack is a good reason for preferring one conceptual scheme, with its standards of judgment, to another. For if all rational appraisal is relative to conceptual schemes, there is no way to appraise conceptual schemes rationally without already having committed oneself to one. So any justification I might supply for the standards I apply in criticizing theism will inevitably beg the question. It would seem to follow that theism is at least no worse off than any other system of beliefs. It fares well by the standards implicit in its own conceptual scheme, but poorly by the standards implicit in others. Theism can even claim the virtue of making explicit the fact that its conceptual scheme, like any other, demands the *faith* of those who would commit themselves to it. If reasons are relative to schemes, then the choice

of a scheme must be a matter of faith and not reasons. Theism
becomes fideism.

The most common, and perhaps the most telling, objection
to a relativism of this kind is that no such relativism can account for itself. Relativism poses as a truth for all schemes,
but in reference to what scheme is relativism to be judged?
Conceptual relativism seems to undo itself. If fideism presupposes relativism, then fideism seems insufficient as a defense of theism. But I still face a difficulty. For my account of
theism's troubles in the modern period does seem to underline
a kind of relativity to changing standards of judgment — a
relativity that can hardly be separated from the generally
historicist orientation of the book as a whole. So the problem
is how to stave off the fideist's argument without relinquishing
the historicism to which I felt driven by the demise of foundationalism. The rejection of foundationalism leads naturally
toward a view of justification as the social practice of giving
reasons for beliefs and plans within some highly specific context. Justification therefore seems *relative* to epistemic context
in just the way the fideist supposes. And if relativism cannot
consistently be maintained, the very possibility of responsible
criticism seems to depend on the Cartesian-Kantian quest for a
perspective beyond, or more basic than, historically conditioned thought.

It is therefore crucial, not only for the criticism of modern
theology but also for the overarching program of this book, to
show that my historicism neither presupposes nor entails the
kind of relativism on which the fideist's reply relies. I shall try
to accomplish this objective, in the final chapter of Part II, by
deploying Donald Davidson's argument against the thesis of
conceptual relativism — the thesis that rationality is relative
to conceptual schemes. It is this form of relativism on which
the fideist leans, and also this form of relativism against which
the charge of self-referential inconsistency is most effective.
Its basic problem, however, is that we have no good reason for
postulating conceptual schemes in the first place. This, I believe, is what Davidson's argument shows. That we can accept
the historicist's contextualist view of justification without
committing ourselves to *conceptual* relativism will be my
major claim. While my defense of this claim will be somewhat
sketchy, as it must be in a book designed more for the purpose
of exemplifying historicism than for that of proving histo-

ricism acceptable, I hope at least to chart the path an acceptable historicism would have to take.

Part II portrays the intellectual dilemma of modern theism as in no small measure moral and political in origin. The secularization of discourse that eventually made trouble for theism was made necessary when, in the wake of the Reformation, theism ceased to provide a vocabulary in terms of which matters of public importance could be debated and decided by Christians of various persuasions without resort to violence. This picture suggests an unorthodox and richly complicated view of the shifting relationship between religion and morality in modern culture. It is not that the demise of theism deprived morality of its foundation. If we reject foundationalism, it seems odd to say that morality ever had, let alone now requires, a foundation. Moreover, the root of theism's modern difficulties seems largely to have been its own inability, during and after the crisis of authority brought on by the Reformation, to secure the terms of a *moral* consensus, and not a purely theoretical matter at all. Part III of this book will elaborate this picture of the relationship between religion and morality and show how such a picture might be related to recent discussions of the same theme in moral philosophy and the comparative study of religious ethics.

Part III will also illustrate in some detail how one might move from the preoccupation with meanings characteristic of analytic metaethics toward an ethical historicism. "Metaethics" was the name linguistic philosophers gave to moral philosophy conceived as the conceptual analysis of moral language and to be distinguished from the work of moralists and historians. But this conception of analysis and of its distinguishing marks presupposed a quite specific philosophy of language. When the central distinctions of this philosophy of language succumbed to the criticisms of Wittgenstein and Quine, so too did the notion of philosophy as linguistic analysis and the rationale for confining moral philosophy to metaethics.

Metaethics required a clear differentiation between matters of substance and matters of meaning, and this was provided in the heyday of linguistic philosophy by the distinction between the synthetic and the analytic. Analytic truths were thought to be sentences true by virtue of meaning alone, unlike the synthetic kind, which were thought to require help from the facts as well as from meanings to attain truth.

If this distinction holds, it must be possible to understand meaning independently from substance or belief, just as a metaethicist would want. If, however, this distinction does not hold, and, as most philosophers of language came to believe, meaning cannot be sharply separated from substance or belief, there seems little point in calling oneself a metaethicist. On the one hand, conceptual analysis has difficulty remaining aloof from normative ethics. On the other, it becomes indistinguishable from historical inquiry. For meaning and belief might well change together.

When metaethicists addressed the issue of morality's relation to religion, they made much of something called the "logical autonomy" of moral discourse. This they treated as a timeless characteristic of moral discourse as such. Yet as conceptual analysis becomes explicitly historical in nature, we want to know precisely where to look to find the form of discourse in question. The discourse of an autonomous morality might prove, on investigation, to be a relatively local phenomenon, one for historians to date and explain. That it is indeed a phenomenon of this kind will be the major thesis of Part III. My defense of this thesis will include a brief critique of metaethical assumptions, a discussion of methodological proposals that would tend to insulate the notion of "logical autonomy" from historical scrutiny, and an outline of the narrative in which my thesis could be more fully developed.

All the leading themes of this book converge on the topic of the autonomy of morals, and it was my interest in this topic that led to the writing of this book. A Kantian could have divided the various themes for independent treatment in separate books and taken the autonomy of morals as the topic of a self-contained treatise. For better or for worse, I found myself wanting to make the Hegelian point that independent treatment would be a mistake — precisely the mistake that makes a Kantian doctrine like "the autonomy of morals" seem so intuitive and so simple. A latter-day Nebridius would bemoan my attempt as inevitably superficial, the ill effect of excessive ambitions. I have risked this criticism in the hope of convincing readers that moral autonomy is in fact a densely historical affair. To understand it well, I believe, one must begin by achieving distance from the epistemological principles that led Hume to question the relation of fact to value and from the myth of autonomous reason we inherit from the tradition of

Descartes and Kant. There is more than a kernel of truth in the notion that morality has become autonomous and even in the notion that morality has lost the coherence it had before the twilight of Christendom. But we shall never be able to grasp this truth unless we learn to view the emergence of autonomy as part of a complicated history in which the crisis of authority, the philosophical quest for autonomy from history, the secularization of public discourse, and the differentiation of cultural domains all play significant roles. The biggest obstacle to be overcome in the attempt to achieve this perspective is the philosophical interpretation our ancestors gave to their genuine accomplishments. To accept their self-interpretation at face value is to preclude the possibility of understanding either their accomplishments or our predicament.

It should be clear by now that one of my aims is to present historicism as a natural successor to analytic philosophy. The concluding chapter of Part III will stand back from the specific controversies in epistemology, philosophy of religion, and ethics with which the book deals, in order to address more generally what this historicism might be and how it differs from earlier representatives of the historicist tradition. Let me conclude this introduction, then, by dwelling for a moment on analytic philosophy itself. I have already hinted, in my discussion of metaethics, that Wittgensteinian and Quinean views in the theory of meaning helped undermine the conception of philosophy as linguistic analysis. These views have been characterized, in a term of art, as *holistic.*[5] I shall not expound or defend a holistic view of language in any detail, but I do wish to exploit the current favor enjoyed by holism in academic philosophy as a source of support for historicism. Anyone familiar with recent developments in the philosophy of science or in the theory of interpretation knows that holism and historicism often seem closely related nowadays. I hope to make much of this relation in the following chapters. Holism is the medium in which conceptual analysis becomes conceptual archaeology. We shall return to holism, to see what it involves, shortly. The first task is to place conceptual analysis within the general account of modern philosophy suggested above.

Modern philosophy has long been caught between two aims. The first is that of providing a special kind of insight — sufficiently powerful to be decisive in fights with skeptics, sufficiently distinctive to promote the philosopher to the role of cultural magistrate, sufficiently secure to remain firm beneath one's feet even during a Kuhnian revolution. This aim was written into the charter of modern philosophy when Descartes decided, given his dim view of the merely probable, that radical skepticism would have to be answered on its own terms. The second aim is that of engaging in fruitful dialogue — the kind that, in principle at least, can generate agreement; the kind that, by virtue of method, makes a discipline seem disciplined. This aim grew, in large part, out of Kant's embarrassment at the spectacle of philosophy as (in Strawson's phrase) a sphere of "maximum pretension and minimum agreement," and it has since been reinforced during subsequent periods of professionalization by the likes of Russell and Husserl.[6]

A professional philosopher who wants good standing in the modern academy needs a way to have a discipline (which involves having intersubjective means for resolving disputes) while remaining something special (by virtue of the philosophical quest). Good philosophy avoids dialectical impasse while maintaining relevance to the concerns that make people turn to philosophy in the first place. But in practice these two aims constitute a dilemma: the dilemma of impasse and irrelevance. For it has never been entirely clear how philosophy could become enough like an empirical discipline to have genuinely rational disputation while retaining enough distinctiveness to be needed. Every great methodological manifesto in philosophy since Kant has sought a way between the horns of this dilemma.

It had become apparent by Kant's time — and not only to Kant but to Thomas Reid as well — that *ideas* (in the sense common to Descartes, Port-Royal, and Hume) could not be the subject of a discipline. They had the virtue of being, on Descartes's view at least, eternal entities of which immediate or intuitive knowledge was possible, and this made them relevant to the quest for certainty. But since knowledge of ideas was a matter of bringing one's mental eye into focus, disagreement about ideas became either hard to explain or impossible to settle. For if we explain disagreement about ideas by saying that some mental eyes just *do* go uncontrollably and unnoticeably out of focus, then the usefulness of the appeal to ideas as a method for resolving philosophical disputes becomes unclear.

Ideas leave the parties to a philosophical dispute in dialectical impasse.

As Ian Hacking has made clear, by the time we reach Frege and the late nineteenth century, *ideas* have had their day and *meanings* are coming into their own.[7] The roots of this new heyday, as Hacking neglects to point out, can be traced back to Kant's treatment of intuitions and concepts, of the understanding as the faculty of rules, and of the judgment as the basic unit of cognition. It became the twentieth-century fashion to sneer at Kant's psychologistic formulations of transcendental arguments while seeking *linguistic* explications of his notion of concept and of his distinction between the analytic and the synthetic. Concepts, construed as meanings, became sets of rules for using linguistic expressions.[8] Analytic propositions became those rendered true by virtue of meaning alone. Thus explicated, many philosophers thought, concepts and analytic truths help us escape the old dilemma. For they represent, not the object of this or that mental eye, but rather (in Frege's phrase) "the common store of thoughts and propositions which is transmitted from one generation to another." This means that they are public enough to be studied in light of shared criteria of identification and classification even while remaining somehow distinct from and more basic than the subject matter of the empirical sciences. Philosophy as conceptual analysis still seemed to yield a priori knowledge — and this set it apart — even though Kant's talk about *synthetic* a priori knowledge fell out. But then so many of Kant's synthetic a priori "truths" had turned out to be not only dependent upon empirical assumptions but plainly false. Better to be rid of the embarrassment by making philosophy analytic, by confining it to the conceptual.

Unfortunately, the dilemma of impasse and irrelevance was not simply left behind during the heyday of meanings. The reason is that one always faces a choice about which of two directions to take in the theory of meaning. *Either* meanings are (like Cartesian ideas) immediately given to the eye of the mind and eternally fixed beyond the history of shifts in thought and practice, *or* what we know about meanings is exhausted by what we know about regularities in the actual use of linguistic expressions. If meanings are immediately given and eternally fixed, then they preserve analytic philosophy's relevance to the traditional quest but sacrifice such philosophy's status as a discipline in which fruitful dialogue can be had. If meanings are not immediately given, if what we know about meanings is exhausted by what we know about use, then it is unclear how they could be known to remain eternally fixed, for use clearly changes. Without immediately given meanings it will be difficult to separate matters of meaning from matters of fact or belief in the way required to give notions of analytic philosophy and conceptual truth their point. This is the background against which Wittgenstein's injunction to look for the use and *not* for the meaning, as well as Quine's attack on the distinction between analytic and synthetic truths, should be seen. Between them, Quine and Wittgenstein succeeded in making the old dilemma seem unpleasant again. In Wittgenstein this realization leads directly to a conception of philosophy as therapy for those quixotic souls still committed to, or at times tempted to undertake, the traditional quest. In Quine it leads simply to a willingness to abandon the idea that philosophy is something special.

If meanings are to play the role assigned to them in analytic philosophy, it will have to be plausible to appeal to knowledge of meanings in order to *justify* beliefs. But if meanings are intuitively known, then the process of justification ceases to be public, and any disagreement that would make one want to philosophize in the first place will be hard to explain or resolve. If, on the other hand, meanings are treated empirically as (in Putnam's phrase) a "coarse grid" we put over use, then it will be impossible to hold them fixed, and it will be circular to appeal to them as justification for beliefs. The reason is that what we know about meanings will, in any event, depend upon assumptions about beliefs held. The meanings of our own words and sentences will depend upon what we in fact believe. So if meanings already *reflect* beliefs, justification of beliefs by appeal to meanings gets us nowhere.

Suppose we are anthropologists, heading off to the hills of West Virginia to study an isolated community. We discover that its people speak a dialect of English. There is no way to separate the task of translating their speech, of finding out what it means, from the task of ascribing attitudes. To take a familiar example, imagine that their use of the words "cat" and "dog" seems deviant. They say that cats fetch the morning paper, chase dogs up trees, and bury their bones, whereas dogs meow, remain aloof, and do the cha-cha on television. Now we can either ascribe strange beliefs to these West Virginians while saying that their words mean roughly what ours do, or reverse the standard translation in order to bring their beliefs into line. The latter option, of course, is the more modest of the two hypotheses. What we cannot do, however, is divorce hypotheses about meaning from ascriptions of belief — unless, that is, we assume immediate knowledge of meanings. Yet if anthropologists had immediate knowledge of meanings, they would not have so much trouble working up their translation manuals from scratch.

The problem, as Quine says, begins at home. Once we confine ourselves, as we should, to intersubjective criteria of identification and classification, we shall have no way to establish a sharp distinction between changes in meaning and changes in belief. If the meaning of a word or sentence is a matter of regularities in the actual use of linguistic expressions, and if we use expressions differently when we change our minds on important matters (such as the existence of God, the validity of Euclidean geometry, or the question of which authorities to accept), then meanings change along with beliefs. They reflect beliefs. How, then, can they figure in the traditional quest for ultimate justifications?

The appropriate response to this question, it seems to me, is not to search for some class of privileged entities that might secure ultimate justifications at precisely the point ideas and meanings failed. Any such entities, it now seems clear, would meet their ruin on the horns of our dilemma. Quinean or Wittgensteinian holism suggests that the traditional quest itself be abandoned. If it is to succeed in its attempt to avoid dialectical impasse, the linguistic turn in philosophy can maintain relevance to the problems of the traditional quest only by dissolving them.

Holism, as I shall use the term, consists simply in the view that language cannot be divided up in the way envisioned by proponents of the distinctions between the analytic and the synthetic, theory and observation, or fact and value.[9] Holists typically hold that once one has said all there is to say about how an expression is used, there is nothing remaining to be said about its "meaning." Some holists, such as Wilfrid Sellars, are happy to put this forward as a positive thesis about meaning: the meaning of an expression depends in large part upon a pattern of intersections in the web of belief. Sellars goes on using the term "meaning" and its cognates, being careful not to imply that meanings are either special or determinate. Others, following Quine, prefer to eliminate talk of meanings altogether, since the postulation of meanings as special and determinate entities is neither necessary nor helpful, and any use of the term can encourage backsliding. But however holism is stated, and whatever choices one makes with respect to details of theory, certain implications follow for the traditional quest.

It follows, first of all, that in order to know or doubt the truth of a sentence, one would have to know a great deal about a lot of different things beyond the sentence in question. The reason is that a sentence has no significance by itself. To assess a sentence's credibility, one must be able to interpret it. To interpret a sentence, one must establish its relation to a context of generally accepted and deeply entrenched sentences in the same domain. This means that both radical skepticism and foundationalist epistemology, at least in their traditional forms, share a mistaken assumption if holism is correct. The radical skeptic claims to be able to doubt meaningfully a great many things all at once. Holists respond by arguing that in order to have this doubt, one would have to be able to assign interpretations to the sentences that express it. They claim that this would be possible only if one had knowledge that implied the truth of most sentences in the domain called into question. The foundationalist proposes some item of knowledge as *basic* in the hope of refuting radical skepticism on its own terms. Holists, already convinced that such skeptics need not be taken seriously, respond that the foundationalist's "basic" knowledge itself presupposes at least enough knowledge to make the interpretation of a proposition possible, which is a great deal of knowledge indeed. One cannot, in other words, know the sense of a supposedly "basic" proposition without already presupposing propositions thought to be "nonbasic." This conclusion makes the very notion of "basic" propositions seem silly. Once these two points have been made — the first against radical skepticism, the second against foundationalist epistemology — a thoroughgoing holist would go on to say (in the spirit of Dewey and Wittgenstein) that epistemology itself, as traditionally conceived, must now seem silly too. In the absence of both its central problems and its trusted tools, the quest for ultimate justifications loses its urgency.

These implications of holism are very striking, and they may even leave one with the impression that there is nothing left for philosophy to do. Suppose, however, we reason as follows. If looking not for the meaning but rather for the use of our words is, as Wittgenstein suggests, a fitting pursuit for philosophy, then the obvious fact that use can change gives a historical dimension to linguistic philosophy. The assumption, articulated by Strawson, that there is "a massive central core of human thinking which has no history" can then be opened to historical scrutiny.[10] Maybe we can discover, in the difference between old sentences and new ones, what it is to be situated in history as we are. Such a discovery, while it would not help much with the quest for autonomy from history, might at least make connection with Socrates' injunction to seek self-understanding or with Aristotle's conviction that philosophy begins in the surprised wonder at everything that is as it is. If philosophy is, as Wittgenstein and Socrates could agree, a kind of therapy, it will be natural to wonder what kind of therapy historical insight into our language might provide. Perhaps it will be a kind that does not leave everything as it is. The ancient city, after all, is ours to repair and renew.

PART I
Philosophy after Authority

1. Descartes, the Father

We still allude to his name or to his metaphor when we need a tag for a theory of knowledge to propose or oppose. Either we are foundationalists, and thus stand within the tradition called Cartesian, or we define ourselves in opposition to all that. These are just two ways of having the same father, and Descartes is, as the textbooks tell us, the father of modern philosophy. Such an image, if Freud had anything right, should not be taken lightly. What is it to have this father, to be Cartesian or anti-Cartesian, to seek foundations for knowledge or to spend a career inveighing against the search?

Not long ago, the featured contest pitted rationalist against empiricist — the heir of Descartes versus the heir of Hume. But now we recognize empiricism as another variation on Cartesian themes, and the question is whether to be Cartesian in this broader sense, not which kind of Cartesian to be. There is also some question, as we shall see, about just how broad this broader sense should be allowed to be.

A modest quest for the historical Descartes will come later. Our topic, at the moment, is not the real Descartes but rather that so-called Descartes whose views can be reconstructed entirely out of what recent philosophers have said about him — the father figure, not the father-in-himself. As evidence of the existence and character of this figure, I cite Frederick Will's portrait of "Cartesian procedure in the philosophy of knowledge" in *Induction and Justification.*[1]

Will takes the problem of induction as his point of departure, but his real topic is the influence of Descartes. Why induction, as opposed to some other point of departure? The answer is autobiographical. Induction was Will's problem, the topic of his never-published magnum opus, which would have come to 700 pages in print.

After completing a draft of that work, and in the process of critically examining the views set forth in it in preparation for publication, I gradually came to realize that the positive view of induction advanced in it was flawed in a way that resisted emendation. What was chiefly wrong with my philosophy of induction was, I finally concluded, that it *was* a philosophy of induction, a kind of philosophy which — Prichard's phraseology seems to fit here — rests upon a mistake.[2]

The mistake was to take up induction without asking what made the problem seem problematical. From what matrix of ideas does the problem drop? Hume's empiricism. To what paternal seed does the problem owe its anatomical design? Descartes's struggle with doubt. Induction is the point of departure for an inquiry into this parentage because it was Will's point of departure from Descartes, the father. The book confesses a conversion, explores the grounds of an apology, and strains for a vantage point beyond Descartes's shadow. It executes a *clinamen,* in the sense Bloom borrows from Lucretius, swerving away from the precursor so as to make change possible in the universe.[3]

Will views the problem of induction as a single manifestation of the general problem of Cartesian epistemology — the problem of how, if at all, we are to "justify" propositions in the various domains of putative human knowledge. The term "justify" deserves scare quotes because of its specialized sense.

> One needs a reminder again and again that what is under consideration is not ordinary variety justification, whatever that may be, but extraordinary, philosophical justification. It was similarly with Luther when he proclaimed the doctrine that justification was by faith.[4]

Just as Luther sought the sort of justification that would be a match for the radical sinfulness he had discovered in his own will and heart, traditional epistemology has sought the sort of justification that would be a match for the radical skepticism implicit in its own Socratic questions and Cartesian doubts.

Cartesian epistemology begins by embracing the challenge of radical skepticism as sufficiently cogent to call for serious attention.

> The problem is thus at bottom how it is possible, having accepted the skeptical questions, and with them the elements of skeptical philosophy from which they arise, to avoid the con-

clusions to which these elements inexorably lead. It is a problem of how, having accepted skeptical principles in order to raise certain questions about knowledge, it is possible consistently to give to these questions any but skeptical answers.[5]

Once this starting point has been accepted, as Will sees it, the remainder of "Cartesian procedure" becomes inevitable. If we deem the skeptic's challenge worthy of straightforward response and we endeavor to defeat the skeptic on a battlefield of his own choosing, we are bound to begin the quest for basic elements of absolutely certain knowledge upon which all justified beliefs might be shown to rest securely. Hence the familiar metaphor. A justification of accepted belief in the face of radically skeptical challenge reconstructs the edifice of human knowledge on a foundation of certainty.

Two sorts of difficulties must be met and overcome if such a rational reconstruction is to succeed. Will calls these *foundation* and *construction* difficulties. First, an absolutely secure foundation must be established and certified as such. Foundational cognitions must therefore enjoy "extreme, large-scale and long-run incorrigibility."[6] They must be "infallible," "indubitable," "self-justifying," and logically independent "from every other possible cognition."[7] Otherwise, they could not play the assigned role in the battle with *radical* skepticism. Second, a way of building upon a foundation of such cognitions must be fashioned such that even the higher levels of the resulting fortress will be immune from skeptical assault. Here it is unclear how the support provided to nonfoundational beliefs can be anything but strictly deductive without failing to achieve Cartesian aims.

Will argues — at great length, often repetitively, and sometimes less than carefully — that these two kinds of difficulty cannot be resolved. He concludes not that skepticism is vindicated, but rather that the all-important first step of the Cartesian procedure, in which hyperbolic doubt is accepted as innocent until proven guilty, must be avoided. It is this step that infects Cartesian philosophy with implicitly skeptical standards for knowledge and in effect guarantees a skeptical result. If the radical skeptic's doubt is itself so extreme that *it* stands in need of justification, we would seem to be within our rights in dismissing both radical skepticism and Cartesian defenses until such justification is provided. Meanwhile, we can use the time we save for less quixotic, more enlightening inquiries into the actual life of our cognitive institutions. Giving up the utopian hopes and abstract strivings characteristic of Cartesian philosophy is no mere exercise in relieving frustration. It has the added benefit of leaving time for better things.

I shall not consider Will's arguments against foundationalism in any detail here. But I do wish to confront these arguments with a highly revealing criticism voiced clearly in William Alston's article "Has Foundationalism Been Refuted?"[8] We have seen that foundationalism, as Will construes it, requires foundational beliefs that enjoy incorrigibility, infallibility, indubitability, self-justification, and logical independence. Alston does not contest Will's claim that such beliefs are not to be found. He argues instead that foundationalists need not and should not require so much of their foundations. Will, like such other antifoundationalists as Bruce Aune and Keith Lehrer, attacks "features of the position that are by no means essential to foundationalism and that do not appear in its most defensible form, which I shall call 'Minimal Foundationalism.'"[9] As James Cornman put the point in his defense of minimal foundationalism as a "prime candidate for the most reasonable theory of empirical justification," "a thesis is refuted only if its minimal version is refuted."[10] So if Alston and Cornman are right, Will and his allies have failed to refute foundationalism.

What is minimal foundationalism? Better to begin by saying what minimal foundationalism is not. Minimal foundationalism does *not* require foundational beliefs that are:

(a) *infallible* (in the sense that such a belief could not be held and fail to be true);

(b) *indubitable* (in the sense that such a belief could not be held without eliminating all grounds for doubting its truth);

(c) *incorrigible* (in the sense that such a belief could not both be held by someone and shown false by someone else);

(d) *self-justified* (in the sense that such a belief is justified just by virtue of being held);

(e) *radically independent* (in the sense that it is nomologically possible for such a belief to stand free of a network of other beliefs or a supporting context of social practices);

(f) *immediately demonstrable* (in the sense that one could show that such a belief is justified without adducing other beliefs as grounds);

(g) *immediately given* (in the sense that what justifies

such a belief is nonpropositional awareness of a particular or a fact); or, finally,

(h) *epistemic* (in the sense that one would not only be immediately justified in holding a specified "first-order" belief, but would also be immediately justified in believing oneself to be immediately justified in holding that belief).

Minimal foundationalism requires only one thing of its foundational beliefs — namely, that they be immediately justified. A foundation of immediately justified beliefs need not include any beliefs of the kinds indicated in (a) through (h). A belief is immediately justified just in case what justifies it does not include other justified beliefs. Minimal foundationalism holds that some beliefs, the foundation, are immediately justified, whereas the remainder depend for their justification on the foundation.

It should be clear that a belief could be immediately justified without being infallible, indubitable or incorrigible. So familiar arguments against infallibility, indubitability, and incorrigibility need not concern a minimal foundationalist. Self-justified beliefs would qualify as one kind of immediately justified beliefs, but only one. So a good argument against self-justification would go only part of the way toward a refutation of minimal foundationalism.

The only kind of independence required of minimal foundations is justificatory: "A minimal foundation *is* independent of every other cognition in that it derives its justification from none."[11] It might be that we cannot possess or understand foundational beliefs without help from a supporting context of presuppositions and social institutions, and the presuppositions themselves may be nonfoundational. But we should not confuse "a requirement for the existence of a *candidate* for justification" with "the requirements for justification" *per se.*[12] So radical independence, one of Will's central targets, may be ignored.

Nor should we confuse the immediately demonstrable with the immediately justified. Alston refers to the "process-product ambiguity" of the terms "justification" and "justified," an ambiguity which tends to blur the difference between "what it takes for a belief to *be* justified" and "what it takes to *justify* a belief in the sense of *showing* it to be justified."[13] An immediately demonstrable belief would be one that could be *shown* to be justified without reference to other beliefs. What such a demonstration could consist in, of course, remains unclear. But an immediately justified belief would *be* justified even though we could not *exhibit* its justification immediately, given what such showing always involves — namely, the presentation of grounds. To require foundational beliefs that were immediately demonstrable would be to require what obviously could never be supplied. Minimal foundations require less.

Appeals to the immediately given are as puzzling as the notion of immediate demonstration. What makes such an appeal puzzling, aside from the idea of nonpropositional awareness itself, depends upon whether particulars or facts are taken as the given. Just what nonpropositional awareness of a fact could be remains unclear, in that facts seem inherently propositional. Nonpropositional awareness of particulars is only slightly less mysterious.[14] In any event, appeals to the given are probably best treated as (probably incoherent) explanations of what makes immediately justified beliefs what they are. There could be immediately justified beliefs even if the given is, as Sellars says, a myth.[15]

Similarly, minimal foundations need not, according to Alston, include immediately justified epistemic beliefs. Inclusion of such beliefs among the requisites of the foundation would yield what Alston calls "iterative foundationalism," a position he attacks in this argument:

> . . . in taking a belief to be justified, we are evaluating it in a certain way. And, like any evaluative property, epistemic justification is a supervenient property, the application of which is based on more fundamental properties. A belief is justified because it possesses what Roderick Firth has called "warrant-increasing properties." Hence in order for me to be justified in believing that S's belief that p is justified, I must be justified in certain other beliefs, viz., that S's *belief that p* possesses a certain property, Q, and that Q renders its possessor justified. (Another way of formulating this last belief is: a belief that there is a valid epistemic principle to the effect that any belief that is Q is justified.) Hence in no case can an epistemic belief that S is justified in believing that p, itself be immediately justified.[16]

While this argument indeed undermines iterative foundationalism, it does nothing to undermine the minimal position. Whenever we evaluate a belief with respect to justification, we presuppose "some general evaluative principle to the effect that all beliefs with a certain property are warranted."[17] Minimal foundationalism must recognize at least one such principle as valid — namely, one to the effect that a belief can be warranted by virtue of some property or set of properties *other than relations to other beliefs*. A belief satisfying such a principle would be immediately justified in the required sense. The property or set of properties indicated in the principle would tell us which kind of immediate justification to consider. A minimal foundationalist, presumably, would be obliged to specify this and to offer some kind of support for the principle thus specified. What kind of support, however, remains an open question. He need not claim, with iterative foundationalism, that the *principle* — or, for that matter, any belief about other beliefs — could be immediately justified. Nor need he claim that the principle could not be overturned as inquiry continues. What now (rightly) counts as immediately justified might someday (again rightly) be the sort of belief that requires mediate justification, if it can be justified at all.[18]

Notice just how minimal the position has become. The foundations need be neither firm nor fixed. Formerly foundational beliefs can become, in the course of time, both nonfoundational and unjustifiable. Whole *kinds* of beliefs can cease to be foundational, for the epistemic principles in reference to which we ascribe immediate justification to kinds of beliefs are not immune to criticism and revision. Imagine, for example, an epistemic principle stipulating that a belief about one's own current state of pain counts as justified "by being formed, or being held, in certain kinds of circumstances, e.g., being wide awake, alert, in full possession of one's faculties."[19] This would give us one, perhaps very plausible, kind of immediate justification. Such a belief would be justified not by virtue of relations to other beliefs, but simply by virtue of relations to circumstances of occurrence—hence its character of immediacy. Given the current state of the relevant sciences, my belief that I am now in pain seems the best available evidence concerning whether I am in pain, provided my belief was formed in "normal" circumstances — hence the principle's plausibility. But the relevant sciences might make progress in the study of pain, making independent checks on the accuracy of such beliefs possible.[20] We might come to view such beliefs as less reliable than we do now, and this might justify abandonment of the epistemic principle. Even this possibility a minimal foundationalist can accept.

Perhaps we should reopen the question of what is "essential to foundationalism." When Cornman wrote that "a thesis is refuted only if its minimal version is refuted," he did not make clear how we should distinguish the minimal version of a thesis from mere impostors. Quinean scruples counsel caution. To think of ourselves as searching for the essence of foundationalism or an analysis of the concept is to presuppose questionable dogma. The task at hand is explication. But what do we do when we explicate a term? Quine answers as follows:

> We do not claim synonymy. We do not claim to make clear and explicit what the users of the unclear expression had unconsciously in mind all along. We do not expose hidden meanings, as the words 'analysis' and 'explication' would suggest; we supply lacks. We fix on the particular functions of the unclear expression that make it worth troubling about, and then devise a substitute, clear and couched in terms to our liking, that fills those functions. Beyond those conditions of partial agreement, dictated by our interests and purposes, any traits of the explicans come under the head of "don't cares."[21]

We shall be returning to this explication of explication time and again in the course of these studies. Quine's comments help us focus on "the particular functions of the unclear expression that make it worth troubling about" and thus on the "interests and purposes" that make some functions worth troubling about and others not. How we should explicate foundationalism depends on what interests and purposes we have that might make one formulation worth troubling about and another fall under the head of "don't cares." In asking whether the minimal position, as described by Alston, captures what is "essential to foundationalism," we are really asking (or ought to be asking) whether this formulation is worth caring about. If foundationalism is, as Will suggests, a human project governed by quite specific interests and purposes, we can ask what is essential (in the sense of *crucial*) to this project. And to answer this question adequately, we need to place the project in a context that makes sense of the relevant interests and purposes.

It is regrettable that Alston, in criticizing Will, fails to attend to Will's account of the interests and purposes that make foundationalism or "Cartesian procedure" interesting. Will writes at great length about *radical* skepticism as the opponent against which Cartesian philosophy struggles. Foundationalism is, according to Will, a strategy for repulsing such skepticism. A thesis that could not plausibly be used to execute this strategy would, for him, lose interest as a formulation of something essential to foundationalism. Minimal foundationalism, as Alston describes it, is simply too weak to satisfy Cartesian dialectical aims, as Will describes them. Alston grants that "the extreme skeptic who refuses to accept anything until it has been shown to be true and who will not allow his opponent any premises to use for this purpose, obviously cannot be answered whatever one's position."[22] If the skeptic is slightly less radical and allows his opponent only indubitable and infallible premises, then a Cartesian response will have to seek foundations considerably stronger than those permitted in the minimal position. If the point is to *establish* such stronger foundations in the face of skeptical objection, then immediate demonstrability seems necessary. If the point is to reconstruct knowledge from the foundations, without presupposing the validity of epistemic principles, then iterative foundationalism seems needed.[23] So if Will is right in characterizing Cartesian aims, Alston's criticisms simply miss the point.

Are there aims and concerns that might make the minimal position worth troubling about? Alston suggests that we do have one good motive for taking the minimal position seriously — namely, the perplexity caused by the spectre of an infinite regress of reasons. If there are no immediately justified beliefs, and only justified beliefs can confer support, and justification cannot be circular, then how can a chain of reasons ever be brought to a halt so as to complete a justification? An argument shaped along these lines, according to Alston, is "the main argument for foundationalism."[24] "And clearly it yields, at most, Minimal Foundationalism."[25]

Let us assume for the moment that the "regress" argument is conclusive. What does it force us to conclude? Only, I take it, that if justification must stop somewhere, we should expect to be able to find in any epistemic context "some stock of well-entrenched beliefs which set the bounds within which current enquiry proceeds."[26] So far as I know, no antifoundationalist has ever denied this. What has divided Cartesians from their opponents at this juncture has been a further issue. As Richard Rorty has written:

> Followers of Wittgenstein reason that since there can be no infinite regress — and thus justification of belief must stop

somewhere — one would expect, given our use of the word "know" to mean "justified belief," that there would be certain conventions dictating that certain beliefs are justified even in the absence of good reasons. For the Cartesian, these conventions reflect introspectable facts about the mind or about entities (such as universals) visible to the eye of the mind; for the Wittgensteinian, they do not reflect anything.[27]

Cartesians characteristically claim that the beliefs we count as justified even in the absence of good reasons necessarily involve some form of privileged access. It is plausible to assume that the insistence on claiming this much has something to do with the desire to refute radical forms of skepticism (even if this desire has been sublimated, as in Chisholm's quest for an analytic science of evidence distinguishable from sociological and historical inquiry, on the one hand, and physiological investigation, on the other).[28]

Consider again the possibility that scientific progress will render questionable some beliefs a Cartesian would be inclined to accept as foundational — namely, beliefs about the contents of our own minds, beliefs involving some kind of "privileged access." Now imagine that *all* such beliefs ceased to be foundational, that, thanks to advances in physiology or some other respectable cognitive domain, we stopped talking about privileged access. Would we be any worse off? It would seem not. Justifiable revision of one set of beliefs would have given us a *better* set. Why mourn the loss of privileged access? A foundationalist who wants to stress privileged access needs to show either that the imagined case is incoherent or that, in such circumstances, we should consider ourselves in danger of cognitive default. If foundational beliefs must be privileged, it will be hard to avoid embracing the possibility of justifiably holding beliefs in the absence of foundations. Foundations neither firm nor fixed but still privileged in some significant way (that is, in some way that goes beyond the idea of being justified even in the absence of good reasons) seem capable of disappearing altogether without taking justification itself along. Foundationalists, whether minimal or not, want to hold that immediately justified beliefs are, *in principle,* required if any belief is to be justified. So it will not do to say simply that we require privileged access if any belief is to be justified *now,* for that would be to neglect saying something about the nature, essence, or structure of justification. It is unclear why anyone would insist on calling himself a foundationalist if he could not tell us something about justification *per se.*

What about the threat of infinite regress? We can assume that, in the imagined circumstances, some classes of beliefs will be deemed acceptable even in the absence of good reasons. One will not have to *show,* in this context, that they are acceptable. They will be immediately justified in the weakest possible sense, a sense that has nothing to do with privileged access of any kind. As the image of Neurath's boat suggests, we will always need some planks in place to stay afloat, and the hope for reconstruction in dry dock is utopian. Which planks will be keeping us afloat at any given moment depends on the course of our voyage, what we are up to, and why. There is nothing deeply philosophical about it. What requires justification and what does not is mainly a matter of context.[29] There is good reason to believe that the relevant features of context vary *far* more than a coherent version of the "foundations" metaphor could accommodate and in ways that only deeply historical thinking could fathom. If we want the best of Neurath and the best of Descartes in the way of imagery, perhaps we should settle for Emerson, who wrote:

> The philosophy we want is one of fluxions and mobility. . . . We want a ship in these billows we inhabit. An angular, dogmatic house would be rent to chips and splinters in this storm of many elements. No, it must be tight, and fit to the form of man, to live at all; as a shell must dictate the architecture of a house founded on the sea.
>
> *(Montaigne; or The Skeptic)*

In introducing Alston's criticisms of Will, I declared them "highly revealing," but I withheld my view of *what* they reveal. They reveal, I think, not so much the weaknesses of Will's presentation as they do the remarkable extent to which Cartesian philosophy, in Will's sense, is a thing of the past. One irony in Alston's exchange with Will is Descartes's role as father figure. For it is Will, as self-proclaimed antifoundationalist, and not Alston, as critic of contemporary antifoundationalism,[30] who maintains the more direct relationship, however oedipal, with the father. On the other hand, if Will executes a *clinamen,* Alston executes what Bloom would call a *tessera,* by so reading the precursor's work as to retain its terms but to mean them in another sense, "as though the pre-

cursor has failed to go far enough."[31] Will blasphemes against
the father, like an Holbach. Minimal foundationalism is more
like Tillichian theology: the former is to the philosophy of
Descartes what the latter is to the Christianity of Aquinas.
Both try so hard to say something unobjectionable that they
become indistinguishable from their opponents. Both use a
traditional vocabulary now emptied of content. Both practice
conversion by redefinition.[32] Both signal the passing of an age.

   Alston accurately points out that the critics of foundationalism have not directed their arguments against the minimal
formulation. He takes this as evidence that they have not
completed their self-appointed task. But why not take it as
evidence that minimal foundationalism is minimally interesting at best? If even a Deweyan historicist — who views justification as mainly a holistic affair carried on under constraints
determined by social context, historical situation, and dialectical setting — can accept the "essence" of foundationalism,
what have we been debating all these years? My intuition is
that Will is basically right about what the issue under dispute
is and that the dispute is virtually over. If, as Alston suggests,
the "regress" argument yields at most the minimal position;
and if, as Alston also suggests, there are in addition strong
arguments against the bolder formulations more directly related to Cartesian dialectical aims; and if, as I have suggested,
there is nothing in the weak sense of immediate justification
the opponents of foundationalist philosophy need have any
stake in denying; then we seem to have reached the twilight of
what has rightly been called the Cartesian period of philosophy.[33] A fitting time for Minerva's Owl and the heirs of Hegel.

   We still need to determine, of course, whether Will's view
of the interests and purposes behind Cartesian procedure
should be adopted. The only way to determine this, so far as
I know, is through historical inquiry. Will's view is, in fact,
already implicitly historical. If he is right, we should be able
to locate the origins of Cartesian philosophy in a historical context that made radical skepticism seem sufficiently cogent and
threatening to motivate a (more than minimally) foundationalist response. Moreover, the passing of Cartesian epistemology and of the central father figure of modern philosophy
should be explicable in terms of changes in context which have
eroded that motivation. In the next three chapters, I shall try
to tell a story along precisely these lines.

2. Placing the Father

Descartes's foundationalism was a human project governed by interests and purposes, which, to be understood, must be placed in a context of inherited traditions, impinging problems, and possible responses. From what traditions of thought and practice did Descartes draw his conception of himself and of his situation? To what problem or network of problems was he responding? With respect to what alternatives should his response be judged? Answers to these questions will not only help make Descartes intelligible as a historical figure, they will also help us see whether Descartes's problem is, in any important sense, *our* problem and, therefore, whether his response still demands the kind of attention it once did.

What, then, was Descartes's problem? We are tempted to answer simply: the problem of knowledge. And this sounds like a problem that could (and perhaps should) occupy any thinker at any point in history, one of the perennial problems of philosophy. But did Descartes have a problem with knowledge? It may seem trivial to point out that our term "knowledge" was not part of the Latin and French vocabulary of Descartes's thought, that his problem was not with *knowledge* but with *scientia*. This point would indeed be trivial if the former term is woven into our discourse in precisely the way the latter was woven into his. But what if the two terms are not strictly equivalent? What if the differences can be rendered intelligible only in a narrative tracing decisive changes in our epistemic vocabulary, changes which themselves reflect a major shift in the problems of cognitive practice? In that event, my point would not be trivial, talk of the "perennial problem of knowledge" would be misleading, and to understand Descartes in context might well be to liberate oneself from the compulsion to be Cartesian.

It is this possibility I wish to explore. I shall not say anything startlingly new about the historical facts. To the contrary, I want to stay as close as possible to established scholarship on Descartes's historical setting, introducing novelty only in my attempt to bring out the philosophical significance of the fact that Descartes wrote in his context and not ours.

Gilson and Koyré many years ago insisted on the importance of Descartes's links to the scholastic tradition.[1] For our purposes, one feature of Descartes's scholastic inheritance is especially important — the Aristotelian distinction between *scientia* and *opinio*. Edmund Byrne has demonstrated the centrality of this distinction in Aquinas's thought.[2] Ian Hacking has noted its broad impact on the thought of early modern Europe.[3] *Scientia,* usually translated without qualification as "knowledge" or "science," is the domain of demonstration. Demonstration is that mode of reasoning which displays necessary connections between a proposition and its principles, as when a geometrical proposition is deduced from or reduced to the first principles of geometrical science. All *scientia,* according to Aquinas, conforms to this deductive model. Even reasoning about cause and effect is conceived as an attempt to display the principle or the source of the effect, an attempt to show essences. We no longer think of causal investigations in this way, of course, but neither do we any longer think of geometrical demonstrations exactly as Thomas did,[4] and these differences are minor when compared with what separates us from Thomas's views on probability and opinion.

All that falls short of scientific demonstration is, for Thomas, mere opinion. "Taken negatively," Byrne writes, "*opinio* . . . connotes 'nondemonstrative,' or, perhaps better, 'not demonstrated.'"[5] Accordingly, one's adherence to an opinion "is based on criteria other than strict demonstration." Opinions must be judged more or less probable. But what is probability? It is not a matter of statistics. Nor is it a matter of evidence speaking up for itself, independently of sacred books and traditional testimony, on behalf of a hypothesis. Probability is a matter of what the authorities approve. Probability "refers to the authority of those who accept the given opinion; and from this point of view 'probability' suggests *approbation* with regard to the proposition accepted and *probity* with regard to the authorities who accept it."[6]

Why does Aquinas lean so heavily upon authority in the
domain of probable opinion? Hacking argues that no other
notion of probability was available in that time and place.
Full-fledged notions of statistical and evidential probability
came into European thought only in the second half of the
seventeenth century — only, that is, in the decades immediately following Descartes's death. Commenting on the implications of Byrne's work, Hacking writes:

> We may expect that an opinion is probable if there are good
> reasons for it, or if it is well supported by evidence. This is not
> the primary sense that Aquinas attaches to probability, and it is
> instructive to see why. In his mind reason and cause are very
> closely related. To comprehend the reason for p is to understand
> the cause, to understand why p. Causes in turn are to be found
> in the real definitions that underlie the science. That is, all
> reasons are demonstrative, because causes are necessary causes.
> We have come to think that deduction is only one way of giving
> reasons, and that much evidence falls short of deduction. For
> the medieval, evidence short of deduction was not really evi-
> dence at all. It was no accident that probability was not pri-
> marily a matter of evidence or reason. Probability pertains to
> opinion, where there was no clear concept of evidence. Hence,
> 'probability' had to mean something other than evidential
> support. It indicated approval or acceptability by intelligent
> people. Sensible people will approve something only if they have
> what we call good reason, but lacking an adequate concept of
> good reason Aquinas could handle only actual approval.[7]

So we encounter a great divide. On the one side, we find
matters susceptible to rigidly scientific demonstration in the
fashion of deductive proof. Only such matters qualify as
"knowledge," which is not explicated as justified true belief.
On the other side, we find matters of mere opinion, susceptible
at best to a kind of proof that rests on what the authorities
approve. Such matters differ completely from science. Thomas
even assigns these two domains to separate habits of the soul.[8]
    Such is the crucial epistemic distinction implicit in the
vocabulary Descartes inherited from his scholastic teachers,
and nothing he did in all his methodical doubt served to call
this distinction into question. But if the two basic categories
continued to be radically distinguished by major thinkers
throughout Descartes's lifetime, it cannot safely be said that
either *scientia* or *opinio* seemed an especially trustworthy
vehicle of thought and persuasion to anyone with a perceptive

eye in the late sixteenth or early seventeenth century. That Descartes can be understood as responding to the "skeptical crisis" of this period is by now a platitude. I want to suggest that this crisis, the setting of Descartes's dialectical problem, consists in the simultaneous disintegration of epistemic categories on both sides of the great divide. Descartes's problem was how to engage in responsible thought and effective persuasion when central categories were in such severe disrepair.

Since the late medieval period various factors had conspired to make trouble for *scientia*. The voluntarists' elevation of divine omnipotence and freedom threatened, as early as the fourteenth century, to narrow the scope of *scientia* to the point of triviality. What, asked Ockham and his followers, can be demonstrated, save the obvious implications of the law of non-contradiction, if God might be intervening at any point, creating the exceptional case or tinkering with the natural order of things? The Ockhamists' nominalistic empiricism raised further doubts, not so much as to the scope as to the possibility of *scientia*. Augustinian doctrines of human nature, especially as expressed by some Protestant Reformers and some Jansenists, added to such doubts still further grounds for limiting the claims made for *scientia*, particularly in ethics and theology. The tension between two strands in the Augustinian tradition — between Augustine's account of human fallenness and his confident Platonic rationalism — contributed heavily to the sense that a more cautious attitude toward *scientia* might be required. Moreover, the discovery and dissemination of ancient skeptical writings in the sixteenth and early seventeenth centuries gave rise to increasingly radical forms of modern skepticism. These writings suggested, in arguments all students of foundationalism know by heart, that any attempt to establish *scientia* will inevitably come to grief in either vicious circularity or infinite regress. Such arguments, originally used in the sixteenth century only in opposition to Protestant views of the rule of faith, before long broke free from Counter-Reformation polemics and fostered the notion that *scientia* is, quite simply, impossible.[9]

But if there were difficulties with *scientia*, doubts about its scope and possibility, these would in effect expand the domain of merely probable opinion. And this expansion would in turn place a heavy burden on the notion of authority, in terms of which probability was then construed. What is more, the notion of authority, now asked to shoulder more social and intellectual weight than ever, proved anything but stable. As competing authorities multiplied and began to diverge more and more sharply, conventional means for resolving disputes arising from such competition became less and less effective. Where probability is a matter of what the authorities approve, and the authorities no longer speak with one voice, it becomes anything but clear which opinions one should accept. This problem, which we may name "the problem of many authorities," is the central social and intellectual difficulty of the Reformation. The domain of *opinio*, no less than that of *scientia*, had entered the sphere of the doubtful.

Descartes had theories to construct and propound. But in what terms? His alternatives were relatively straightforward. He could, in the first place, submit to a sweeping form of skepticism, concluding both that *scientia* is impossible and that no opinion can finally be judged more or less probable than another with anything like good reason. This would be to abandon his intellectual hopes altogether, to conclude that there were no terms in which his theories could be constructed and propounded without failing to carry conviction or win reasonable assent. Short of this despairing conclusion, Descartes could only attempt to restore a major portion of the inherited epistemic vocabulary to health. His choice, of course, was to refurbish *scientia* and the related notion of demonstration. But to understand why this choice was reasonable we must deepen our understanding of why *opinio* must have seemed beyond repair. We therefore need to rehearse the sixteenth-century debate over the problem of many authorities, the crucial features of which are treated in Popkin's *History of Scepticism*. We may begin where Popkin begins, in Luther's Wittenberg, 1517.

Luther's Ninety-Five Theses were not grounded in a full-fledged critique of the traditional hierarchy of authorities. In fact, Luther's early arguments lean heavily on appeals to papal decrees and conciliar rulings. As Popkin sees it, "in the Ninety-Five Theses, and in his letter to Pope Leo X, he tried to show that, *judged by the standards of the Church for deciding such issues,* he was right, and certain church practices and the justifications offered for them were wrong."[10] But within only a few years, the momentum of the early protests carried Luther into a full-scale attack on the traditional rule of faith. It became increasingly difficult to give positive support to his conclusions by citing earlier papal decrees and conciliar rulings in their favor. This strategy could be used to shift the burden of proof to his opponents on specific points of controversy or to exploit specific instances of incoherence in his opponents' positions. But why should one papal decree or conciliar ruling count as positive support for Luther's position when there were obviously decrees and rulings that could be cited against his position as well? This question raises Luther's version of the problem of many authorities.

His solution was to narrow down the number of authorities he would recognize — the strategy of contraction. Aquinas himself had granted Scripture a privileged place at the top of his hierarchy of authorities. Luther would simply dispense with the hierarchy, leaving Scripture to stand on its own. The problem of many authorities cannot, by definition (according to Luther), arise with respect to truly *divine* authority. God's word is one. Papal decrees and conciliar rulings must therefore belong to the domain of merely human authority. They can support judgments of probable opinion, perhaps, but they do not have the authority of faith. Here is Luther relegating Christian tradition to the realm of mere opinion:

> . . . I saw that the Thomist opinions, whether they be approved by pope or by council, remain opinions and do not become articles of faith, even if an angel from heaven should decide otherwise. For that which is not asserted with the authority of Scripture or of proven revelation may be held as an opinion, but there is no obligation to believe it.[11]

Nor does Luther stop there. Referring to his examiners at the 1519 Leipzig disputation, he wrote:

> Here too, not to prove ungrateful to such learned men, I acknowledge that I have profited much from their labors. For while I (even then) denied the divine authority of the papacy, I still admitted its human authority. But after hearing and reading the super-subtle subtleties of these coxcombs, with which they so adroitly prop up their idol (the Pope) (for my mind is not altogether unchangeable in these matters), I now know for certain that the papacy is the kingdom of Babylon. . . .[12]

The pope is no authority at all, divine or human.

Now consider what may be Luther's most famous sentences, his refusal to recant at the Diet of Worms in 1521:

Unless I am convicted of error by testimony of Scripture or (since I put no trust in the unsupported authority of Pope or of councils, since it is plain that they have erred and often contradicted themselves) by manifest reasoning I stand convicted by the Scriptures to which I have appealed, and my conscience is taken captive by God's word, I cannot and will not recant anything, for to act against our conscience is neither safe for us, nor open to us. On this I take my stand. I can do no other. God help me.[13]

Notice that the problem of many authorities is precisely what is at issue here. Traditional authorities have often contradicted each other and themselves, so they must have erred, and this makes them undependable in matters as important as faith. Luther's solution is radical, designed to eliminate the possibility of those conflicts of authority that drain the certainty from faith: Scripture *alone* will be the rule of faith. The words *"sola scriptura"* thus became the battlecry of the Reformation.

But will Scripture do all by itself? Luther's critics, led by Erasmus of Rotterdam, argued that it will not. To begin with, since the time of Augustine, theologians had been finding more and more doctrinal points on which Scripture is silent.[14] More important, however, Scripture is by no means easy to interpret. Erasmus responded to the difficulties of scriptural interpretation by combining cautious skepticism with a reliance on traditional means for settling disputed points of interpretation. One cannot rely on Scripture alone, for Scripture does not interpret itself and many passages are unclear. This may mean that our faith falls short of certainty, but that, according to Erasmus, only goes to show the folly involved in the intellectual's quest for certainty. We should abandon that quest and rest content with the virtues of a simple faith and the guidance of tradition.[15]

Luther's response was that only certainty suffices in matters as crucial as faith. He argued, moreover, that all Christians have "the power of discerning and judging what is right or wrong in the matters of faith."[16] John Calvin, who led his own challenge to authority in the 1520s, made the Reformation's claim to certainty still more explicit, even while granting that he had no arguments capable of swaying his opponents. The faithful are illuminated through the activity of the Holy Spirit. The resulting inner persuasion consists in absolute certainty — certainty that Scripture alone is the rule of faith, certainty about what is revealed therein. Scripture is self-validating. Faith is self-authenticating.

From this point on, fruitful debate became more and more difficult. For many Reformers felt bound to interpret opposition to their views as evidence of God's decision to withhold illumination from some. The matter is beyond debate and in God's hands. It is in this spirit of inner persuasion that the Calvinists condemned the heretic Miguel Servetus to death for his anti-Trinitarian views. At least one Reformer, however, drew back from the claim of absolute certainty in the face of such intolerance. I refer to Sebastian Castellio of Basel, who sought to combine the Protestant tactic of contraction with a mildly skeptical attitude not entirely unlike that of Erasmus. Castellio trusted the human intellect a good deal more than Erasmus did, but agreed that many things pertaining to religion, including the interpretation of crucial scriptural passages, were too obscure to leave room for certainty. This was not, for Castellio, a reason to glorify simple Christian piety or simple-minded reliance upon tradition. It was, however, a reason to withdraw claims of absolute certainty, even while applying sound human judgment ever more diligently in the hope of learning more. As Castellio saw it, the presence of long-standing differences on religious issues could just as easily count as evidence against the Calvinist claim to certainty as it could count in favor of the Calvinist theory of illumination through the Holy Spirit. As for the heretics, "who is so demented that he would die for the denial of the obvious?"[17] The Calvinist theory of selective illumination can be sustained only *within* the Calvinist position taken as a whole.

What weakened the Reformers' dialectical position far more than the counterclaims of certainty made by heretics like Servetus was the extent of disagreement within their own camp. Who is right about Scripture: Luther, Calvin, Zwingli, or someone else? The Protestant appeal to the individual conscience and inner persuasion in effect produces yet another version of the problem of many authorities. But now we have far more authorities than before, for *every* man recognizes his own inner light. Every conscience constitutes a separate authority. We are left with no means to settle disagreements about matters of public importance. What started out as an appeal to the single authority of scriptural revelation now seems to recognize, implicitly at least, ten authorities in every pew. The potential for anarchy did not go unnoticed by the Catholic critics.

The greatest of these was François Veron of La Flèche.
Popkin introduces Veron with these words:

> ... Veron became so successful at debating and demoralizing
> Protestants, that he was freed of his duties as a teacher, and
> later from those of his order, so that he could be the official
> arguer for the Faith for the King of France. He was given free
> rein to attend Calvinist meetings and services, and to debate
> with Reformers, anywhere and anytime, always with the King's
> protection. Thus he rapidly became the scourge of the French
> Protestants who tried desperately to avoid him and his
> attacks.[18]

Paul Feyerabend, who has applied Veron's tactics in his own
battles with empiricism, recently restated the gist of Veron's
critique in a passage worth quoting at length:

> ... Luther and Calvin (1) declare Holy Scripture to be the
> foundation of all religion. This is the new Protestant Rule of
> Faith from which everything else is supposed to proceed. But
> we are also urged (2) to put aside, and never to use, what cannot
> be justified by this rule. Now this second step clearly voids the
> first, or to express it differently, the Protestant rule of faith as
> expressed in (1) and restricted in (2) is *logically vacuous.* The
> argument, briefly, is as follows.
>
> (a) The rule does not provide any means of identifying scrip-
> ture (no version of scripture contains a passage to the effect that
> "the preceding ... and the following ... pages are Scripture").
> We are told what the basis of the right faith ought to be; but we
> do not receive any indication of how we can find this basis
> among the many books and tales in existence.
>
> (b) Given scripture we do not know how to *interpret* it (no
> version of scripture contains a grammar and a dictionary of the
> language in which it is written. Such a grammar and such a
> dictionary are of course available, and often unnecessary; for
> example, they are unnecessary when we understand the lan-
> guage of the bible. But then our traditional understanding of a
> particular language is added to scripture whereas the rule of
> faith, and especially the second principle enounced above, wants
> scripture to be the only authority. We see how much more rea-
> sonable, *and human,* the Roman position had been).
>
> (c) Given scripture and a certain reading of it we have no
> means of deriving consequences (no version of scripture con-
> tains a logic or a more general system for the production of
> statements on the basis of other statements). Even if we recog-
> nize the basis of our faith, and even if we know how to interpret
> it, still we have no means of going beyond it, not in the simplest

> matter. For example, we cannot apply it to contemporary problems.[19]

The idea here is that one *cannot* give up tradition entirely, in favor of a single authority, even if one wants to. One needs to rely on traditional means even in reaching a judgment about what books belong to the canonical scriptures. The Calvinist appeal to inner persuasion merely begs the question. What we need to be told is how to tell genuine inner persuasion from the other kind. And this pushes us once again toward reliance upon traditional means. On the other hand, Veron's brilliant attack does not diminish the problem of many authorities to which the Protestant rule of faith had addressed itself. The problem of many authorities remains.

The most important moment in the Catholic response to the Reformation challenge came at the Council of Trent, which sat in three sessions between the years of 1545 and 1563. What happened there was not so much a justification of the Church's authority as an exertion of it. The challenge to authority was answered by conciliar fiat. Dogmas were defined. Differences from the Reformers were delineated sharply. Catholicism took on its modern shape. The intellectual standoff between Protestants and Catholics was soon to be played out at another level. For over a hundred years, beginning roughly at the end of the last session of the Council of Trent and continuing throughout most of the seventeenth century, Europe found itself embroiled in religious wars.

But if the Protestant strategy of radical contraction will not work, and if the traditional means can be used to assert authority but not to justify it, we should not find it surprising that appeals to authority were more likely to heighten conflict than to resolve it. The fragmentation of authority constituted a dialectical impasse of the first order, and gave the young Descartes, who as a student at La Flèche could take in Veron at first hand, legitimate grounds for treating all merely probable opinions with suspicion.

Descartes's discovery of doubt, though not always his means of expressing it, is standard fare for the period:

> I have been nourished on letters since my childhood, and since I was given to believe that by their means a clear and certain knowledge could be obtained of all that is useful in life, I had an extreme desire to acquire instruction. But so soon as I had

achieved the entire course of study at the close of which one is usually received into the ranks of the learned, I entirely changed my opinion. For I found myself embarrassed with so many doubts and errors that it seemed to me that the effort to instruct myself had no effect other than the increasing discovery of my own ignorance.[20]

As for philosophy, Descartes grants that "it has been cultivated for many centuries by the best minds that have lived," but regretfully concludes "that nevertheless no single thing is to be found in it which is not subject to dispute, and in consequence which is not dubious."[21] The difficulty signaled by the extent of philosophical disputation, of course, is the problem of many authorities, as Descartes goes on to say in the next sentence:

And also, considering how many conflicting opinions there may be regarding the self-same matter, all supported by learned people, while there can never be more than one which is true, I esteemed as well-nigh false all that only went as far as being probable.[22]

Probability still amounts to no more than approval by authorities, but the authorities are many, and they do not speak with one voice. To say that an opinion is probable might have been a way to recommend that opinion for Aquinas. But now the entirety of probable opinion has entered the sphere of the radically doubtful. All that is merely probable Descartes is prepared to deem "well-nigh false."

When Descartes speaks up on behalf of probability, he damns it with faint praise, and takes back with ironic inflection what he seems to give in the literal sense. The methods of probable reasoning are well suited for scholastic polemics and for sharpening the wits of youths. It is better, at any rate, to teach these methods than to leave the young to their own devices.

For thus through lack of guidance they might stray into some abyss; but as long as they follow in their master's footsteps, though they may diverge at times from the truth, they will yet certainly find a path which is at least in this respect safer, that it has been approved of by more prudent people.[23]

You have little assurance of discovering the truth through the methods of probable reasoning, but you will at least stay out of trouble with your teachers, whose opinions define probability. Probability is prudent, for students anyway. Descartes goes on to say, in effect, that probability loses even this advantage once one is freed from the prospects of schoolroom discipline.

> We ourselves rejoice that we in earlier years experienced this scholastic training; but now, being released from that oath of allegiance which bound us to our old masters, and since, as becomes our riper years, we are no longer subject to the ferule, if we wish in earnest to establish for ourselves those rules which shall aid us in scaling the heights of human knowledge, we must admit assuredly among the primary members of our catalogue that maxim which forbids us to abuse our leisure as many do, who neglect all easy quests and take up their time only with difficult matter; for they, though certainly making all sorts of subtle conjectures and elaborating most plausible arguments with great ingenuity, frequently find too late that after all their labours they have only increased the multitude of their doubts, without acquiring any knowledge whatsoever.[24]

Descartes releases himself not only from his oath of allegiance to his Jesuit teachers but also from dedication to the study of ancient authorities. He is happy to have worked on the ancients in his youth, but mainly because this has taught him "what in the various sciences is still left for investigation."[25] Faint praise quickly gives way to stern warnings:

> But yet there is a great danger lest in a too absorbed study of these works we should become infected with their errors, guard against them as we may. For it is the way of writers, whenever they have allowed themselves rashly and credulously to take up a position in any controverted matter, to try with the subtlest of arguments to compel us to go along with them. But when, on the contrary, they have happily come upon something certain and evident, in displaying it they never fail to surround it with ambiguities, fearing, it would seem, lest the simplicity of their explanation should make us respect their discovery less, or because they grudge us an open vision of the truth.[26]

Once again, the conflict among authorities is brought forward as the crucial symptom:

> . . . since scarce anything has been asserted by any one man the contrary of which has not been alleged by another, we should be eternally uncertain which of the two to believe. It would be no use to total up the testimonies in favour of each, meaning to follow that opinion which was supported by the greater num-

ber of authors; for if it is a question of difficulty that is in dispute, it is more likely that the truth would have been discovered by few than by many.[27]

The problem of many authorities reveals the unreliability of authority *per se*. Even if all the authorities agreed on some point, Descartes concludes, "what they teach us would not suffice for us."[28]

It is with this in mind that Descartes pins all his hopes on *scientia*, and begins the quest for certainty now associated with his name. He vows, "I ought no less carefully to withhold my assent from matters which are not entirely certain and indubitable than from those which appear to me manifestly to be false."[29] This is the step of Descartes's response to the skeptical crisis which, according to such antifoundationalists as Will, actually guarantees a skeptical result. For even the most sweeping forms of doubt are here declared innocent until proven guilty, and implicitly skeptical standards of judgment have therefore been assumed from the start. The category of *scientia* is the only available notion retaining strong enough connections with certainty and indubitability to be at all useful to Descartes once he has granted this much. Has something close to genuine *scientia* been achieved in any area of human inquiry? Only, Descartes concludes, in arithmetic and geometry, which can now become the model for all science. And Descartes remains optimistic (in all but a passage or two) that the tools are at hand for making all would-be science conform to a rigid standard of certainty.

> No doubt men of education may persuade themselves that there is but little of such certain knowledge, because, forsooth, a common failing of human nature has made them deem it too easy and open to everyone, and so led them to neglect to think upon such truths; but I nevertheless announce that there are more of these than they think — truths which suffice to give a rigorous demonstration of innumerable propositions, the discussion of which they have hitherto been unable to free from the element of probability.[30]

Where Descartes's project takes him from here is familiar territory to any modern philosopher: the *cogito*, the various arguments for God's existence, talk of mental eyes, and what Quine has called the "idea" idea. For Descartes, as for Luther before him, what most matters in life is no longer played out in the dimensions of community and tradition. One discovers truth in the privacy of subjective illumination, and this truth is underlined by a kind of self-certifying certainty. Community, tradition, authority: these have all started to give way to the individual, his inwardness, his autonomy. But we have already seen how the inner persuasion of the Reformers encountered a series of devastating criticisms to which little could be said in response.

A long tradition, often eclipsed from view (even, for much of its history, hidden from itself), has raised analogous questions about Cartesian subjectivity. The problem comes down to this: intuitive certainty looks useful only when not needed. When we need a disagreement settled, inner persuasion, whether philosophical or theological in kind, contributes nothing. Appealing to intuition as the basic tool for the reconstruction of *scientia,* Descartes lands in the same kind of dialectical corner as the Protestant proponents of inner persuasion. In both cases we want to know how to tell genuinely objective certainty from mistakenly heartfelt conviction. But we are told, in effect, that when it comes to objective certainty, either you have it or you don't. Rational disputation grinds to a halt, its gears stripped of what intersubjective norms of discourse would provide. Nothing goes further toward the undoing of Descartes's philosophy than the propositions he confidently presents as intuitive which most of us, several centuries later, are inclined to judge obviously false. This is true not because the propositions in question are essential to essential arguments in his philosophy, but rather because of what historical change tells us about the reliability of intuition, which *is* essential to his philosophy. Without it, his case against radical skepticism cannot be prosecuted.

But keep in mind above all else that, if Hacking is right, Descartes lacked our notion of nondemonstrative evidence, which did not become available until later in the seventeenth century. This means that part of what it is to place Descartes correctly is to place him *before* what Hacking calls the emergence of probability. The new probability, more than anything else, is what separates us from Descartes, making his problem — and therefore his response as well — seem dated. It was *reasonable* for Descartes, in a way it could not be for us, to view the category of probable opinion with the gravest kind of suspicion and to turn instead to the quest for certainty, even as a prelude to empirical inquiry.

The radical skeptic gives no assent whatsoever, not even assent of the most tentative kind, to any proposition or set of propositions that leaves any room for doubt. Or rather, that is how the radical skeptic describes himself. We want to say that one's degree of assent should be perfectly proportioned to the available evidence and that the available evidence might render a proposition probable, though not certain. There seems little question to us that we have more reason to accept such a proposition, even while granting that we may someday have good reason to change our minds, than to treat it as if it were "well-nigh false." Radical skepticism and Cartesian dogmatism alike seem unreasonable extremes. The former asks too much, the latter mistakenly tries to supply it — and in failing to do so makes radical skepticism look misleadingly good. Yet in thus brushing skeptics and Cartesians aside in a single stroke, we are the beneficiaries of the conceptual breakthrough of the 1660s. It is no accident that radical skeptics became hard to find after that decade, at least outside philosophy.

What made this breakthrough possible? This is the question I shall try to answer in the remainder of this chapter. We have seen that Descartes responded to the erosion of *scientia* and *opinio,* and to the doubts engendered by this erosion, by attempting to refurbish *scientia.* He rejected the domain of *opinio* as hopelessly tied up with the problem of many authorities, and fell back on an ancient ideal of demonstration, which he reworked in light of metaphors and concepts drawn from the Platonic-Augustinian tradition. Other thinkers, however, convinced that skeptical arguments are more powerful than Descartes's attempt to rebut them, sought instead less quixotic standards of judgment. This involved giving up on *scientia,* except perhaps as a distant ideal, while trying to salvage probable opinion. Popkin refers to such thinkers as "mitigated skeptics" — *skeptics* because they abandon claims to *scientia, mitigated* skeptics because they are content to settle for less, for the probable opinions certified by tradition or by what Castellio called "sound human judgment." It was the "constructive" strand in the tradition of mitigated skepticism derived from Castellio that helped prepare the way for the new probability, which required a theory of how sound human judgment might weigh the probability of an opinion without direct appeals to authority.

Consider William Chillingworth, Descartes's contemporary. Like Castellio before him, Chillingworth wanted the advantages of the Protestant response to the problem of many authorities but without the dialectical disadvantages of appeals to inner persuasion. So, once again like Castellio, he appealed to sound human judgment — the sort of judgment a thoughtful person reaches after fairly considering all features of the case at hand. He invokes the old distinction between knowledge and opinion, yet proceeds to distinguish grades of certainty ranging from absolute infallibility through conditional infallibility to moral certainty.[31] Chillingworth advances beyond Castellio mainly in articulating a notion of moral certainty that itself admits of degrees. Yet, as H. G. Van Leeuwen has pointed out, "Precisely where the lines are to be drawn between the several degrees of moral certainty . . . and what the standard is by which the degrees are measured, are not made clear."[32]

It is not simply that he fails to draw distinctions or measure degrees of credibility; for Chillingworth cannot say anything insightful about how the various features of a case are to be weighed in reaching a sound judgment. As Van Leeuwen puts it, "it is not clear whether certainty is wholly subjective — solely a matter of a feeling of confidence — or whether it is in some way objective — determined by features of the object believed."[33] Moreover, for Chillingworth, the degree of moral certainty appropriate to belief about a given matter of fact is still determined by "excellence of testimony."[34] Probable opinion, here under the title of moral certainty, remains a matter of testimony. Chillingworth's mitigated skepticism seeks an explication of sound human judgment, but is brought up short by the priority of authoritative testimony. He cannot yet say why one authority's testimony might be *intrinsically* more probable than another's. *Internal* evidence, in the sense distinguished at Port-Royal, has not yet arrived.

If the tradition of mitigated skepticism requires a clear notion of nondemonstrative evidence which does not involve direct appeal to authorities before the case against radical skepticism and Cartesian dogmatism can be made convincing, where did such a notion come from? Hacking's answer is that the Renaissance notion of *sign*, as understood by empirics like the physician Paracelsus, may be viewed as "something that is not probability but which was, through something like a mutation, transformed into probability."[35] Paracelsus takes what we would call a medical symptom as a sign to be read and interpreted. A symptom is like a word or sentence, not by dint of metaphor but by virtue of belonging to the same natural kind. For bodily symptoms, like all natural events, are part of a book authored by God. If nature is a book and God its author, then events, like linguistic expressions, are signs. To study them is to decipher meanings, to search for their real names. The firmament, writes Paracelsus, "is like a letter that has been sent to us from a hundred miles off, and in which the writer's mind speaks to us."[36]

It is easy to miss the import of this comment by reducing it to poetic flair. The distinction between natural and conventional signs arrived hand-in-hand with the new probability in the years flanking 1660. So Paracelsus is not taking two distinguishable kinds of thing and establishing an interesting analogy by calling them both *signs.* The word "smoke" is a sign of actual smoke, for him, in exactly the sense that real smoke is a sign of real fire. He is a century and more too early to see the distinction. Hacking argues that for us

> . . . the names of the stars are arbitrary and the points on the antler are not. For Paracelsus both are signs and there are true, real, names of things. He often rants against his contemporaries and the ancients who called things by their wrong names, having forgotten, perhaps in Babel or at The Fall, what the names really are. For example, Paracelsus knew that the metal mercury, in the correct dosage, would cure syphilis, and he thereby established medical practice for three centuries. He knew this despite the fact that his colleagues were killing their patients by randomly treating syphilitics, among others with mercury. Syphilis is signed by the market place where it is caught; the planet Mercury has signed the market place; the metal mercury, which bears the same name, is therefore the cure for syphilis.[37]

Here we have just one typical example of the medical reasoning of an earlier age. Our inclination is to find Paracelsus not merely bizarre or alien but guilty of irrationality. He prescribes cures that, time and time again, kill patients. He does not take these deaths as evidence against the proposition that mercury cures syphilis. Instead, he reasons in strange ways, reading signatures in the firmament, searching out the *real* names things had in paradise. Paracelsus reads the book of nature, searching for cures by getting God's signatures straight. Probability and testimony remain intertwined, but now, as Hacking puts it, "A new kind of testimony was accepted: the testimony of nature which, like any authority, was to be read. Nature now could confer evidence, not, it seemed, in some new way but in the old way of reading and authority."[38] Testimony, given this new twist, will become internal evidence before long.

We do not have too much farther to go. A natural event can now speak up on its own behalf; it need not await the testimony of an authority, either person or book. If nature is a book, it can give its own testimony, be an authority in its own right. Moreover, the connection between probability and statistical frequency is about to fall in place. For some of Paracelsus's contemporaries, convinced that some signs were more trustworthy than others, will seek the relevant distinctions in patterns of frequency.[39] The famous duality of probability is not far to find once nature speaks up for itself through signs that vary in reliability. Degree of evidential credibility will soon be linked to the calculated frequency of the sign's reliability — as modeled on games of chance. One difficulty, however, still needs to be overcome. Nature, construed as a book, can speak up for itself. But it remains one authority among many. The problem of many authorities seems as intractable as ever.

The crucial reversal, according to Hacking, is the work of Pascal and his associates at the Jansenist retreat in Port-Royal. The Port-Royal Jansenists, especially Antoine Arnauld, were strongly influenced by Descartes, in particular by his theory of ideas. It is not, however, his antiskeptical strategy that they find persuasive. In Pascal's fragments, we find a subtle interweaving of fideist and constructivist strands in the tradition of mitigated skepticism. The fideist strand is more important for understanding his theology; the constructivist is more important for understanding the emergence of probability. At times Pascal seems uncertain whether he wants a fideist stress on the necessity of faith as redemption from human folly and wretchedness or a constructive, optimistic portrayal of the habits of sound human judgment. It is perfectly clear, however, that he rejects both radical skepticism and Descartes's response. In Pascal's view, "humanly speaking, there is no such thing as human certainty, only reason" (#837).[40] He finds Descartes "useless and uncertain" (#887). Skeptical thinkers, like Montaigne and Charron, suffer from the "defects of a rigid method" (#780), a method Descartes in effect shares.

We should not, in other words, take the rigidly demonstrative knowledge of *scientia* too seriously.

> . . . [D]emonstration is not the only instrument for convincing
> us. How few things can be demonstrated! Proofs only convince
> the mind; habit provides the strongest proofs and those that
> are most believed. . . . [W]e must resort to habit once the mind
> has seen where the truth lies, in order to steep and stain our-
> selves in that belief which constantly eludes us, for it is too
> much trouble to have the proofs always present before us. We
> must acquire an easier belief, which is that of habit. (#821)

What, then, about probability? If probability is a matter of
what the authorities approve, then that will not do either.
Pascal compares reliance upon authority to reliance
upon hearsay:

> Hearsay is so far from being a criterion of belief that you should
> not believe anything until you have put yourself into the same
> state as if you had never heard it. It is your own inner assent
> and the consistent voice of your reason rather than that of
> others which should make you believe. (#505)

And he specifically rules out the use of authority in his attempt
to persuade others of the truth in important matters (#820).

Pascal does not, however, abandon probability. His decision is to try to loosen the connection between the notion
of probability and the question of what the authorities approve.
But, unlike Castellio, Pascal feels the need to say something
specific about sound human judgment, as this is reflected in
nondemonstrative reasoning:

> One must know *when* it is right to doubt, to affirm, to submit.
> Anyone who does otherwise does not understand the force of
> reason. Some men run counter to these three principles, either
> affirming that everything can be proved, because they know
> nothing about proof, or doubting everything, because they do
> not know when to submit, or always submitting, because they
> do not know when judgment is called for. (#170; my emphasis)

Pascal wants a middle way between the Cartesian quest for
certainty and the skeptical resignation that often grows out
of failure in that quest. We need to know *when* to doubt, to
affirm, to submit. That requires sound human judgment, an
ability to weigh evidence falling short of absolute proof. But
if the evidence falls short of absolute proof, and is not a matter
merely of authoritative testimony, in what does its evidential

status consist? What might a new notion of probability be?

Hacking underlines the duality of the new probability, its connection with statistical frequencies on the one side and with evidential credibility on the other. One of Pascal's major contributions is on the aleatory side — related, specifically, to the so-called problem of division. Suppose a game of chance has been interrupted. How shall we divide the stakes? Pascal's correspondence with Fermat on this problem brings us into the age when people fully understand averages, binomial coefficients, and the arithmetical triangle. More important for our purposes is Pascal's wager (#418) where, according to Hacking, decision theory was born. Pascal's accomplishment was to show how "the structure of reasoning about games of chance can be transferred to inference that is not founded on any chance set-up."[41] Decision theory

> is the theory of deciding what to do when it is uncertain what will happen. Given an exhaustive list of possible hypotheses about the way the world is, the observations or experimental data relevant to these hypotheses, together with an inventory of possible decisions, and the various utilities of making these decisions in various possible states of the world: determine the best decision.[42]

Pascal's interlocutor has a decision to make. Either he will choose the Catholic way of life in order to incline himself toward belief, or he will not. As for the way things are, either the God of whom Catholics speak exists, or he does not. How to decide? To reach a decision, Pascal argues, we need only add one more set of considerations — namely, the various utilities of making one decision or the other in the two possible states of affairs. Hacking summarizes the final stage of the argument:

> The decision problem is constituted by two possible states of the world, and two possible courses of action. If God is not, both courses of action are pretty much on a par. You will live your life and have no bad effects either way from supernatural intervention. But if God exists, then wagering that there is no God brings damnation. Wagering that God exists can bring salvation. Salvation is better than damnation. Hence the wager, "God is," dominates the wager, "He is not."[43]

Actually, as Hacking shows, this is but the first of three related arguments Pascal gives in #418. The important feature of these arguments for our purpose is that the premises are designed to make the actual likelihood of God's existence irrelevant or indecisive. So Pascal invents decision theory, but the wager calculates only utilities. The next, still more important, step will involve more explicit attention to (and even primitive calculation of) probabilities.

This next step was taken by the authors of *Logic, or the Art of Thinking.*[44] The authorship of the crucial chapters on probability remains uncertain, though Antoine Arnauld and Pierre Nicole were probably the major contributors. The *Logic* appeared in 1662, near the time of Pascal's death. As for deductive demonstration, Port-Royal stands pat on Descartes's *Rules for the Direction of the Mind.* The probability chapters, however, break new ground. Whereas Descartes had eschewed probable opinion, Port-Royal gives it a prominent place and seeks a "rule for the proper use of reason in determining when to accept human authority."

Chapter 13 of Part IV begins the treatment of probability. Its first nine paragraphs introduce the problem. The vocabulary is drawn entirely from the tradition of Castellio and Chillingworth. We must, in matters pertaining to everyday life, rely on sound human judgment. When we must decide whether to accept testimony as to the occurrence of an event, we ask initially whether the putative event is even possible. If so, we need to know whether we have grounds for believing or not. Nothing new so far. The tenth paragraph, however, asks exactly what should settle the issue. Then come two paragraphs in reply:

> In order to judge the truth of an (alleged) event, and to decide whether or not to believe it, it need not be considered abstractly (*nuement*) and in itself, as a proposition of geometry would be; but all the circumstances that accompany it, internal as well as external, need be considered. I call internal those circumstances pertaining to the fact itself; and external those pertaining to the people whose testimony leads us to believe it. This being done, if all the circumstances are such that similar circumstances never or very rarely accompany falsehood, our mind is naturally led to believe it is true; and it is right to be so led, above all in the conduct of life, which demands no greater certainty than this moral certainty, and which should content itself on a number of occasions with the greatest probability.
>
> But if, to the contrary, it is not the case that such circumstances are only seldom found in connection with falsehood, reason determines, either that we remain in suspense, or that we deem false what we have been told when we see no indication of its being true, even though we do not see an utter impossibility.

There follow several paragraphs in which this maxim is applied to a historical puzzle, a qualification is placed on application of the maxim, and further examples are considered. Chapters 14 through 16 apply the maxim to miracles, historical events, and predicting the future.

The treatment of miracles largely concerns the quality of testimony. We must avoid the two extremes of believing either all stories about miracles or none at all. Our standards of judgment must be neither too rigid nor too lax. And this means we must attend to specific details in each case, treating the details not in isolation but in conjunction. St. Augustine, as opposed to certain pagan authors, makes a good witness. First of all, we have evidence of Augustine's prudence, his desire for the success of Christian religion, and the public nature of many of the miraculous events to which he gives testimony. To give false testimony about matters so public would surely bring disgrace upon Christianity, which a prudent advocate would never do. Second, we have evidence from the rest of Augustine's career of his steadfast commitment to the truth. So Augustine's testimony can be accepted. Moreover, the events he describes are so wondrous that only God's intervention could explain their occurrence. Therefore, the external evidence and the internal evidence, when integrated in the right way, lead naturally to belief in certain miracles. That is, the quality of Augustine's testimony, combined with the nature of the events described, makes the hypothesis that these events were both actual and miraculous highly probable.

Chapter 15 relies not only on the distinction between internal and external evidence but also on the connection between the epistemological and aleatory sides of probability. Some combinations of circumstances are very rarely found in connection with falsehood. Others are very often found thus. And so on. This suggests that degrees of probability in the epistemological sense can be calculated. Notaries, who have high stakes in their own reputations, certainly post-date the contracts they notarize only very rarely. It is fair to say that no more than one out of every thousand contracts is post-dated. Therefore, if we have a contract before us but lack information about the characters of the notaries who witnessed its signing, the probability that the date is correct will be at least .999. To obtain information about the notaries, of course, would be to improve our epistemic standing. We could then adjust our calculation accordingly, depending upon *what* we found out. Evidence of criminal association might lessen the probability considerably. The chapter goes on to apply such reasoning to historical events.

The final chapter takes up future events — the question of what one ought to expect from the future, given limited evidence. But while this chapter ends with a statement of Pascal's argument from dominating expectation, the third argument deployed in the wager fragment, the *Logic* expresses as much interest in calculating probabilities as it does in utilities. The crucial phrase comes in the tenth paragraph: ". . . therefore, the fear of an evil (happening) ought to be proportionate not only to the magnitude of evil, but also to the probability of the event. . . ." The *Logic* does not, of course, tamper with Pascal's premises in presenting its version of the argument from dominating expectation. But it does assemble all the tools subsequent authors will use to determine the intrinsic probability of hypotheses relating to the existence of specific sorts of God, a matter to which we shall return in Part II.

Note well what has happened here. Not only has probability been calculated, it has been applied to crucial religious questions pertaining to miracles, the authenticity of testimony, and the problem of reconstructing history. As Hacking puts it, "The author not only counted degrees of probability but knew how to use them."[45] More important, the distinction between internal and external evidence has been drawn clearly. It is now possible, therefore, to treat the observed character of a natural event as a special, independent kind of evidence. From this point onward, external evidence — the testimony of authoritative persons and books — will be treated as evidence at one remove, as it were, second hand. And this forever alters the problem of many authorities. For if the authorities are many and fail to speak with one voice, we can judge the quality of their testimony both in light of frequency of reliability and in terms of the intrinsic likelihood of the factual claims put forward. Port-Royal, needless to say, does not carry this very far. The *Logic* does not calculate, for example, the probability of this or that kind of God. Nor does it make much of internal evidence when it considers Augustinian reports of miracles. But the Jansenists at Port-Royal do, thanks to these four slim chapters, open the door to another age.

What made the distinction between internal and external evidence possible? What made the distinction between the evidence of natural signs and the evidence of testimony seem like a difference in kind? We have seen that Paracelsus drew no distinction between natural and conventional signs, between the signatures written upon the firmament and the sorts of signs inscribed in books or uttered in verbal testimony. Hacking suggests, and here the influence of Michel Foucault is clear, that the distinction between internal and external evidence followed immediately upon the distinction — worked out in the years from 1640 to 1660 — between natural and conventional signs:

> Paracelsus, remember, classed words with comets, halos, and statues. He thought that the (true) names of the stars are signs in exactly the way in which the points on a stag's antlers signify the animal's age. Of course it had always been realized that we can choose names at will, but wilful names were not true signs at all. The physician, chemist and astronomer must aim first and foremost at discovering the correct names of things. There is no element of convention in that. The discovery that all names are conventional thunders us into modern philosophy.[46]

It is no accident that Arnauld was both the great grammarian of his century and an inventor of the new probability, or that the Port-Royal *Logic* includes the distinction between kinds of sign as well as between kinds of evidence. For if we can distinguish between the two kinds of sign, if it occurs to us that conventional signs are subject to arbitrary manipulation in a way natural signs are not, then we shall need two kinds of theory — one for inscriptions and utterances, the other for what natural events tell us about themselves.

> In the Renaissance there were signs, real signs, written by God on nature. People spoke with signs, but so did the world around us. The testimony of man and of nature was one. Then the sign became divided into "natural" and "arbitrary." . . . But just as there was required a theory of the conventional side of signs, so there was needed a theory of their natural side, which is internal evidence and probability.[47]

Once internal evidence has been distinguished from the testimony of persons and of books, once observation of a natural event seems to give a different *kind* of warrant to an opinion from that conferred by testimony, it becomes possible to assess testimony on relatively independent grounds. The authorities are many and they do not speak with one voice. How shall we decide among them? The answer, according to the Port-Royal *Logic,* is clear. We must consider all the circumstances surrounding not only the testimony at our disposal but also the events in question themselves. This procedure will make our opinions probable.

Notice the reversal. Our opinions are no longer made probable by virtue of what the authorities approve. Our opinions about which authorities ought to be followed are now rendered more or less probable largely by *our* judgments about *internal* evidence.

The Port-Royal *Logic* was but one part of an explosion of theorizing on probability in the second half of the seventeenth century, an explosion Descartes had no way to anticipate when he eschewed the merely probable as "well-nigh false." The new probability, often connected with Chillingworth's theory of moral certainty, immediately became central to the practice of the new "science." *Scientia,* despite its etymological associations, became the name for an increasingly distant and irrelevant ideal.

3. Displacing the Father

I have thus far been treating Descartes as a historical figure whose accomplishment must be understood as a response, chosen on reflection from among the available alternatives, to a "prephilosophical" problem. As Richard Rorty has put it, Descartes was "fighting (albeit discreetly) to make the intellectual world safe for Copernicus and Galileo."[1] He had, moreover, a specific version of mathematical physics to defend, one that incorporated his own most original discoveries and took inspiration from the mystical vision of his twenty-third year.[2] His problem was how to be genuinely persuasive (to himself as well as to others), given the "skeptical crisis" which was the European intellectual's dialectical predicament in the early seventeenth century. I have tried to show that Descartes's decision, in response to this problem, to eschew the merely probable was, under the circumstances, not unreasonable. But it will be obvious that my motives in so "placing" Descartes are not entirely innocent with respect to the figure of the father. For I have also suggested that the "skeptical crisis" which constituted the "prephilosophical" problem motivating Cartesian philosophy ceased to exist when the new probability caught on in the second half of the seventeenth century. As the new probability was integrated into scientific practice, doubts about *scientia* were bound to seem less urgent and the difficulties of Descartes's antiskeptical strategy mattered less. It began to make considerably more sense to seek not absolute certainty, but a strength of assent perfectly proportioned to the evidence.

Ian Hacking has written that "Descartes and Gassendi were both apostles of the new science, but they were pulling in opposite ways."[3] Descartes was pulling it toward *scientia*, Gassendi toward probability. The latter's doubts about the

Cartesian quest made him a skeptic as a young man, but the emergence of probability later made skepticism seem to him the wrong conclusion to draw. Suddenly the ancient distinction between knowledge and opinion had been blurred: "We use the expressions 'to have an opinion' and 'to know' interchangeably. . . ."[4] So wrote Gassendi less than a decade after Descartes's death. Henceforth, radical skepticism increasingly became a matter of merely academic interest — a concern for philosophers, but not an impediment to the new science. Moral certainty and high probability were good enough for Gassendi and, as Van Leeuwen has shown,[5] for Boyle, Newton, and Chillingworth's followers in the Royal Society of London. As it happened, the chief vehicle for the transmission of Cartesian ideas by the end of the century was none other than the Port-Royal *Logic*, which as a widely used textbook did more for the *bon sens* of the new probability than for the method of hyperbolic doubt.[6]

It needs now to be added that Descartes's response to his own dialectical problem created *new* problems — problems which were in turn responsible for the irony that, just as radical skepticism ceased to be a major cultural concern, it became the *philosophical* concern *par excellence*. For the "idea" idea, which Descartes had invented for his own antiskeptical purpose but which nonetheless was given a major role to play in the Port-Royal *Logic* and in Locke, gave rise to its own, still more radical, forms of skepticism. When philosophers and scientists started to become more easily distinguishable in the eighteenth and nineteenth centuries, scientists ignored radical doubt as beside the point while getting on with the business of keeping strength of assent in line with strength of evidence. Meanwhile, philosophers began to take preoccupation with the implicitly skeptical subjectivity of the veil of ideas as their own professional obligation and distinguishing mark. The triumph of this self-image was made possible by a series of developments leading from Descartes to Kant, was secured in the metaphilosophy and historiography of Kant's followers in the later nineteenth century, and was reinforced by analysts and phenomenologists in the twentieth. The upshot of philosophy's differentiation and professionalization and of the specific historical conditions in which this process was carried out was the orthodox picture of philosophy as a foundational discipline with epistemology as its most basic part. This picture was complemented by the story that makes Descartes, who did not think of himself as a philosopher in the modern sense at all, the father of modern philosophy. I shall not, however, try to narrate the rise of modern philosophical orthodoxy here,[7] but will instead turn briefly to the dynamics of the corresponding heresies — the struggle to overcome Descartes's influence, to displace the father. If we have in fact reached the twilight of the Cartesian period, how was it that Descartes's influence was diminished and finally resisted?

To answer this question, I shall borrow some categories from our most provocative theorist of literary influence, Harold Bloom. I am, for present purposes, more interested in Bloom's categories — his descriptions of the literary devices poets use to struggle with the influences of their precursors — than in his Nietzschean and Freudian speculations on the psychology of anxiety or in such dubious Bloomian doctrines as the view that *all* reading is misreading.[8] But Bloom is right in holding that critical understanding is largely the art of knowing the "hidden roads" that go from one text to another,[9] and it seems to me that he has followed the hidden roads of modern poetry with great descriptive insight. I hope to show that his categories may have considerable utility well beyond the confines of poetic theory and that this fact, if it is indeed a fact, raises interesting questions about the relations between modern poetry and philosophy and about why influence might be a source of anxiety for those who take Descartes and Milton as their fathers.

Bloom's theory, simply stated, is that father is the necessity of invention. Strong poets must accomplish something new. But to do this, they must struggle to overcome the influence of their most powerful precursors. One becomes a poet by being gripped by another poet. The artistic problem, for the strong poet at least, is to transcend indebtedness to the precursor, which would express itself in mere imitation. Artistic creation is therefore largely a struggle against influence and is born in the anxiety of having been influenced. Poetry can be read, then, as involving mechanisms of defense against the power of earlier poems. Bloom's categories offer a typology of such mechanisms — "revisionary ratios" or "tropes upon the precursor's tropes."

If there has in fact been a struggle to overcome Descartes's influence as chief progenitor of "modern philosophy," it would be interesting to find something like the poetic mechanisms of defense in philosophical writing as well. And I have already hinted at this possibility by using two of Bloom's categories in my treatment of Will and Alston in chapter 1. Will executes his *clinamen* with respect to Descartes, his swerve away from the father's influence, by refusing to take Descartes's first step in the duel with skepticism — by refusing, that is, to allow the skeptic his own choice of weapons. Acceptance of radical doubt tilts the contest in the skeptic's favor from the start. Fairer terms would disarm the skeptic and make the elaborate procedures of Cartesian self-defense unnecessary. Will was not the first, of course, to articulate this response to Descartes's foundationalism. Descartes's earliest critics, Pascal included, made much the same point. But I have tried to show how the rationale of the Pascalian *clinamen* was fortified by the emergence of the new probability.

Alston's criticisms of Will, I argued, can be viewed as a *tessera* with respect to Descartes. For the minimal foundationalism Alston proposes as a possible alternative to Will's antifoundationalism seems to restore the possibility of continuity with the precursor but in fact loses contact with Cartesian dialectical aims altogether. Descartes's metaphor of "foundations for knowledge" is retained but deprived of its original role as part of a strategy for repulsing skeptical assault by *reconstructing* the edifice of knowledge on foundations of *certainty*. Such marks of certainty as indubitability and incorrigibility, and even the image of reconstruction itself, are declared inessential to the foundationalist position. We are left with the confusing image of a building the foundations of which can be in constant flux, and without reason for preferring this image to the Neurathian metaphors Will finds more illuminating. We are also urged to abandon the imagery Descartes used as a model for the kind of certainty a foundational belief should possess — the notion of a mental eye which brings the objects immediately given to it into clear and distinct focus. The Platonic-Augustinian metaphor of knowledge as vision, on which Descartes worked his variations, falls away. Only a truncated notion of immediate justification remains.

Yet this *tessera*, by only barely disguising the extent of its discontinuity with the precursor's original intent, does at least force us to confront more squarely the question of what is "essential" to foundationalism. I have tried to show that this question leads in turn to questions one can answer only by "placing" the precursor in his historical context — questions about how his project, including his choice of metaphors, can be rendered intelligible as a human response to the problems and traditions impinging upon him. I now hope to bring out how historical "placement" of foundationalism can itself be "a movement toward discontinuity with the precursor" of the kind Bloom discusses under the heading *kenosis*.[10]

"Placing" Descartes's philosophical endeavor may sound like nothing but a favor, the charity that strives for better understanding. It is a favor, of sorts, but it can also be an operation self-consciously designed to break the compulsion to be Cartesian. We both distort the precursor and place ourselves in his shadow by raising him above his age. To be free of him, we must put him in his place, place him back in his age. To place him is to displace one source of his power over us — namely, his own claim to have transcended the influence of tradition.

This is not to say that Descartes was no genius, but only that genius, to be understood, must be given a context of problems and choices. Talk of genius tends to mystify, to inflate the precursor beyond understanding, to divinize. Then the presence of the precursor cannot be avoided, and the repetition begins. No precursor can be avoided until his godhood has been voided. *Kenosis* is the method of deflation. We need to bring Descartes back to earth. That would do him the favor, if it is a favor, of better understanding him (by making the categories of understanding relevant again). It would do us the favor of diminishing the shadow he casts. If Descartes "transcends his age," as the saying goes, that is because his problems and choices endure. If they do not, we can safely keep our distance.

If anyone could transcend his age in the strongest sense, Descartes could. That is our problem. To deflate Descartes, we must also deflate ourselves. We must say that by virtue of being human we are all *situated* more radically than poets and philosophers typically pretend. Descartes *seemed* to transcend his situation in part because he thought he could. Historicism says he could not because no one can. That means we cannot. The first step toward discontinuity with the precursor is to empty *oneself* of the hope for a perspective above history.

Bloom has this to say about *kenosis*:

I take the word from St. Paul, where it means the humbling or emptying-out of Jesus by himself, when he accepts reduction from divine to human status. The later poet, apparently emptying himself of his own afflatus, his imaginative godhood, seems to humble himself as though he were ceasing to be a poet, but this ebbing is so performed in relation to a precursor's poem-of-ebbing that the precursor is emptied out also, and so the later poem of deflation is not as absolute as it seems.[11]

The historicist humbles himself by confessing his own historicity — his finitude. In so doing, he may seem to cease to be a philospher, though only because the search for absolute foundations, the perspective of eternity, has been taken for so long as the essence of the philosopher's task. To deny the possibility of transcendental perspective therefore seems antiphilosophical. And indeed the risk of *kenosis,* in philosophy as in poetry, is that one will find nothing appropriately humble to do when the *kenosis* itself has been carried through. The genre seems to destroy itself. The difficulty is to avoid obsession with the "end," to find (as Wittgenstein put it) a suitable "heir" to the newly dead.

The point of *kenosis,* of course, is not only to humble oneself but also to humble the precursor as he would rather not be humbled. This "ebbing," as Bloom writes, must be "so performed in relation to a precursor's poem-of-ebbing that the precursor is emptied out also." Descartes's *Meditations* — and, for that matter, such works as Kant's first *Critique* — must be made to seem historically conditioned in ways that belie the author's claims to transcendence. "However plangent or even despairing the poem of *kenosis,*" Bloom notes, "the ephebe takes care to fall soft, while the precursor falls hard."[12] The historicist falls from the perspective of eternity, but onto a bed of humbled assumptions. This is where he expects to land and where he thinks he belongs. The precursor falls, also from eternity or the hopes thereof, but onto hard ground. The fall dashes expectations to which he has tied his quest and without which this quest comes to nothing.

Descartes's quest for certainty was born, I have argued, in a flight from authority. The crisis of authority made an absolutely radical break with the past seem necessary. Methodical doubt therefore sought complete transcendence of situation. It tried to make the inheritance of tradition irrelevant, to start over again from scratch, to escape history.[13] But is this possible?

Descartes, according to Alasdair MacIntyre, "radically misdescribes" his own epistemological crisis, "and thus has proved a highly misleading guide to the nature of epistemological crises in general." What goes wrong?

> First of all he does not recognise that among the features of the universe which he is not putting in doubt is his own capacity not only to use the French and Latin languages, but even to express the same thought in both languages; and as a consequence he does not put in doubt what he has inherited in and with these languages, namely, a way of ordering both thought and the world expressed in a set of meanings. . . .
> What thus goes unrecognised by Descartes is the presence not only of languages, but of tradition — a tradition that he took himself to have successfully disowned. It was from this tradition that he inherited his epistemological ideals. . . . Thus Descartes also cannot recognize that he is responding not only to the timeless demands of scepticism, but to a highly specific crisis in one particular social and intellectual tradition.[14]

To say what MacIntyre says here is to bring Descartes down to earth and to separate oneself from him temporally. Descartes fails to transcend the problems and alternatives of his age; those problems, and therefore his choices, need not be ours. Descartes fails because anyone must fail at that. It is like wanting to be one's own father.[15]

Before the age of Gilson, Descartes often seemed like a completely novel departure in the history of thought. But consider Valéry's warning:

> We say that an author is *original* when we cannot trace the hidden transformations that others underwent in his mind; we (should) say that the dependence of *what he does* on *what others have done* is excessively complex and irregular. There are works in the likeness of others, and works that are the reverse of others, but there are also works of which the relation with earlier productions is so intricate that we become confused and attribute them to the direct intervention of the gods.[16]

Historical investigation in the tradition of Gilson has gone a long way toward dispelling any such confusion in Descartes's case. Descartes can now be located squarely within the Platonic-Augustinian tradition. Indeed, it was this tradition which supplied most of the concepts and images he used in his attempt to transcend all tradition. Once the unacknowledged debt is recognized, it should no longer be surprising that the attempt did not succeed. It was inherently paradoxical — and self-deceptively so.

"Placing" the precursor historically has the added benefit of bringing competing traditions, which had tended to be eclipsed by the precursor's inflated stature, into view. When the precursor's achievement is treated as a response to a problem, this particular response can be juxtaposed with other responses actually found in the historical record — responses which, once given their due, can command respect at the precursor's expense. Thus do Chillingworth, Arnauld, and Gassendi gain stature as Descartes shrinks to merely human proportions. Bloom speaks of *daemonization,* a "movement towards a personalized Counter-Sublime, in reaction to the precursor's Sublime."

> The later poet opens himself to what he believes to be a power in the parent-poem that does not belong to the parent proper, but to a range of being just beyond that precursor. He does this, in his poem, by so stationing its relation to the parent-poem as to generalize away the uniqueness of the earlier work.[17]

Daemonization functions "by absorbing the precursor more thoroughly into tradition than his own courageous individuation should allow him to be absorbed."[18] Not only does Descartes's problem belong to a specific epoch now past, not only is his response to this problem more decisively shaped by tradition than he can afford to allow, but his problem's eventual dissolution must be credited to the labors of a competing tradition — the proponents of probability.

Only two of Bloom's central categories remain. But if we could not find within contemporary philosophy authentic parallels to the final ratios of Bloom's typology, I could not help suspecting that Descartes's influence had not really been overcome, that the truly strong sons of this father were still to be born. Yet I think we can see, in Wittgenstein and in Heidegger, the closing of the circle and of the Cartesian period — fitting applications for the categories of *askesis* and *apophrades.*

Bloom defines *askesis* in these words:

> . . . A movement of self-purgation which intends the attainment of a state of solitude. . . . The later poet does not, as in *kenosis,* undergo a revisionary movement of emptying, but of curtailing; he yields up part of his own human and imaginative endowment,

so as to separate himself from others, including the precursor, and he does this in his poem by so stationing it in regard to the parent-poem as to make that poem undergo an *askesis* too; the precursor's endowment is also truncated.[19]

I take Wittgenstein to be executing an *askesis* in reference to Descartes and also in reference to the entire Platonic-Augustinian tradition unconsciously carried on by Descartes. That Augustine appears as a major antagonist at the beginning of the *Investigations* is surely no accident. But the movement of *askesis* requires the solitude of inner dialogue. Historical references are therefore for the most part deeply allusive, brought *within* a dialectic of self-purgation. In this dialectic, the solipsism always implicit in the veil of ideas is pressed to its extreme and finally undone. The metaphors of Platonic-Augustinian metaphysics and epistemology — the metaphors Descartes failed to question — are subjected to ruthless examination, handed over to thought experiments that threaten the security of the intuitive. The familiar language of *presence* and *representation,* of *subject* and *object,* of knowledge as *vision,* is radically curtailed. No *askesis* has ever been undergone more thoroughly or in the face of more risk. *Askesis,* in Wittgenstein as in Stevens, goes as far as one can go into the hopeless solipsism of dualism — the inwardness that loses the presence of the object and retains only representations, the phenomenal without noumenal reality, the subjective without objective contact. The world is lost. But dualism, taken to this extreme, consumes itself (and consumes the philosophical self given to dualism as well).[20] The world lost was well lost, "a world without kinds or order or motion or rest or pattern — a world not worth fighting for or against."[21] A world worth having returns.

Dualism gives way, in *apophrades,* to the theme of belated arrival, to the sense that *we* have come too late to be philosophers. This is what Heidegger expresses when he speaks of "the end of philosophy" and what Wittgenstein expresses when he aims for the "dissolution" (and not the solution) of philosophical problems. Bloom describes *apophrades,* or "the return of the dead," as follows:

> The later poet, in his own final phrase, already burdened by an imaginative solitude that is almost a solipsism, holds his own poem so open again to the precursor's work that at first we might believe the wheel has come full circle, and that we are

back in the later poet's flooded apprenticeship, before his strength began to assert itself in the revisionary ratios. But the poem is now *held* open to the precursor, where once it *was* open, and the uncanny effect is that the new poem's achievement makes it seem to us, not as though the precursor were writing it, but as though the later poet himself had written the precursor's characteristic work.[22]

This is, roughly, what the history of philosophy becomes at Heidegger's hand, as he makes even the ancient dead return on cue to speak their lines as if Heidegger had written them. Suddenly, all the precursors, from Plato onward, seem to be speaking the same language of dualistic imagery that Wittgenstein's *askesis* curtails.

Bloom sees the truly strong modern poets as preoccupied with their own belatedness.[23] To be a modern poet is to be, sometimes to the point of terrible pain, *after* Milton. Western philosophers, likewise, are *after* Descartes, *after* Plato, and essentially so. The poetic movement from *askesis* to *apophrades*, according to Bloom, is typically "an imagistic movement from inside/outside polarities to early/late reversals."[24] A similar movement is clearly exhibited in the philosophical transition from Cartesian dualism (in any of its forms) to the historicism of Hegel, Dewey, and Heidegger. It is equally present, though more latently, in the images of belatedness that periodically interrupt Wittgenstein's *askesis*.

This and the other similarities between modern poetry and philosophy suggested by my application of Bloom's categories raise several interesting questions. Why, for example, are both poets and philosophers in the modern period so drawn to polarities between the inner and the outer? Surely, the answer to this question must lie in the common traditions out of which modern poetry and philosophy arose. The Romantic poetry that has always been Bloom's central concern has been called "a continuation of Protestantism by other means." One need only think of Coleridge to begin to understand why. Perhaps the point goes deeper. Bloom has portrayed Milton as the Romantic tradition's great father figure. Shakespeare, according to Bloom, wrote before "the Flood" — before, that is, Milton transformed the universe.[25] Influence has been a source of poetic anxiety ever since. But why did influence become a problem at just this point in history? Bloom does not say. Taking a more broadly historical view of the matter, however, we can see that both Milton and Descartes were using resources, made available to them for the most part by sixteenth-century Augustinians, to create an inner refuge from the turbulence of seventeenth-century Europe. They were, in effect, taking Protestant inwardness a step further, widening the gap between inner and outer reality, and radicalizing the solipsistic tendencies of various metaphors whose roots can be traced deep into our Greek and Christian past.

When Milton wrote poetically of that "Paradise within thee, happier far" or theologically of the "supreme authority . . . of the Spirit, which is internal and the individual possession of each man,"[26] and when Descartes took the image of knowledge as vision behind the veil of ideas, they were both reworking themes from the Augustinian tradition, themes which had been given fresh expression in the previous century's struggle with traditional authority. These men thus helped create the potentially solipsistic intuitions with which the theologians, poets, and philosophers have been doing battle ever since. This historical background explains why *askesis,* the overcoming of an inner/outer polarity inherited from the precursor, is, in Bloom's phrase, "the contest proper"[27] — and also why the anxiety of this particular influence should become prominent only after the Flood. Moreover, if we view the retreat to inner persuasion as an attempt to escape the problem of influence implicit in the seventeenth century's crisis of authority, we can see why the fact of influence — its unavoidability — should create anxiety in modern writers. Descartes asked himself, "By whom should I be influenced?," and, given the fragmentation of authority, concluded that he had better be influenced by no one. Since the attempt to escape influence, to negate the ways in which one has been shaped by the inheritance of a tradition, is also an attempt to escape history, it should not be surprising that genuinely *historical* thinking plays a crucial, but essentially antithetical, role in modern letters. Historicism, with its imagery of early and late and its sense of belated arrival, is the deconstruction of an intellectual tradition for which the fact of influence must remain a paradox and a source of anxiety.

Stanley Cavell has written that

Innovation in philosophy has characteristically gone together with a repudiation — a specifically cast repudiation — of most of the history of the subject. But in the later Wittgenstein (and, I would now add, in Heidegger's *Being and Time*) the repudiation of the past has a transformed significance, as though containing the consciousness that history will not go away, except through our perfect acknowledgment of it . . . and that one's own practice and ambition can be identified only against the continuous experience of the past.[28]

The historical fact that I have been and will continue to be influenced will not go away. But a more nearly perfect acknowledgment of history can at least help me liberate myself from specific kinds of self-deception I inherit from the tradition that would rather not have to be a tradition at all — the *traditio* for which the given has not been *handed over by someone* but is rather the unmediated presence of reality itself.

Heidegger, according to Richard Rorty, made his "greatest contribution" to philosophy by helping us view notions like the "foundations of knowledge" as "the fruit of the Greek (and specifically Platonic) analogy between perceiving and knowing."[29] Heidegger's work suggests "that the desire for an 'epistemology' is simply the most recent product of the dialectical development of an originally chosen set of metaphors," metaphors which are "optional" in the sense that they can be left behind when they become "outworn." Rorty continues:

To describe this development as a linear sequence is of course simplistic, but perhaps it helps to think of the original dominating metaphors as being that of having our beliefs determined by being brought face-to-face with the object of the belief (the geometrical figure which proves the theorem, for example). The next stage is to think that to understand how to know better is to understand how to improve the activity of a quasi-visual faculty, the Mirror of Nature, and thus to think of knowledge as an assemblage of accurate representations. Then comes the idea that the way to have accurate representations is to find, within the Mirror, a special privileged class of representations so compelling that their accuracy cannot be doubted. These privileged foundations will be the foundations of knowledge, and the discipline which directs us toward them — the theory of knowledge — will be the foundation of culture. . . . The neo-Kantian consensus thus appears as the end-product of an original wish to substitute *confrontation* for *conversation* as the determinant of our belief.[30]

What fostered the "original wish" behind Descartes's use of this imagery? It makes sense that one would want to substitute something for conversation when social and intellectual forces conspire to make conversation break down. Descartes turned to the image of knowledge as vision — and to the myth that something must be *immediately given* to the eye of the mind if genuine knowledge is possible — when he became convinced that ordinary (conversational) appeals to traditional sources of insight (the authorities) had proven inherently and fatally problematical. Only sheer confrontation with the object of knowledge, unmediated by the inheritance of tradition, would secure reasonable assent in the face of skeptical objections that then seemed plausible.

But if it now seems clear that Veron was right when, in his refutation of the Protestant rule of faith, he declared the inheritance of tradition indispensable, and if it seems equally clear the Veron's arguments are as telling against Cartesians as they were against Protestants, how can we avoid the conversational impasses to which Veronian traditionalism is prone in times of crisis? Does not Veron's appeal to tradition leave us with the very authoritarianism which brought on the crisis Descartes and others quite rightly sought to resolve? Were not the proponents of *internal* evidence trying, every bit as much as Descartes had, to circumvent the appeal to traditional authority by supplying epistemic considerations they thought to be more *basic?*

It is worth recalling at this point that the authors of the Port-Royal *Logic* were reaching for a theory of rational tradition, that despite their commitment to the "idea" idea, they did not follow Descartes toward antitraditionalism. They wanted a notion of tradition rich enough to account for why the testimony of one or another authority should be accepted. Unfortunately, when the notion of internal evidence was taken over by the empiricist tradition and explicated in terms of Locke's version of the "idea" idea, the suggestion that natural events can speak up on their own behalf without mediation by the testimony of persons and books seemed to beg for completion in a new kind of foundationalism. To empiricist eyes, internal evidence and the first cognitions of sense seemed made for each other. So long as empiricism thrived, the notion of rational tradition was bound to seem hopelessly paradoxical. But when the analogues to Veron's criticisms of Protestant inner persuasion are brought to bear on the empiricist transformation of Cartesian philosophy, it becomes clear that the notion of rational tradition may have represented the more promising point of departure for understanding internal evidence after all.

There is indeed no reasonable way back to the authoritarianism of the Counter-Reformation. We can, however, be Veronians with a difference if we view rational tradition as (in Sellars's phrase) "a self-correcting enterprise which can put *any* claim in jeopardy, though not *all* at once."[31] A neo-Veronian would maintain the inescapability and indispensability of tradition, but he would treat traditions as historical entities capable of substantial change when faced with new problems, altered circumstances, interior disintegration, and external challenge. And he would recognize no transcendental restriction, whether by appeal to external authority or to inner persuasion, on the continuing process of critical revision. Thus, on the one hand, the claims of traditional authority would be accorded no special epistemic privilege and would instead be subject to critical assessment and possible rejection. Nor, on the other hand, would claims of some other kind, of say the "immediately given" presentations of sense, be granted the special forms of epistemic immunity they have enjoyed in foundationalist philosophy.

From this vantage point we can see, as Feyerabend pointed out in his discussion of Veron,[32] that both theological and philosophical antitraditionalists retained precisely the feature of authoritarian traditionalism that made it vulnerable in the first place — its insistence on bestowing epistemic privilege. Their divergence from the proponents of traditional authority merely substituted one class of privileged claims for another. They were in Weberian terms, exchanging traditional authority for charismatic inwardness. They were not disputing the epistemic necessity of *something like* sacred authority.

How, then, should the priority of internal over external evidence be explicated if not as the epistemic privilege made possible by "greater proximity to the immediately given"? Beyond saying that it reflects one of the seventeenth century's reasonable alterations of the norms we inherit as part of our epistemic tradition, it need not be explicated at all. The relaxation of epistemological concern implied in this conclusion becomes possible, of course, only after the imagery of the seventeenth century has lost its grip. I have tried in this chapter simply to describe some of the devices by means of which thought in our century has tried to work itself free — not free from tradition, but free from the metaphors of another age's attempt to escape it. Could it be that philosophy moves along

not so much by proof and disproof as by a kind of poetic struggle with a legacy of traditional metaphors? Perhaps that is why
Wittgenstein spoke of the source of philosophical perplexity as
a "picture which held us captive."

4. Explicating Knowledge

As Michael Dummett sees it, the Cartesian period of philosophy ended with Frege.

> Because philosophy has, as its first if not its only task, the analysis of meanings, and because, the deeper such analysis goes, the more it is dependent upon a correct general account of meaning, a model for what the understanding of an expression consists in, the theory of meaning, which is the search for such a model, is the foundation of all philosophy, and not epistemology as Descartes misled us into believing. Frege's greatness consists, in the first place, in his having perceived this.[1]

Descartes made epistemology the basic level of inquiry for generations of philosophers, but Frege made the theory of meaning seem more basic still. It is easy to see why epistemology might seem basic. If I want to know what we know about God, the moral law, or the structure of the universe, it would seem that I need first of all to learn what knowledge is and whether knowledge is possible, and these are the central topics of epistemology. Whether knowledge is possible, of course, depends on what knowledge is, on what kind of standard we invoke when awarding the title. But how can we tell what knowledge is? After Frege, this has seemed more and more like a question in the theory of meaning, a question, to be specific, about the meaning of the expression "knowledge." How should we explicate "knowledge"?

The displacement of epistemology at the basic level of philosophical inquiry was, however, less total than some (but not all) of Dummett's remarks imply. How one explicates "knowledge" depends in turn on how one explicates "explication," and that depends in part on one's view of what and how we *know* about meanings, which brings us back to episte-

mology. This might sound like vicious circularity to a
Cartesian, but—provided we take the kind of dependence we
find here as interdependence — the circularity is innocent. A
contemporary philosopher's views on knowledge and meaning
are bound to interlock in all sorts of complicated ways that
cannot be captured in talk about "basics." Before concluding
my reflections on the genealogy of modern philosophy, I wish
to explore some of these connections, especially as they might
bear on my suggestion that Cartesian epistemology (and therefore epistemology-centered philosophy) may even now be a
thing of the past.

I need to explore these connections to make my suggestion about the passing of Cartesian philosophy plausible in the
face of likely objections. What I have said seems to imply that
traditional epistemology and radical skepticism are phenomena
of a specific time and place now past, but the need for analysis
of "knowledge" and responses to skepticism seems both timeless
and timely. If, even after the demise of Cartesian philosophy,
I want to know what we know about God, the moral law, or the
structure of the universe, why should I not ask at the outset
what knowledge is and whether knowledge is possible? Would
not my answer be a contribution to something rather like traditional epistemology? Moreover, even if I avoid asking whether
knowledge is possible, giving as my reason this question's
relation to Cartesian doubt, does not the analysis of "knowledge" remain on the agenda? If so, it seems foolish to speak of
the passing of epistemology.

The debate over what to do about Edmund Gettier's
counterexamples to the traditional analysis of knowledge as
justified true belief has little to do with Cartesian philosophy,
but nevertheless seems to provide both a motive and a task for
contemporary epistemology of a kind that harkens back to
Plato. Finally, have we really established that skepticism and
and antiskeptical epistemology belong to another period and
not our own? Peter Unger's writings seem to work against my
conclusions in two ways: both by giving evidence of sincere
skepticism in our own day, far removed from the skeptical
crisis of the seventeenth century, and by showing how legitimately skeptical worries can be derived simply from careful
analysis of the expression "knowledge" in English, a matter to
which the emergence of the new probability as documented by
Hacking would seem irrelevant.

These objections are crucial; if they cannot be met, much

of what I have said so far would deserve rejection. In particular, my sweeping historicism would reduce to the kind of wishful thinking one associates with cargo cults and French philosophers.

In that all these objections hang in one way or another on a general question about the procedure and point of analyzing or explicating "knowledge," let me begin my response by returning to Quine's remarks on explication. It seems perfectly natural to seek an explication of knowledge, but what could such an explication be after Wittgenstein's attack on essentialism and Quine's attack on analyticity? Surely, an explication of knowledge would not be a statement about the essence of knowledge or a conceptual analysis of the term, as if essences or underlying meanings were to be discovered by bringing Cartesian ideas into clear and distinct focus before the eye of the mind. Wittgenstein and Quine invite us to eschew entities like intuited essences and underlying meanings as insufficiently public to sustain fruitful discourse. If such entities exist, they must be deemed too private to matter, for we have no means to settle disputes about them. The term "knowledge" in English is, however, open to public scrutiny. We can ask about "the particular functions of the unclear expression that make it worth troubling about, and then devise a substitute, clear and couched in terms to our liking, that fills those functions."[2] Here is a kind of explication worth pursuing.

The procedure of explication, thus construed, gives us a recipe for dissolving problems, for getting the kinks out of theory and the impasses out of conversation, by eliminating troublesome terms. As Quine puts it in a slogan worth remembering, *"explication is elimination."*

> We have, to begin with, an expression or form of expression that is somehow troublesome. It behaves partly like a term but not enough so, or it is vague in ways that bother us, or it puts kinks in a theory or encourages one or another confusion. But also it serves certain purposes that are not to be abandoned. Then we find a way of accomplishing those same purposes through other channels, using other and less troublesome forms of expression. The old perplexities are resolved.[3]

Quine proceeds to relate his notion of explication to Wittgenstein's conception of philosophy:

> According to an influential doctrine of Wittgenstein's, the task of philosophy is not to solve problems but to dissolve them by

showing that there were really none there. This doctrine has its limitations, but it aptly fits explication. For when explication banishes a problem it does so by showing it to be in an important sense unreal; viz., in the sense of proceeding only from needless usages. [4]

Such problems, concludes Quine, are "dissolved in the important sense of arising from usages that can be avoided in favor of ones that engender no such problems."[5]

So an explication of knowledge, carried out in the spirit of Quine and Wittgenstein, will attend to the use of the term in our language and to the "particular functions" of the term that make its use interesting. It will, moreover, aim for dissolution of problems and confusions that are, at root, verbal, by eliminating the troublesome term in favor of less troublesome substitutes. Notice that explication as elimination already prepares the way for the elimination of epistemology itself, where that means the theory of *knowledge*. For when the explication has been worked out, we shall have a new way to identify our topic—if the old topic survives at all after the dissolution of verbal difficulties.

With this view of explication in mind, consider briefly the literature inspired by Gettier's examples. It is noteworthy that most of this literature, including Gettier's original article,[6] seeks an analysis of knowledge in precisely the sense of "analysis" that Quinean and Wittgensteinian scruples would have us avoid. The dominant strategy has been to use intuitions about hypothetical cases to help formulate necessary and sufficient conditions for knowledge. Michael Williams expresses his doubts about this project in Wittgensteinian terms:

> The history of the various attempts to formulate necessary and sufficient conditions for knowledge suggests that, although we may share reliable linguistic intuitions about which cases are to count as cases of knowledge, there may be no way to codify these intuitions in the form of a definition, any more than there is a way to codify our intuitions about what activities count as games. I do not find this an especially disturbing position to be in.[7]

Williams goes on to raise questions about just how reliable our intuitions are in judging cases of Gettier's kind. What may be more troubling is the way the idea of conceptual analysis deflects attention away from what might make the topic of knowledge worth worrying about. Gettier's problem, as Williams points out, has little or nothing to do with questions about justification. It is of course clear why justification might attract our interest. If we ask what beliefs we ought to accept (and desire an answer less trivial than "the true ones"), our answer will depend on the stringency of our standards of justification. Just how stringent these standards should be is a good question. But it remains unclear how a satisfactory fourth condition for knowledge will meet any need we have except those thrown up by a misleading doctrine of analysis.

Gilbert Harman takes Gettier's examples seriously, but follows Quine away from the enterprise of conceptual analysis.[8] He professes skepticism about the possibility of providing an analysis of knowledge "in part because I am skeptical about all attempts at philosophical analysis and in part because in this particular case it seems to me that the . . . terms in which knowledge is supposedly to be analyzed . . . are themselves relatively obscure . . ."[9] He adds that his own strategy "does not depend in any way on any analysis of knowledge." So Harman's work provides a more challenging case for anyone interested in what epistemology could be *after* Quine.

What, then, is his strategy?

> The basic assumptions of my approach are (N) that our ordinary judgments about when people know things are, for the most part, right; (O) that reasoning that can give someone knowledge is justified reasoning; and (P) that reasoning that depends essentially on a false proposition cannot give one knowledge. My strategy is to try to devise a theory of inference or reasoning which is compatible with these three assumptions and which accounts for Gettier examples. A Gettier example is a pair of cases in which someone is equally justified in believing something true although he or she knows in the one case and not in the other.[10]

The strategy is to use intuitions about Gettier examples, to formulate not an a priori analysis of knowledge, but rather an empirically oriented theory of inference. To the extent that epistemology, as a distinctively *philosophical* endeavor, is identified as a priori and not empirical, Harman's post-Quinean project leaves epistemology behind. Relatively little hangs on whether we speak of this development as the "naturalization of epistemology" (in Quine's phrase) or as the "elimination of epistemology," provided we realize how little of the traditional conception survives once a priori standing has been abandoned.[11]

If Harman's work challenges or diverges from any conclusion I have offered here, it does so mainly in preferring psychology to history as an interest to be pursued after more traditionally epistemological concerns have been given up. "What is being suggested here," Harman writes, "is a kind of *psychologism:* the valid principles of inference are those principles in accordance with which the mind works."[12] To a historicist, Harman's psychologism is bound to seem a naïvely unhistorical approach to the study of inference, and one therefore especially unprepared to achieve critical insight into the deficiencies of contemporary cognitive practice. "After all," writes Williams, "what seems right to us now has not always seemed right, and this is a fact an empirically grounded theory of inference should take note of."[13] But Harman speaks, without defending his choice of words, of "those principles in accordance with which the mind works," as if these principles were timelessly engraved in the human psyche—an assumption I take to be undermined by, among other things, Hacking's account of the new probability. Harman does not sufficiently specify *to whom* the mind he investigates and the intuitions he uses belong.[14]

For our purposes, Unger's skepticism, precisely because of its attempt to retain relevance to the reasons that draw people to philosophy in the first place, must command more interest that Gettier's problem or Harman's program. The literature spawned by Gettier's examples is either too open to Quinean objections or too unlike traditional epistemology to pose a real threat to my central theses. Unger's *Ignorance*,[15] on the other hand, derives its radically skeptical (and therefore traditionally epistemological) stance from a subtle study of the linguistic behavior of the term "knowledge" in English. He differs from Quine on analyticity, "real" meanings, and related matters, but it is not immediately obvious how Quinean objections might be used to dismantle his arguments, and his project seems too closely related to traditional epistemology to be dismissed as irrelevant. So Unger merits closer scrutiny.

Unger argues that nobody knows (much of) anything about anything.[16] The basic argument is, roughly, that since no one can be certain of more than hardly anything, and since knowing something involves being certain of it, there can be (at most) hardly anything that any given person knows. This argument is obviously valid, but is it good? Unger's major contribution to the skeptical tradition is the ingenious support he gives to his major premise by invoking a sophisticated theory of the meaning of *absolute* terms (like "certain" and "flat") as distinguished from *relative* terms (like "confident" and "bumpy"). I shall not dispute Unger's major premise or its supporting linguistic theory. But what about the minor premise? Does knowing something involve being certain of it (in the *absolute* sense explained in Unger's linguistic theory)?

Oliver Johnson has argued, against Unger, that knowledge does not necessarily involve certainty—at least not certainty of Unger's absolute kind.[17] To be more precise, sentences of the form "*S* knows *p*" do not, according to Johnson, imply sentences of the form "*S* is (absolutely) certain that *p*" in English. Johnson gives four reasons for rejecting Unger's definition of "knowledge":

> (1) It is not, as he claims it to be, the traditional conception of knowledge. (2) It forces us to conclude . . . that we should not apply the term *knowledge* to situations in which most of us would find this term appropriate, hence is a faulty definition. (3) It seems to be designed to accomplish Unger's aim of substantiating epistemological skepticism. (4) Other, better definitions of knowledge—definitions that do not lead to skepticism but *do* reflect more accurately what most people mean by the term than his does — are available to us.[18]

Johnson concludes that "It is no feature of the English language which yields Unger's skeptical conclusion, but only his own peculiar definition of the term *knowledge*, which is shared neither by the ordinary user of our language nor by most philosophers."[19]

I wonder, though, whether the matter is as simple as Johnson suggests. He wants to explain Unger's skeptical conclusion by appealing to "Unger's misuse" of English, but he never explains why or how Unger comes to be muddled in the use or study of English. My hunch is that both philosophers are right, or rather that each is half right, about the behavior of "knowledge" in contemporary English. This hypothesis would, at least, help explain why both Johnson and Unger have ample supplies of examples and counterexamples to draw on in defending their definitions. My point is not that some third definition will do better, but rather that the term "knowledge" in contemporary English is troublesome in ways that defy straightforward attempts at definition—in ways that can be uncovered by what I have called conceptual archaeology and avoided by what Quine calls explication as elimination. To develop this hunch, I need now to turn to the passages in Unger's book I find most striking, those in which he opens the door to historicism.

Unger is not terribly happy with his skeptical conclusions, which he occasionally refers to as "crazy." The difficulties revealed in his book are, he says, "great," but his aim is "to bring us to the point where we might face these difficulties openly." These difficulties are, he adds, not "of my own making," but rather "originate from quite another source."[20] "How did we come to be in such a conceptual mess, to be, as it were, trapped in it? As it has to other philosophers, there occurred to me the idea of a theory of things embodied in our language, inherited from an ancestor language, or languages."[21] It is worth quoting Unger now at some length:

> I often continue to conceive of these things along the following bold, shall we say, anthropological lines. This embodied theory, with its rigid theorems, was the developed view of certain persons who were instrumental in creating an important ancestor, or ancestors, of our language, of English. I place no strict limit on how far back these thinkers go, but I should be surprised if they did not operate, and complete (at least most of) their contribution, a very long time before the Greek thinkers who are commonly taken to represent "ancient" philosophy. In trying to make sense of things, and in trying at the same time to satisfy certain other deep needs or drives, they developed a theory which in certain respects badly failed in various places, of necessity, to fit the world. While new meanings have sometimes been added, the central meaning of our common words does not differ from theirs, however much pronunciation may differ. While syntax has shifted, deep syntactic relations have been preserved. Accordingly, even if it is without our realizing the fact, their incorrect theory is always on the tips of our tongues. . . . .[22]

> Now, vague as they are, these hypotheses are still quite bold, I realize, and hardly what one would expect from a contemporary American philosopher. . . . (I)t is of importance to me that the sort of empirical research here indicated be undertaken with some vigour and with a friendly seriousness of purpose. But my research inclinations are too typical of one with my training and social associations. Accordingly, with a hope which may well be vain, I leave that work to philosophically inclined anthropologists, linguists, and others . . .[23]

I think I have already done some of the work Unger wants done. And I believe there is, indeed, *something* to his hypotheses. Whether his hypotheses, properly extended and emended, lead toward radical skepticism and the concerns of traditional epistemology is another matter.

Unger is right, I think, in supposing that his own skeptical conundrum derives from certain features of contemporary English inherited from ancestors reaching as far back as ancient Greek. These features relate to the distinction between genuine *scientia* and mere *opinio* which Aquinas inherited from Greek philosophy. *Scientia* (and its equivalents), during periods of skeptical crisis in Western history (especially in the years leading up to Plato and Descartes), took on connections with extremely rigorous standards of judgment and conceptions of certainty relevant to Unger's category of an *absolute* term. Our term "knowledge" still owes something to the career of *scientia*. It has been the favored translation of *scientia* throughout the modern period and the focal point of English-language debates over skepticism. There is also good reason to believe, with skeptics and with the likes of Pascal and Dewey, that knowledge in the sense Cartesians give to *scientia* is in very short supply, if not impossible.

Unger is also right to suppose that "meanings have sometimes been added" to the ancestors of our term "knowledge." He is probably wrong, however, in supposing that "the central meaning" of the concept has not been substantially altered by these additions. My hypothesis would be that the emergence of the new probability in the seventeenth century helps explain the linguistic intuitions Johnson uses against Unger's definition. As the successful completion of Descartes's antiskeptical project became an aim increasingly peripheral to modern culture and as the new science grew in cultural prestige in the eighteenth and nineteenth centuries, it became less and less common to use "knowledge" in ways that had anything to do with the ancient ideal of *scientia*, at least in ordinary life and actual scientific practice. We came to award the title "knowledge" in accordance with the finer grained standards of acceptance implicit in the new probability, with its subtle distinctions between degrees of evidential credibility and its notion of nondemonstrative evidence. Radical skepticism haunted conversation, after a certain point, only when philosophers, stumbling across old connections to ancient ideals or entangled in the veil of ideas, asked questions like: "But do you *really* know that?"

and "Are you *absolutely* certain?"

If I am right about this, Johnson is probably wrong when he says that Unger's definition fails to reflect "the traditional conception of knowledge." The *traditional* conception probably was *scientia*. The new probability, comparatively speaking, is a newcomer. Johnson is also probably wrong to call Unger's motives into question, as when he charges that the stringent definition "seems to be designed to accomplish Unger's aim of substantiating epistemological skepticism." For Unger is responding to something genuinely perplexing about our language—and even pointing the way toward the historical inquiries that might remove the perplexity. Johnson is right, however, to call attention to functions of the troublesome term that make the term worth troubling about, functions that have nothing to do with radical skepticism or with *scientia* but everything to do with the best of contemporary cognitive practice. Nothing forces us to conclude, with Unger, "that we should not apply the term *knowledge* to situations in which most of us would find this term appropriate." If we find connections to both *scientia* and the new probability in our use of "knowledge" in contemporary English, why should we follow Unger's advice by retaining the ties to *scientia* while cutting the others, thus accepting the cost of radical skepticism and its impoverishment of our vocabulary of cognitive assessment? If something must be cut, why not the ties to *scientia* and to the tradition that takes radical skepticism seriously?

Michael Williams remarks that Unger's kind of skepticism amounts "to little more than carping about the use of the verb 'to know.'"[24] He therefore finds Unger's conclusion "remarkably uninteresting."[25] It is probably too strong to say that Unger is carping; he is simply caught, as he himself admits, in a "conceptual mess" from which he does not know how to free himself. Unger does advise that, "to solve our problems, either a new language should be developed and made available or at least an existing language should be radically changed in creative ways."[26] He calls upon "dextrous logicians" who have "a subtle appreciation of the function and workings of a natural language" to execute the constructive task. But all that is needed is an explication of "knowledge." Such an explication will preserve those functions of the term that make it worth troubling about and provide rules for eliminating the term in favor of less troublesome substitutes when its use leads us into anything like Unger's "conceptual mess." The insight in Williams's remark is reminiscent of Quine on explication: Unger's mess is purely verbal "in the sense of proceeding only from needless usages" and is therefore "in an important sense unreal."

What functions of the term "knowledge" make it worth troubling about? In the early seventeenth century, a Cartesian answer to this question would have made sense. To stress the rigid standards of *scientia* was to respond directly to the skeptical crisis of the day—and thus to speak to a pressing social and intellectual problem. But if these standards are in effect skeptical, as Hume became convinced, if they sweep aside all beliefs, good and bad alike, as unjustified, this is itself a reason for ceasing to trouble about these functions of the term. By the end of the seventeenth century, the means for arguing that many of the beliefs being swept away by application of these standards were innocent beyond a *reasonable* doubt were entirely at hand, if at times unnoticed by philosophers who considered straightforward battle with a now-waning skepticism a professional obligation and a sign of seriousness. The functions of the term that today make it worth troubling about have to do largely with the notion of nondemonstrative evidence and distinctions between degrees of evidential credibility enshrined in the practice of, among other things, science and law as they entered the eighteenth century.

But when we want to ask about degrees of evidential credibility and the standards of justification appropriate to each, we are free to proceed directly to these topics without speaking of *knowledge* at all, thus saving ourselves from troubling with the historical residues that make that term the scene of many a conceptual mess. Explication is, after all, elimination — whenever we want it to be. On the other hand, when there are obviously no skeptical dragons in the vicinity to worry about, we can, as Quine puts it, allow elimination "the gentler air of explication,"[27] by using the old term while being careful not to mean too much by it. Pierre Gassendi was the first, so far as I know, to take this milder tack when, at the dawn of the new probability, he proposed treating "to know" and "to have an opinion" as something more like synonyms than the ancient distinction would allow.[28] After several centuries of Ungerian muddles, elimination of the term may be more prudent, at least for the purposes of philosophy. The irony is that the term has recently been used in a sense stronger than Gassendi's only *within* philosophy: to eliminate the term there would be to sever completely our ties to the ancient ideal without which Cartesian philosophy and traditional epistemology cannot survive.

William Rozeboom finds the same connections between "knowing" and "being absolutely certain" that Unger makes so much of, and this leads him to what initially looks like Unger's conclusion: that his "conception of 'knowledge'—and presumably yours as well—is so impossibly idealized that no real-life belief episode ever satisfies it."[29] But, unlike Unger, Rozeboom takes this as a reason for eliminating the term from philosophy. If "knowledge" imposes impossible standards, it imposes uninteresting standards, which derive from the "cognitive crudities" of ordinary language. "In particular, there is no more reason for us to agonize philosophically over the esoterics of everyday knowledge-talk . . . than for geometricians to puzzle over why some common-sense spheres have a larger cubed-surface-to-squared-volume ratio than do others." Rozeboom continues:

> . . .I propose that the subject of "knowledge" is no longer of serious philosophical concern. . . . With problems of "How strongly should X believe p?" lying dark and unfathomed before us, we stand to profit from continued epistemological preoccupation with the nature of "knowledge" to just about the same extent as would psychology from a return to the study of the "soul."[30]

Wittgensteinians may protest that Rozeboom's attitude toward ordinary language, however Quinean, is certainly not "in the spirit of Wittgenstein." But such a protest would, I think, quite drastically miss the point of Wittgenstein's work. Wittgenstein never proposed to leave everything in *philosophy* just as it is, and "explication as elimination" is itself a tool available in ordinary language. When Wittgenstein calls us back to the ordinary uses of "knowing" and "being certain," the ordinary uses he has in mind are post-seventeenth-century uses. After the mid-seventeenth century, what used to be ordinary usage *became* merely philosophical usage from which we needed to be called back. The now merely philosophical usage became residual when it lost its ordinary point. The question, as Rozeboom and Wittgenstein and Humpty Dumpty could all agree, is which will be master, the words or us. Nothing could be more Wittgensteinian than to seek cures for linguistic bewitchment, and that is what Rozeboom does.

I have already suggested that the disagreement between contemporary foundationalists and their antifoundationalist targets is largely verbal. Now I am suggesting that disputes between contemporary skeptics and their critics are largely verbal as well. Epistemology is disappearing before our eyes. Perhaps a more explicit treatment of verbal disagreement will make my theses more convincing. Harman has used Quine's account of translation in formulating an account of verbal disagreement as follows:

> Ordinarily a person interprets the words spoken by other speakers of the "same language" in the same way that he interprets his own words, i.e., he takes the obvious translation scheme to apply, call it the "identity scheme." He can do this because the identity scheme ascribes to others roughly the same beliefs he has and roughly the same methods of belief formation (and similarly for desires and other psychological attitudes), because there is no obvious alternative that does as well, and also because of an epistemological conservatism that favors assumptions one has been making all along. Occasionally there are reasons for overriding this conservatism. Sometimes a relatively obvious modification of the identity translation will translate beliefs, etc., that appear to diverge from one's own beliefs, etc., into beliefs, etc., similar to one's own. If so, one will accept the modified translation scheme and take the apparent disagreement in belief to be "merely verbal."[31]

If, to return to an example from the Introduction, another community uses the words "cat" and "dog," but in roughly the reverse of the ways we do, we would not conclude that the members of this community substantively disagree with us on the essence of cats and dogs. We would simply modify the identity scheme, ascribe to them roughly the beliefs we hold, and treat the difference as merely verbal. My point is that we can do the same with skeptics.

Compare David Hume and Thomas Kuhn. The former is famous in our century for his doubts about induction and for passages like this one, which I call Hume's lament:

> The *intense* view of these manifold contradictions and imperfections in human reason has so wrought upon me, and heated my brain, that I am ready to reject all belief and reasoning, and can look upon no opinion even as more probable or likely than another. Where am I, or what? From what causes do I

derive my existence, and to what condition shall I return? Whose favour shall I court, and whose anger must I dread? What beings surround me? and on whom have I any influence, or who have any influence on me? I am confounded with all these questions, and begin to fancy myself in the most deplorable condition imaginable, inviron'd with the deepest darkness, and utterly depriv'd of the use of every member and faculty.[32]

Kuhn, in contrast, is famous for his philosophically relaxed attitudes about human knowledge, attitudes that seem as far away as they could be from Hume's dark night of the soul.[33] But on what, exactly, do Hume and Kuhn disagree? They both agree that absolute certainty cannot be achieved even in the most respectable domains of scientific inquiry. Both hold that we can and should get on with the best of our cognitive endeavors anyway. Each proceeds to study actual cognitive practice under the categories (which we have already met in the tradition of Pascal) of custom and habit. It may be unfair to say that the disagreement is *entirely* verbal, but it *is* largely so. Hume and Kuhn do not disagree about the essence of knowledge so much as they have different attitudes toward the impossibility of achieving genuine *scientia*. Hume is nostalgic for *scientia* whereas Kuhn is not. What makes Hume differ from more recent skeptics is the simple fact that nostalgia for *scientia* no longer makes sense. It still made sense for Hume to treat the new science and the new probability as in need of justification *in terms of scientia*—hence the problem of induction, Hume's lament, and the nostalgia that actively wishes *scientia* would work as Descartes thought it did. Hume is, however, one of the last outposts of the tradition for which such nostalgia made sense. His own attempt to pull back from this nostalgic despair into a Pyrrhonic equilibrium open to the relative certainties of actual cognitive practice, as understood under the categories of custom and habit, marks part of a transition to another age — one in which disputes over skepticism would become increasingly verbal and culturally marginal.

The surprising thing is that Hume himself saw this as clearly as anyone has. I am pleased to find him saying, in a note to the *Dialogues,* exactly what I would have him say:

It seems evident, that the dispute between sceptics and dogmatists is entirely verbal, or at least regards only the degrees of doubt and assurance, which we ought to indulge with regard to all reasoning: And such disputes are commonly at the bottom, verbal, and admit not of any precise determination. No philosophical dogmatist denies, that there are difficulties both with regard to the senses and to all science: and that these difficulties are in a regular, logical method (that is, as viewed from the vantage point of *scientia*), absolutely insolveable. No sceptic denies, that we live under an absolute necessity, notwithstanding these difficulties, of thinking, and believing, and reasoning with regard to all kind of subjects, and even of frequently assenting with confidence and security. The only difference, then, between these sects, if they merit that name, is, that the sceptic, from habit, caprice, or inclination, insists most on the difficulties; the dogmatist, for like reasons, on the necessity.[34]

Descartes could not have taken such a relaxed view of the dispute a century earlier. Hume's contemporaries were not fully prepared to do so. Looking back, we can.

Nothing is more significant in the completion of this shift than the rise of the new science to a position of immense cultural prestige during the intervening two-hundred years. For evidence of how the triumph of the new science contributed to the dissolution of all but merely verbal forms of skepticism, look at what has happened by the time we reach A. J. Ayer in our own century. Ayer accepts the Humean principles that lead toward the problem of induction, but he cannot bring himself to take the problem at all seriously: "It is time . . . to abandon the superstition that natural science cannot be regarded as logically respectable until philosophers have solved the problem of induction."[35] The success of the new science, now hardly new, is too obvious and valuable—too deeply entrenched in custom and habit—to be called into question by failure to solve Hume's problem. If Hume's problem is beyond solution, as Ayer also grants, then that is good reason to abandon empiricist preoccupation with residues of *scientia* that make the problem seem problematical. This is Will's point against the likes of Ayer, by now generally accepted.

We can reject the way positivists used the prestige of the new science against, say, religion and morality without denying the extent to which the prestige was truly earned and remains richly deserved. The irony of positivism was its insistence upon using the standards Ayer would not use against science in its criticisms of less fortunate aspects of culture. The cognitive status of ethics, for example, fell into the abyss separating "is" from "ought," even while formally identical doubts about induction were being treated as superstition. As we shall see, what came to be known as Hume's gap between "is" and "ought" is really just another manifestation of the Cartesian compulsion to reconstruct the edifice of human knowledge on secure foundations—just so much more nostalgia for *scientia*. The time seems right for a fresh look at those aspects of culture positivism found cognitively deficient, a fitting task for the remainder of this book to begin. Thanks to Kuhn and his inter-locutors, we now have a fairly clear idea of what science might look like after we relax the philosophical concerns that define the Cartesian period. How religion and morality might look in the absence of such concerns we have only begun to ask.

PART II

Theism after Authority

5. Unfounded Criticism

Philosophers of religion used to be in the business of applying to a specific range of judgments and concepts the more general findings of epistemology and the philosophy of language. What do we know about God? We can answer this question properly, it was thought, only by first establishing what we know about knowledge and meaning. A theory of knowledge will tell us, among other things, what standards of justification to apply when appraising a specific belief, such as the belief that God exists. A theory of meaning will tell us, among other things, how to determine the meaning of the proposition in question (the better to appraise its acceptability) or even whether talk about God *has* meaning of a kind that qualifies it for cognitive appraisal — that is, whether its sentences manage to express propositions at all. For a thrilling moment or two, many philosophers thought that conceptual analysis had simply done away with theology as a serious intellectual enterprise by establishing its cognitive meaninglessness. But the demise of the positivists' criteria of meaningfulness meant that philosophical critics of theology could no longer so easily dismiss the question of justification as beside the point. Moreover, the same holism in linguistic theory that contributed heavily to the demise of the positivists' criteria had also undermined the leading accounts of justification. So just as one could no longer ban theology from the realm of serious cognitive endeavor by applying a theory of meaning, neither could one establish its unacceptability by pointing to the gap between theological propositions and the putative foundations of knowledge. Quine, Wittgenstein, and Kuhn had, virtually overnight, destroyed the confidence of criticism. Philosophers of religion lacked an epistemology to apply. And the theory of meaning they felt justified in applying seemed to do more for something called "charity" than for criticism. It was not long before theologians (and all varieties of enthusiasts) could be heard referring to their most controversial beliefs as "deeply entrenched in the language game of an alternative paradigm."

Philosophers of science, philosophers of religion, and social-scientific students of witchcraft and magic suddenly found themselves pushed together in one conversation — a conversation apparently as consequential as it was confusing and exasperating. In the first place, the very possibility of critical thought seemed to hang in the balance. No one really believed that any theory is as good as any other or that anything goes in the life of thought once foundationalism can no longer be held with conviction. But many feared that, in the absence of firm foundations for knowledge, critical thought in fact *seemed* unfounded. Unless one could produce universal criteria for preferring one conceptual scheme to another, unless one could show (by performing philosophical miracles with words like "about," "refer," and "true") that some schemes make better contact with the Real than others, conceptual schemes seem to become ideological havens for even the most scandalously hideous views and deeds. Where relativism reigns, rationality and human decency cannot.

Furthermore, whenever Polanyi spoke of the "faith" of the scientist, or Kuhn mentioned "conversions," or Feyerabend referred to himself as a "church historian," it seemed that a self-consciously secular subculture had blurred the contrast between religious thought and scientific rationality essential to its own self-understanding. It had lost the distinction required for telling its own story as the triumph of rationality over superstition. What solace this spectacle offered to theologians was, however, diminished by having to be shared with magicians and witches — hardly the kind of company to keep when intellectual respectability is at issue (as John Watt pointed out in his response to Peter Winch). Savage minds were the only ones with real reason to be happy, and even the ethnographers grew uneasy, despite their professional sympathies for savages, when it seemed that all the social science anthropologists are taught in graduate school might have to be discarded as insufficiently sensitive to the boundaries separating conceptual schemes. Meanwhile, the interdisciplinary seminar thrived, Anglo-Americans discovered hermeneutics, and Hilary

Putnam became the spinning weathervane of philosophical opinion.

We can pose the problem more concretely by taking up a single essay as an exemplary case. Let me turn, therefore, to Alasdair MacIntyre's essay, "The Fate of Theism," originally delivered as one of his Bampton Lectures at Columbia University in 1966.[1] Theism, as MacIntyre tells the story, is a traditional mode of thought and practice faced with the decision of how to respond to a modern situation. But how can it respond to modernity without becoming either incomprehensible to it or so much like it as to sacrifice the claim to distinctiveness? Reformulations of traditional theism like Deism and liberal Protestantism have tended to shade off into atheism, unable to retain enough distinctiveness to justify the use of traditional vocabulary or sustain the interest of the host culture. Less thoroughgoing reformulations maintain distinctiveness, but only by holding onto features of traditional theism that seem indefensible or unintelligible in modern terms. The horns of this dilemma constitute the dialectical situation that is the fate of modern theism. The emergence of religion's cultured despisers can be explained in terms of the evolution of a kind of thought that is distinctively modern — and therefore essentially inhospitable to theism in the traditional mode. The subsequent movement of debates about God to the periphery of the culture — the virtual disappearance of the cultured despisers — can be explained in terms of the inability of theism to find a way between the horns: neither thinly disguised atheism nor Kierkegaardian unwillingness to argue makes a vital and interesting opponent in debate, the sort of position a cultured atheist would want to spend time despising.

This is, I think, a highly interesting and deeply attractive account of the fate of modern theism. There may be a number of problems with the details of MacIntyre's story that engender minor doubts.[2] More important, however, are the difficulties related to MacIntyre's category of the *modern*, for this category creates the central contrast in terms of which the narrative itself is cast. It should not be surprising to find MacIntyre explicating this contrast by directing attention to an anthropologist on the one hand and a philosopher of science on the other:

> As Mary Douglas has shown in her book *Purity and Danger*, primitive thought is characteristically reluctant to tolerate

whatever is anomalous or exceptional to its own established classificatory schemes. . . . The primitive's concept of dirt, of uncleanliness, is one of "matter out of place," of disorder. The unclean is that which violates his notion of order; his rites for dealing with pollution are techniques for preventing it from harming him; they enable him to recognize its existence and yet to resist revising or abandoning his beliefs and his conceptual schemes in the face of it. If we set Mrs. Douglas's analysis of the primitive mind beside Karl Popper's analysis of science, we immediately see that one view is the "photographic negative" of the other. Primitive man acknowledges the existence of the anomaly, of the exceptional, of that which constitutes a counter-example to his conceptual generalizations, only in order to out-law that anomaly; and he thus avoids having to revise or re-formulate his prevalent beliefs. The scientist, however, accepts anomalies and exceptions as a basis for either abandoning or revising the theories which he has hitherto accepted.[3]

"There is therefore," MacIntyre concludes, "a sharp line to be drawn between these two modes of thought, and I want to situate theism in relation to them." The story of the fate of theism thus becomes a tale about a mode of thought caught between a traditional attitude toward the anomalous and the modern demand that all beliefs be subjected to Popperian standards of refutability. Since MacIntyre says little more than what I have already quoted in elaboration or defense of the theoretical commitments he takes on from Douglas and Popper, the first step toward critical assessment of his narrative is to look more carefully at his sources.

Mary Douglas's theory focuses in part on how anomalous beings are treated in different cognitive and cultural contexts. Take any system of classification. The system will sort the objects within its domain into kinds in accordance with criteria which may or may not be made explicit. But, presumably, the classification is bound to work better for some objects than for others. Some objects, for example, may show the marks of more than one class, where the classes are meant to be mutually exclusive. Other objects may possess some salient character-istics of a given class but not enough to qualify as a fully fledged member of any class. In either case, the objects in question would be anomalous in the required sense. Their behavior would be difficult to predict with laws phrased in terms of the recognized kinds of objects. The appropriate form of behavior toward the objects in question would not be prescribed in the standard way either. Popper, of course, would take the appearance of such an anomaly as a compelling reason for revising or rejecting the presupposed system of classification, as well as the theories and norms that make essential use of it. But many societies respond differently, setting aside anomalous objects and events as abominations or as signs of the sacred, to be treated with respect and trepidation.

The Mosaic dietary laws, according to Douglas, are a case in point. Far from being primitive attempts to legislate public health through better hygiene, these laws single out anomalous creatures for avoidance and counsel against mixing members of discrete classes. To see this, compare the abominations of Leviticus with the cosmology of Genesis and its threefold system of classification.[4] The Lele also set their anomalies aside as dangerous and powerful, but are more apt to see them as sacred than to abhor them as abominations. Hence their cult of the pangolin, which bears the marks of a fish (scales) but dwells on land. Examples like these could be multiplied many times over by anyone familiar with ethnography. Douglas suggests that we can learn much by trying to correlate variations in the treatment of anomaly with types of social context.

Wayne Proudfoot has shown how Douglas's suggestions can be developed into a full-blown theory of religious experience. How are experiences of defilement and spiritual elevation generated? Precisely, according to Proudfoot, by frustration of the attempt to classify and explain experience.

> Douglas's work suggests that the sense of the sacred or mysterious is inextricably bound up with the anomalous. A mystery is something that defies explanation or classification. Mystery and awe result when no appropriate label or explanation is available to satisfy inquiry. Schachter manipulated the cognitive context of his experiments so that different labels or interpretations were salient. What would happen if the context were arranged so that every candidate for a determinate interpretation was discredited, and no labels were present by which to make sense of the experience? The more the need for interpretation is aroused and is frustrated, the greater the sense of unease and mystery that would be created. As Douglas reports, such situations often lead to the behavior of respect and awe toward the "objects" of these experiences. Whether they are classified as objects of worship or taboo, they are set apart from the world of profane objects and actions.[5]

Nature will seem enchanted, in Weber's sense, to someone who finds the course of natural events punctuated by anomalous happenings ("miracles") and who is disposed by his context to respond with awe, religiously labeled. The anomaly arouses emotion, the cognitive context frustrates the search for standard explanatory categories, and tradition makes religious labels available. Likewise with ritual contexts, which often serve to heighten the experience of anomaly by prohibiting discursively coherent application of categories only to reinforce the offended system of classification with religious shaping of the emotions thus aroused.

It is a truism that religious traditions often allow objects of worship to be described only in negative, vacuous, or paradoxical terms. Proudfoot's point is that this kind of rule can only serve to heighten the sense of mystery we often associate with religious experience. The function of such terms as the Hebrew "YHWH" and of such doctrines as the mysteries of traditional Christian faith "is served precisely by the rules that deny them any representational role. Their opacity maintains a sense of ineffability."[6] Religious thinkers typically explain the ineffable as experience beyond the limits of language and therefore as experience of the sacred. "Perhaps, however," Proudfoot writes, "it is not that the experience is intrinsically beyond the limits of language, but it is an experience of an event or phenomenon for which one does not have available an adequate interpretation or explanation. The mystery consists in the fact that the search for labels or interpretations is frustrated."[7] Mystical rapture is *ineffable*, according to Proudfoot, but only in the perfectly down-to-earth sense that should surprise no one who is aware of the elaborate procedures mystics use to make *effing* difficult or impossible. As Proudfoot puts it, "the fact that it is ineffable IS the emotion."[8]

So it would seem that Douglas's suggestions can be taken rather far. They are, of course, highly controversial, and I shall not try to appraise them here. Assume, for present purposes, that Douglas and Proudfoot give us a reasonably adequate picture of one aspect of primitive and traditional thought. What, then, about Popper's contrasting portrait of the scientist as the person who treats anomalies not as abominations or as signs of the sacred but simply as refutations of hypotheses, as reasons for rejecting theories? Can we rest content with refutability as the mark that distinguishes science, the quintessentially modern mode of thought, from its prescientific ancestors and pseudoscientific competitors? That depends, of course, on what the doctrine of refutability consists in — by no means a noncontroversial matter, but one on which MacIntyre provides little guidance (either in "The Fate of Theism" or in other writings of the same vintage). MacIntyre does make clear that the issue is not falsification in the sense associated with the positivist charge that theism, at least in some forms, is cognitively meaningless. Popper's criterion of demarcation is not a criterion of meaningfulness. To rule out the positivist misreading of Popper does not, however, answer all the relevant questions.

Popper originally defined his own position by contrasting it with logical empiricism. As a form of foundationalism, logical empiricism sought to erect scientific theory on a base of purely observational statements. It thus faced two sorts of difficulties — in Will's terminology, *foundation* and *construction* difficulties. The former pertain to the sense in which observational statements might be epistemologically basic and uninfected by theory. The latter pertain to the problem of using such a meager base to support scientific theories (the problem of induction). Popper began his career by rejecting foundationalism and, with it, the problem of induction. Science makes progress, he argued, not by erecting theories on foundations of observation, but rather by a process of conjecture and refutation. Theories do not follow from observation; they are invented and then tested against experience. But what is the character of the test?

Suppose that the process of refutation "consists of deducing observable results from our theory (in conjunction with appropriate initial and boundary conditions) and then deducing the falsity of our conjectures when the predicted observable results are shown not to be the case."[9] This suggests the following picture. Deductive logic is the only logic of science, and all the crucial arguments have the form of *modus tollens*. Crucial arguments follow crucial experiments, turning unwanted findings against theory. The scientific attitude may be defined by its avoidance of ad hoc revisions of theory and its insistence upon the power of observation to refute decisively. Refutations can and should be decisive and final.

Refutability, thus construed, gives us a sharp line between scientific and prescientific modes of thought, and supplies the kind of contrast with Douglas's primitives that would sustain MacIntyre's narrative. Traditional theology, confronted by the demand for refutability embodied in the modern critical mentality, must either accept this demand or reject it. To accept the demand is to put one's most cherished beliefs at risk by specifying clearly conceivable conditions in which these beliefs would be falsified. This would be to treat theism as a collection of hypotheses, or rather to transform theism, which had been "elaborated in the light of that prescientific culture where the anomalous and the exceptional are not permitted to falsify existing beliefs,"[10] into Deism — and therefore to accept a steady erosion of theism's traditional content. To reject the demand is to treat theism either as something to be believed in the face of the evidence or as something to which evidence is not really relevant — in either event as something essentially removed from the critical rationality central to the culture. If evidence is treated as irrelevant, then the traditional theoretical content of theism is diminished just as radically as it would be in Deism. But if theism retains its traditional content while being believed in the face of evidence any genuinely critical intellect would consider a decisive refutation, it thereby sacrifices any serious claim for attention from the culture upon which it would like to have an influence.

This version of the narrative is powerful, but can the interpretation of refutability on which it depends withstand critical scrutiny? I think not. It seems clear that refutations could be final and decisive in the required sense only if observational statements were roughly what the logical empiricists said they are — that is, both theory-independent and in some sense incorrigible. Popper has, throughout his career as an author, always (rightly) rejected this aspect of the logical empiricist's foundationalism. It follows, then, that "no conclusive disproof of a theory can ever be produced."[11] What, then, becomes of refutation? His early answer was this: "From a logical point of view, the testing of a theory depends upon basic statements whose acceptance or rejection, in its turn, depends upon our decisions. Thus it is decisions which settle the fate of theories."[12] Decisive refutation results only when scientists agree to accept the relevant observational statements. A refutation's decisiveness is therefore relative to the firmness of an agreement and the decisions that led to it.

Kuhn's response was to ask why anyone would want to

follow Popper in stressing "the role of *modus tollens*, the privileged status of falsification over corroboration, and the special role of basic statements in the methodology of science" once this relativity has been pointed out.[13] Kuhn then contented himself with mapping the variables of this relativity in social and historical space. But Kuhn's contentment struck many philosophers as an unwillingness to take seriously the irrationalist character of the relativism that had been unleashed. How does the primitive *bricoleur* or the traditional theologian differ from the modern scientist if refutability is a function of decision and acceptance within a community? If refutation is never absolute, then how is a theologian being unscientific when, in accordance with the agreements of his community, he treats some highly theoretical beliefs as more deeply entrenched than this or that bit of putative counterevidence and tinkers with theory (as opposed to rejecting major hypotheses) to bring evidence into line? In short, has not the central contrast of MacIntyre's story collapsed?

Normally, according to Kuhn, scientists do make room for the anomalous, guard deeply entrenched assumptions, and spend the greater part of their time tinkering and puzzle-solving. Does not this make normal science sound altogether too much like traditional theology for MacIntyre's purposes? If, as Kuhn puts it, "no theory ever solves all the puzzles with which it is confronted at a given time,"[12] then why should theology be singled out as an object of criticism at all? Why should we not agree with the fideist who claims that the relativity of refutability makes the community of faith the only appropriate court of appeal for judging the acceptability of theological propositions?

As Popper and his followers recoiled from what seemed the most vicious kind of relativism, they began a search for objective constraints upon rational decision, a quest for "the scientific method." Success in this quest would hold out the hope that MacIntyre's narrative could be recast without losing its power and attractiveness. But MacIntyre has recently reached this verdict on the quest:

> . . . Popper has rightly tried to make something of the notion of rational tradition. What hindered this attempt was the Popperian insistence on replacing the false methodology of induction by a new methodology. The history of Popper's own thought and of that of his most gifted followers was for quite

a number of years the history of successive attempts to replace Popper's original falsificationism by some more adequate version, each of which in turn fell prey to counterexamples from the history of science. From one point of view the true heir of these attempts is Feyerabend; for it is he who has formulated the completely general thesis that all such attempts were doomed to failure. There is *no* set of rules as to how science *must* proceed and all attempts to discover such a set founder in the encounter with actual history of science.[15]

Must we, then, abandon MacIntyre's rendition of "The Fate of Theism" even by the logic of his own later pronouncements?

I have now done my best to pose the problem I want to address in Part II of this book. My thesis will be that we need *not* abandon the basic structure of MacIntyre's narrative or succumb to irrationalist relativism even if the quest for universal criteria of rationality fails. I shall begin, in chapters 6 and 7, by reformulating the narrative such that the explanatory power is preserved but no assumptions about the success or failure of the "quest" are made. And I shall conclude, in chapter 8, by trying (with a little help from my friends) to dissolve the problem of rationality seemingly implicit in all cultural criticism since the demise of foundationalism. The following passage from MacIntyre's recent remarks on Popper may serve as our point of departure:

> Any attempt to show the rationality of science, once and for all, by providing a rationally justifiable set of rules for linking observations and generalizations break (*sic*) down. This holds, as the history of the Popperian school shows, for falsification as much as for any version of positivism. It holds, as the history of Carnap's work shows, no matter how much progress may be made on detailed, particular structures in scientific inference. It is only when theories are located in history, when we view the demands for justification in highly particular contexts of a historical kind, that we are freed from either dogmatism or capitulation to scepticism.[16]

Perhaps, then, the historical details themselves will provide precisely the therapy we need.

6. From Mystery to Paradox

Suppose we accept the sketch of primitive and traditional religious thought I have taken from the work of Douglas and Proudfoot, and also accept something like Kuhn's portrait of "normal" scientific rationality. Need we then conclude that traditional theologians and "normal" scientists do not differ significantly with respect to the treatment of anomalies? Several authors have recently suggested that we need not.[1] Only careful attention to the historical details seems capable of settling the issue.

In what follows, I want to develop a proposal of John Skorupski's:

> One does not need to insist that no scientific theory ever has any conceptually anomalous features, or that scientists will never put up for a moment with incoherence or anomaly, however peripheral, in an otherwise usable theory. . . . There is a real and important difference between a system of thought in which the recognition of logical paradox among accepted beliefs about the world generates attempts to replace the affected parts by new theories at the first-order level, and one in which paradoxical beliefs can be defused by a second-order or philosophical, reinterpretation of the relationship between meaningfulness and intelligibility.[2]

I think Skorupski is basically right about this. Incoherence, anomaly, and paradox do not always force immediate rejection of a scientific theory or revision of its central tenents. As Jay Rosenberg has put it, "what it takes to dislodge an accepted theory turns out to be a *better theory*" — where a better theory is (roughly) one that gives us an improved account of the strengths and weaknesses of its predecessors.[3] But incoherence, anomaly, and paradox *always* count as weaknesses in a scientific theory. And this appears not to be the case for primitive and traditional religious thought.

As evidence for this last claim, Skorupski cites not only the paradoxes in African religions made famous by Lévy-Bruhl, but also the "supernatural mysteries" of the Roman Catholic doctrines of the Trinity, the Eucharist, and the Incarnation.

> These doctrines are accepted as "supernatural mysteries in the strict sense": an expression which has since at least Vatican Council I had a technical use. In a nutshell, a "mystery" is a doctrine whose truth cannot be demonstrated but must be taken on faith; a mystery "in the strict sense" is a doctrine such that not merely the fact that it is true, but also the fact that it has a definite, coherent sense, must be taken on faith.[4]

These doctrines are all, according to Skorupski, paradoxes of identity. How can God be one being and yet three persons? How can a piece of bread be the whole Christ? How can more than one Host be identical with the whole Christ? What is the relation between Christ's divine and his human nature?[5] Skorupski also refers to another set of paradoxes, including the traditional problem of evil, as the consequence of "putting various parts of Church teaching together."[6]

Now, so far as I am concerned, the crucial matter is not whether Skorupski is justified in calling any or all of these doctrines and theological problems *paradoxes* in the sense of this term proper to logic. What matters is that traditional theology seems to have had means for "defusing" whatever central paradoxes it might have had. What we might deem a "paradox," and therefore a *weakness*, traditional theology christens a "mystery," to be accepted on faith. So even *if* a given doctrine turns out to be a logical paradox, such that its intelligibility or comprehensibility must be taken on faith, a traditional theologian would not treat this as a potential obstacle to belief. MacIntyre writes as follows:

> It is obvious that the internal incoherences in Christian concepts did not go unnoticed in the Middle Ages. The antinomies of benevolent omnipotence and evil, or of divine predestination and human freedom, were never more clearly and acutely discussed. But it is not the case in general that mediaeval thinkers who were dissatisfied with the solutions offered to these antinomies differed in their attitude to belief in God or belief in Christ from thinkers who believed that they or others had offered satisfactory solutions. So the problem becomes: why do the same intellectual difficulties at one time appear as difficulties but no more, an incentive to enquiry but not a ground for disbelief, while at another time they appear as a final and

sufficient ground for scepticism and for the abandonment of Christianity?[7]

How, in other words, did *mysteries* become *paradoxes*? To answer this question, we shall have to learn what argument traditional theologians might have given for accepting "mysteries in the strict sense." Perhaps we can then discover something in the emergence of modernity that undermined this argument and thereby transformed "supernatural mysteries" into paradoxes of a kind that constituted potential grounds for disbelief. We can find what we are looking for, I think, if we return to a topic introduced in Part I — the history of *authority* and *probable opinion*.

When we engage in theology, according to Aquinas, we begin by accepting principles marked out by revelation, just as "optics starts from principles marked out by geometry, and harmony from principles indicated by arithmetic."[8] Christian theology begins by taking its principles on faith, that is, on "the authority of the men through whom divine revelation has come down to us, which revelation is the basis of sacred Scripture or doctrine."[9] Aquinas has this to say about appeals to authority in theology:

> Argument from authority is the method most appropriate to this teaching in that its premises are held through revelation; consequently it has to accept the authority of those to whom revelation was made. Nor does this derogate from its dignity, for though weakest when based on what human beings have held, the argument from authority is most forcible when based on what God has disclosed.
>
> All the same Christian theology also uses human reasoning, not indeed to prove the faith, for that would take away from the merit of believing, but to make manifest some implications of its message. Since grace does not scrap nature but brings it to perfection, so also natural reason should assist faith as the natural loving bent of the will ministers to charity. . . . Hence holy teaching uses the authority of philosophers who have been able to perceive the truth by natural reasoning. . . .
>
> Yet sacred doctrine employs such authorities only in order to provide as it were extraneous arguments from probability. Its own proper authorities are those of canonical Scripture, and these it applied with convincing force. It has other proper authorities, the doctors of the Church, and these it looks to as its own, but for arguments that carry no more than probability.[10]

These remarks represent, of course, precisely the attitude

toward authority Holbach would later condemn as childish credulity. What was for Aquinas the virtue of faith became for the Enlightenment the vice of gullibility, soft-mindedness, and superstition. What Aquinas found authoritative the *philosophes* came to denounce as merely authoritarian.

But recall that, if Hacking is right about the history of probability, Aquinas lacked our notion of probability. For him probability could consist only in actual approval by recognized authorities. There was no notion of *internal* evidence, in the sense distinguished at Port-Royal, to be brought to bear in self-conscious appraisal of which authorities to recognize. That is, Aquinas was not in position to argue *from* the intrinsic unlikelihood of a recognized authority's testimony *to* the rejection of that testimony as false. Conflict with the testimony of superior or otherwise weighty authority did tend to diminish the credibility of an authority and his testimony,[11] but this was *external* evidence in Port-Royal's sense. Even an event we would deem intrinsically improbable — such as a virgin birth — would be deemed *highly probable* by Aquinas, provided only that it had the right kind of authority speaking up on its behalf. If the authority in question is God's word, as revealed in *sacra scriptura*, then "probable" is too weak a word.

Thomas does not deny that people have entertained doubts about articles of faith. But how, he asks, can we finally doubt the word of God? Whatever momentary doubts we might have simply reveal our own imperfections. If we have trouble comprehending the articles of faith, it "is not because the reality is at all uncertain, but because the human understanding is feeble."[12] "There is nothing," Aquinas writes, "to stop a thing that is objectively more certain by its nature from being subjectively less certain to us because of the disability of our minds, which, as Aristotle notes, blink at the most evident things like bats in the sunshine."[13] We do well to believe even the most mysterious article of faith on divine authority. On such authority we can be certain that the articles of faith are true, though we cannot see clearly how it is that they are true. God's revelation "joins us to him as to an unknown."[14] Aquinas continues:

> The assent is not due to what is seen by the believer but to what is seen by him who is believed. In that it lacks the element of seeing, faith fails to be genuine knowledge, for such knowledge

causes the mind to assent through what is seen and through an understanding of first principles.[15]

Theology is a science, but only because, like optics, it inherits its first principles from another science — in this case, God's own knowledge of himself. The prior acceptance of an authority elevates the apparently incoherent, anomalous, and paradoxical to the status of supernatural mystery — incomprehensible, but nonetheless certain or acceptable. Divine authority is, for Aquinas and his contemporaries, the best conceivable warrant for belief. It follows, as he sees it, that whatever we encounter in another science that is incompatible with theological truths passed on by established tradition "should be completely condemned as false."[16]

If the articles of faith were to come to seem intrinsically improbable, if their mysteriousness or incomprehensibility was to count against them, the notion of authority would first have to suffer erosion. We have already noted, in chapter 2, the character of this erosion in late medieval and early modern Europe. We are now in a position to see how this erosion affected religious experience as construed by Proudfoot and traditional thought as construed by Skorupski. To loosen the connection between credibility and authority is to clear the path that leads toward criticism of all thought which treats anomalies as credible and thus toward the disenchantment of experience. Even as early as the fourteenth century, the notion of authority has become sufficiently problematical to encourage relatively radical innovations in traditional thought, especially those emerging out of the city republics of medieval Italy and pertaining to the art of persuasion. By the time we reach Valla and Machiavelli, much has changed. Genuine precursors of a new notion of probability give discourse of a new, less distinctively Christian shape.

The revival of ancient skeptical writings in the sixteenth century at first does as much to reinforce the attractiveness of traditional means for settling disputes as it does to raise doubts about religion, and whatever doubts it raises about religion tend to be placed on an equal par with doubts of other kinds. Only a nuanced notion of nondemonstrative evidence will make religious doubts seem especially severe. But in Descartes's work, theology has already become the handmaiden of philosophy, reversing the Thomistic order of things. In addressing the "Dean and Doctors of the Sacred Faculty of Theology in Paris," Descartes argues that questions about God and the soul "ought to be demonstrated by philosophical rather than theological argument."[17] He grants — and here we are not sure how much he is holding back — that

> . . . although it is absolutely true that we must believe that there is a God, because we are so taught in the Holy Scriptures, and, on the other hand, that we must believe the Holy Scriptures because they come from God . . . , we nevertheless could not place this argument before infidels who might accuse us of reasoning in a circle.[18]

The final clause glistens with irony. The problem of many authorities and the emergence of full-blown skepticism about *scientia* have combined to make theology seem needful of philosophical support. Infidels no longer keep their distance, as they did in Aquinas's time. They now animate our own mental lives, in ways beyond medieval imagination, voicing doubts we ourselves entertain.

Yet it seems unfair to say that Descartes's methodical doubt actually shifts the onus of proof to the believer, for Pascal and others seem warranted in dismissing Descartes's radically skeptical standards of judgment as excessively rigid. Early modern thought about religion does not advance far beyond the critical maneuvers practiced in antiquity, and in fact largely derives from the Pyrrhonism of Sextus Empiricus and the Epicureanism of Lucretius. The revival of classical writings is an important part of the background to Enlightenment critiques of religion, but it does not account for what makes these critiques distinctive. Radically skeptical standards of judgment have as much to do with fideism and traditionalism as with the climate of criticism. Lucretian anticlericalism is as much a mainstay of religious reformers as of critics of Christianity. The distinctiveness of Enlightenment criticism consists mainly in its increasingly rigorous application of the new notion of evidence worked out at Port-Royal.

Pascal sets up the problem of belief as a case for decision theory, but his premises are designed to make the actual likelihood of God's existence irrelevant (as in the argument from dominance) or indecisive (as in the arguments from expectation and dominating expectation). Doubts about Pascal's premises or about the point of his procedure make the actual likelihood of the existence of a specific kind of god seem more important. And the Port-Royal *Logic*, though of course without intending to do so, makes available the conceptual means for pursuing the matter rigorously. The connection between probability and authority has been loosened, thus opening the articles of faith to possible question. A new notion of probability has been fashioned that might allow *us* to judge the quality of testimony and authority even in those areas falling radically short of demonstrative certainty.

The consequences of such developments in the area of biblical interpretation have been documented with great skill by Hans Frei, whose work meshes beautifully with Hacking's study of probability.[19] Before the late seventeenth century, as Hacking would have it, the Bible stands in the still-privileged sphere marked off by the authority of books. It remains, as we have seen, the one authority all Christians can agree upon as an authority. It may be difficult to interpret, but its authority as God's word is final. The Renaissance complicates matters by radicalizing the doctrine that nature too is a book authored by God. We have traced the steps by which nature's signs become indications of internal evidence. Internal evidence provides a way .to test the Bible against a historical realm to which we have access independent of the sphere of authority.

Against this background, Frei's discussion of the change from "precritical" to "critical" interpretation of the Bible makes perfect sense. Before the emergence of internal evidence, biblical interpretation was a matter of making oneself conform to the book. Henceforth, however, another element enters in and turns things around. For we can now ask, without presupposing a ready-made doctrine of authority, whether the book conforms to the evidence. We can evaluate the quality of its testimony. We can try to determine whether its historical claims violate accepted canons of reasonable assent. We can, in other words, read the Bible critically. Books used to be primary, by virtue of authority, and authority made judgments more or less probable. Then people started *reading* nature more and more seriously as if it were a book, contributing to the fragmentation of authority. The book of natural signs gave birth to the new notion of internal evidence, which outlived the heyday of the book of nature. Internal evidence then became primary and came back to haunt the one book that still claimed absolute authority: the Bible.

Spinoza's *Tractatus theologico-politicus* (1670), according to Frei, foreshadows the mode of interpretation that comes to dominate the following century. This mode takes on something like its full form as early as Anthony Collins's *A Discourse of the Grounds and Reasons of the Christian Religion* (1724). Speaking in terms reminiscent of Hacking, Frei notes that "The transition from Luther and Calvin to Collins's *Grounds and Reasons* is a voyage from one world to another. The logical, hermeneutical difference bespeaks a chasm between worlds of thought and imagination."[20] Nor is the change in interpretation confined to the thought of radicals like Spinoza and Collins; it extends into the work of conservatives like Johannes Cocceius and Johann Albrect Bengel as well.[21] As Frei describes the change,

> it was a kind of detachment of the "real" historical world from its biblical description. The real events of history constitute an autonomous temporal framework of their own. . . . Instead of rendering them accessible, the (biblical) narratives, heretofore indispensable as means of access to the events, now simply verify them, thus affirming their autonomy and the fact that they are in principle accessible through any kind of description that can manage to be accurate either predictively or after the event. . . . The depicted biblical world and the real historical world began to be separated at once in thought and in sensibility, no matter whether the depiction was thought to agree with reality (Cocceius and Bengel) or disagree with it (Spinoza).[22]

"The point," as Frei sees it, "is that the direction of interpretation now became the reverse of earlier days."[23] No longer does interpretation consist in the attempt to make oneself and one's vision of reality conform to the text; it now consists in the attempt to discern the text's meaning and determine the truth of its claims by considering all the relevant evidence, internal and external.

Similar consequences ramify throughout the religious (and antireligious) thought of the period, most clearly in Britain.[24] Three stages of development can be distinguished; I shall illustrate each with examples from the British discussion. The first stage can be seen in the theology of the Royal Society divines and in the Latitudinarianism of Locke, the second in the controversies over Deism, the third in Hume's critique of religion. If I may anticipate my discussion with a bit of oversimplification, the Deism that stands at the center of the British controversies is what happens when the new notion of evidence breaks free from traditional religious commitments and tries to draw up a system of religious beliefs from scratch. Deism, in other words, is the probability section of the Port-Royal *Logic* minus the Jansenism of its authors and without the Anglicanism of its first British defenders. The history of the controversies, from their incubation in the Royal Society of the late 1660s to the demise of Deism in Hume's critique of religion, is that of a revolution of diminishing expectations as to what religious tenets can be reached by way of probable reasoning. The new probability was the lamp of Enlightenment criticism.

The notion of internal evidence was from the start closely related to the theological and epistemological tradition descendant from Castellio and Chillingworth. Its appeal is the leverage it provides in seeking a resolution to the problem of authority. But the new notion of evidence does not immediately recast the entirety of theology. It must first make its way slowly among the traditional categories. The Port-Royal authors use internal evidence in limited ways to settle specific disputes arising from the fragmentation of authority. They remain, however, the most rigorous of Jansenists, fully committed to theological tenets not entirely unlike those found in Calvinism. Though the patterns of influence remain ambiguous, Chillingworth's followers among the early members of the Royal Society of London make a similarly delimited use of internal evidence over the next several decades. Internal evidence must, here as elsewhere, establish its foothold among the traditional categories before its far-reaching consequences can be discerned. John Tillotson begins this process by integrating the new probability with Chillingworth's theory of moral certainty, thereby giving a new sense and wide circulation to Aristotle's maxim about seeking only the sort of proof and precision of which the subject matter at hand admits.[25]

John Wilkins, the first secretary of the Royal Society, carries this development further.[26] Hacking makes much of the transition from Wilkins's early works, written in 1640 or so, to his later works, written in the late 1660s. This transition illustrates the emergence of both the distinction between natural and conventional signs and the new notion of probability. In 1640 Wilkins, following Chillingworth, can already appeal to the reader's sound human judgment as an indication of probability. In the late 1660s he can make explicit use of internal evidence. He does so in his presentation of the argument from design. Hacking elaborates as follows:

> Wilkins is the first representative of what I shall call "Royal Society theology" and whose most familiar doctrine is the argument from design for the existence of God. The argument proposes that the way things are, constitutes evidence for the existence of a supreme being. A universe so well constituted could only be the work of a sublime artisan. Aquinas also had a teleological argument, but his is quite different. It supposes that everything in the world is acting purposefully, and so seeks an agent to endow matter with intentions. In the Thomistic teleological argument, the world is an agent, which, since it is not in itself active, demands a Supreme Agent. In the argument from design, the world is passive. We hunt not for an agent but an artisan. The world is not "external evidence" written by God, but "internal evidence" which can be explained only by the existence of a God. In confirmation of this thesis we find that Wilkins, first propounder of an argument from design, begins by presenting the new categories of evidence.[27]

Wilkins inherits the categories of demonstration and testimony. Between these stands another category, that of "mixed" evidence, which relates both "to the senses and the understanding, depending upon our own observation and repeated trials of the issues and events of actions or things, called experience."[28]

> Wilkins may be our best witness to the fact that what Port Royal called "internal" evidence is new. In twentieth century epistemology there is only one fundamental kind of evidence, namely internal evidence. In the mid seventeenth century this kind of evidence could make its way only as a sort of wedge between demonstration and testimony. Yet the decisive feature of this wedge is that, by being conceived of as in the middle, it united what had hitherto been utterly disparate. . . . Probable evidence enters the same league as demonstration.[29]

Internal evidence is still making its way between demonstration and authority, yet its relevance to apologetics is already clear. An argument from design, at least in a context shaped by the image of God as author of the book of nature and by newly popular mechanistic models of the universe, provides a way to avoid extensive commitments and disagreements in metaphysics without sacrificing central theistic beliefs.[30]

Once this move has been made, however, Deism is not far to find. The liberal Anglicans, as Van Leeuwen calls them, seek simplicity in theology. They strive for common ground and toleration as antidotes for religious conflict. Application of the new probability in the argument from design establishes at least some area of agreement. As the Port-Royal authors sensed, disputes over accounts of miracles can also be reformulated in ways less likely to divide the faithful. Royal Society theology makes as much of miracles as it makes of design. A few, like Spinoza, sense tension between belief in God as the perfect artisan and the idea that God might find it necessary to intervene in the course of natural events, but Newton's powerful influence reinforces the notion that God's active relation to creation is needed to keep the created order from falling apart. The crucial difficulty lies elsewhere: in the problem of relating the category of revelation to the theological findings of probable reasoning. The growing sense that the very notion of revelation poses a central theological problem is not a reaction to deistic critiques of liberal Anglicanism. Deism, to the contrary, inherits its interest in revelation, together with its preoccupation with design and miracles, from latitudinarian theology.[31] The same could be said in reference to the other problems given special emphasis during this period, such as the problem of theodicy and the critique of Augustinian positions on original sin.

Of all the Latitudinarians, Locke exerts the most pervasive influence on the eighteenth-century controversy. Both Deists and their opponents appeal to his authority, which is rivaled only by Newton's. It is important not to misread Locke by reading him backward, as it were, through the later invocations of his name. For in Locke's apparent reliance on the probability chapters of the Port-Royal *Logic* and his explicit attempt to bring the new probability together with Chillingworth's theory of certainty, he remains a child of the seventeenth century. For Locke the relation of revelation to probable reasoning is a problem to be addressed, and a crucial one at that. But he assigns probability a carefully delimited place amid the traditional categories, a place easily misconstrued if his comments about the role of reason as the guarantor of revelation are not interpreted with special caution.[32]

For the most part, Locke works within the traditional distinction between demonstrative knowledge and the sphere of mere belief or opinion. The two grounds of assent short of the certainty of demonstrative knowledge are revelation and probability. Revelation takes precedence over probability in the sense that evident revelation requires assent even when the content of such revelation runs against its likeliness to be true. Reason is the guarantor of revelation in two senses. First of all, no true revelation could contradict the absolutely certain results of truly demonstrative knowledge. Second, reason must determine whether the putative revelation in question is indeed revelation, which must be done in accordance with probable reasoning. If it is probable that the putative revelation in question is the work of God's hand, then the proposition commands our assent whether or not its *content* expresses a probable truth. One mark of divine authorship, besides compatibility with what we already know and with what has already been certified as revelation, is the attendant presence of miraculous signs. Hence the importance of miracles for Locke.

The next stage of the British discussion arrives when Deists, marching behind Locke's dictum about reason as the guarantor of revelation, ask why, if *all* evidence is to be taken into account (as Arnauld and Nicole had urged), the content of a putative revelation should not bear more directly upon our decision to accept or reject the proposition in question. If the proposition itself is inherently improbable, does this not make it less likely that the proposition is revelatory? As for miracles, does not the unlikelihood of the events described in any miracle account constitute internal evidence against the account itself? Armed with questions like these, the Deists proceed to whittle down latitudinarian theology until little besides the argument from design remains. Frei asserts that

> Two issues were at stake from the beginning. The first was of a predominately philosophical nature. It concerned the inherent rationality or credibility of the very idea of a historical revelation. Was it conceivable or intelligible? Is it likely, it was asked, that a perfectly good God should have left mankind without decisive guidance for so long, only to grant the privilege finally to a tiny, rude, and isolated fraction of the human race? . . . Furthermore, is the appeal to the "mystery" of revelation anything other than an admission that the idea itself is unintelligible, a token of that unwarranted intrusion of imagination or, worse yet, sheer ignorant superstition into matters religious, which the new intellectual rigor must repel?

The second question was: Even granted the rationality or inherent possibility of revelation, how likely is it that such a thing has actually taken place? . . . The immediate question was whether there are good grounds for believing in the actual occurrence of the miraculous events constituting the indispensable evidence for historical revelation.[33]

It is easy enough to see how the central problems of the period, from theodicy to miracles, form an interlocking set. The important point to notice is that the deistic response to the latitudinarian stress on revelation in effect unleashes internal evidence from the carefully delimited place Locke accorded it. Deism, in short, accepts only those tenets of traditional theology that can be established independently as probable hypotheses. Deists divide mainly on the question of whether their work purifies or obliterates Christianity. In Locke revelation retains its status as an independent ground of assent. Revelation and reason confirm each other. In Deism reason renders revelation either improbable or redundant. The supernatural mysteries of faith, in particular, are declared paradoxical and, therefore, improbable. Hence the significance of John Toland's title, *Christianity not Mysterious* (1696).

Deism is not, however, an especially stable position. As Bishop Atterbury points out early in the debate, Deism tends to collapse into either orthodoxy or outright atheism if pressed hard enough.[34] Deism asks religion to pass muster in a court governed by new canons of appraisal. The question is whether anything worthy of the title "religion" can pass muster in this court.

This question becomes unavoidable after Hume. Hume applies the new canons of appraisal to Deism itself, to the immediate and great misfortune of Deism. This critique of Deism he couples with a deistic critique of the latitudinarian appeal to miracles as warrant for belief in revelation. While Hume sometimes expresses, or seems to express, assent to the hypothesis that the origin of the universe probably bears some remote analogy to human intelligence, and while he refers to this qualified assent as "genuine theism" or "true religion," the theism or religion professed here is absolutely minimal. Neither theoretical nor practical consequences, according to Hume, follow from such assent. Nor is the probability of the "religious hypothesis" high. Several alternative explanations of the phenomena are nearly as good, if not equally good or better. Why one should insist upon calling this minimal position "theism" or "religion" — apart from worries about censorship, harassment, and unemployment — is unclear.

Holbach and his circle of atheists in Paris used this question to poke fun at Hume, though not without great affection for his person and respect for his accomplishment. It is also a question Hume's theistic opponents used in denying him professional positions he dearly wished to hold. Hume's subtle use of irony and the dialogue in response to this crossfire of mild and harsh rebuke makes his final answer hard to discern. I shall, in what follows, largely ignore the notorious problems of interpretation surrounding Hume's views about religion. My interest, like that of Hume's atheistic admirers and clerical opponents, pertains less to his intentions than to the critique of religion his writings make possible. The issue here is historical significance, not the ambiguity and relative secrecy of mental life. Hume's historical significance for subsequent religious thought — from the vantage point not only of Parisian atheists and Scottish clergy but also of Hamann, Kant, and Kierkegaard — rests in the methodical critique of religion that can be extracted from his works. This critique sets the direction of future inquiry by making clear the severely limited character of any religious system that embraces the new probability. This closes lines of development that had been open. Whatever Hume's view of absolutely minimal theism might be, the position is not *religiously* satisfying, for nothing in the way of ritual or moral action follows from it. Readers are therefore bound to treat it as the conclusion of a *reductio ad absurdum* of latitudinarian and deistic premises. So Hume's importance as the third stage in the emergence of Enlightenment criticism of religion can be brought out most effectively if he is read as his contemporaries read him. About the negative thrust of his work they entertain no doubt.

Hume's critique of religion, as I shall reconstruct it, begins with an endorsement of deistic criticisms of the appeal to miracles. Hume is far from a Deist in sensibility; he would never express the confidence in reason so evident in the deistic writings. Yet on the issue of miracles, Hume shares with Deism a negative intent.

The issue itself is novel. In the Middle Ages, no one was expected to *become* a theist because of the authority of this or that account of a miracle. The authenticity of certain miracles came part and parcel with an entire network of beliefs and commitments not yet called in question. One became a theist as a matter of course. Latitudinarian theology, however, requires miracles as marks of revelation. Revelation itself is on the defensive, requiring certification by reason. Miracles become central when revelation becomes problematical.

Hume's essay "Of Miracles" belongs to this dialectical setting.[35] As several commentators have pointed out, Hume makes no attempt to prove that miracles cannot occur.[36] He is responding directly to latitudinarian claims. Latitudinarian theology appeals to miracles to solve a problem. Hume's point is that the solution does not work. He argues that "a miracle can never be proved, so as to be the foundation of a system of religion."[37] The point is epistemological. We could never have *reason to believe* that a miracle has *probably* occurred.

Hume defends his thesis with two sorts of arguments. The first kind, which restricts itself to consideration of external evidence alone, does not move significantly beyond Port-Royal. If we ignore (for the purposes of argument) the *content* of the testimony, what considerations would make a purported miracle highly probable? Certainly, we should give *great* credence to a piece of testimony only if the alleged witnesses are numerous, intelligent, well-educated, evidently honest, in the position of having something to lose if the account proves false, and operating publicly in a well-known part of the world. Weakness on any of these points weakens credibility of testimony, whether the issue is the miraculous or not. Crime detection employs such criteria. So does historiography (more radically so after Hume). Arnauld and Nicole had used such criteria to cast doubt on pagan witnesses while praising Augustine. Hume concludes, after reflecting on a handful of cases, that few (if any) reports of supposedly wondrous events can survive such scrutiny of witnesses. Moreover, time takes its toll. Each retelling introduces new possibilities for deception, hyperbole, and delusion. Ancient miracles, witnessed only by the vulgar, recounted over the generations in the secrecy of the cult, would be hard to believe. They would surely make slim evidence for revelation.

But that is not the end of it, for internal evidence remains to be taken into account. The other sort of argument deployed against the appeal to miracles, the sort Hume finds decisive, brings internal evidence into prominence. The crucial point to notice, Hume argues, is that the *content* of testimony that

endeavors to establish a miracle always diminishes the reliability of that testimony. "Suppose, for instance, that the
fact, which testimony endeavors to establish, partakes of the
extraordinary and the marvellous; in that case, the evidence,
resulting from the testimony, admits of a diminution, greater
or less, in proportion as the fact is more or less unusual."[38] Tall
tales are not likely stories, no matter who tells them. "*I should
not believe such a story were it told me by Cato*, was a pro-
verbial saying in Rome, even during the lifetime of the philosophical patriot. The incredibility of a fact, it was allowed,
might invalidate so great an authority."[39] The taller the tale,
the less likely the story. Tales of miracles, of supernatural inter-
ventions in the normal course of nature, are, by definition, the
least likely stories possible. For if we are confident enough of
the regularity of our experience to postulate a natural law,
then all the weight of our prior experience counts against the
likelihood of the miracle. "A miracle is a violation of the laws of
nature; and as a firm and unalterable experience has established these laws, the proof against a miracle, from the very
nature of the fact, is as entire as any argument from experience can possibly be imagined."[40]

Hume's methodological insight, already implicit in the
Port-Royal *Logic* but fully understood only in Hume's time and
later, is that by the now "commonsensical" canons of internal
evidence, miracles are *prima facie* unlikely. These canons make
even the best witness's report of truly extraordinary events
seem questionable. The less likely the alleged event, considered
in itself, the more likely it is that a report of the event involves
error, fabrication, or hyperbole. The doubts raised by such a
report must then be integrated into our assessment of the witness, thus diminishing his authority. "There must, therefore,
be a uniform experience against every miraculous event, otherwise the event would not merit that appellation. And as a
uniform experience amounts to a proof, there is here a direct
and full *proof*, from the nature of the fact, against the existence
of any miracle. . . ."[41]

Hume makes common cause with Deists against Latitudinarians, who, without grounds for deeming specific events
probably miraculous, lack criteria for distinguishing revelation.
He concludes, as some Deists would, that his method of reasoning "may serve to confound those dangerous friends or disguised enemies to the Christian Religion, who have undertaken

to defend it by the principles of human reason."[42] Christianity, as a religion of revelation, cannot successfully defend itself by appeal to probable reasoning. It rests on sheer faith or nothing at all. "And whoever is moved by Faith to assent to it, is conscious of a continued miracle in his own person, which subverts all the principles of his understanding, and gives him a determination to believe what is most contrary to custom and experience."[43] What, then, about religion without revelation? What about Deism itself? Short of the miracle of faith that *makes* one affirm revelation, which is, of course as unlikely as any miracle, what could sway us to accept the hypothesis that a personal God exists? Deists answered this question by arguing from the apparent design of the universe to the postulate of an intelligent creator.

It is easy, in retrospect, to see why the Deists were so taken by the argument from design, given the currency of the image of God as author of the book of nature and given the popularity of mechanistic models among the new scientists. Especially for the early Deists, the notion of internal evidence was only barely loosened from the idea of a divine signature in the book of nature. It would have been hard, in this setting, even to imagine nature as something unlike a book authored by God or a machine created by a supremely intelligent designer. The new probability, in early stages of the controversy over Deism, remained tied to the circumstances of its birth.

By Hume's day, however, the new probability has had time enough to loosen its connection with divine authorship and intelligent design. For Hume, the argument from design is no longer *obvious*. Well into the eighteenth century, Hume can treat God's existence as one among several possible explanations of the origin of the universe. This hypothesis will have to compete with others in light of all the evidence. It no longer seems tied up with the very idea of evidence itself. Hume can treat the relation between the world and artifacts as mere analogy.

Hume's critique of the argument from design, expressed by Philo in the *Dialogues Concerning Natural Religion*,[44] underlines the analogical structure of the argument and then undercuts the analogy. Is the suggested analogy between machines and the world all that strong? Philo suggests that the universe may be more like an organism than like a machine, in which case it may be plausible to suppose that the world was

produced by propagation. This analogy, unlike that to machines, does not push us toward acceptance of an *intelligent*
creator. All this is intended to muddy the waters, to make
design seem less simple than it once did. Consideration of other
analogies brings out the fact that we are here engaging in
inference to the best available explanation. Alternative hypotheses, perhaps founded on less remote analogies, must be
brought in for scrutiny and comparison.

Arguments by analogy establish a bare probability at
best. The final verdict on the proposed conclusion will depend
upon a wide variety of factors, only one of which is the strength
of the analogy. As the authors of the Port-Royal *Logic* argued,
all relevant considerations must be brought to bear before the
actual probability of a conclusion can be determined. This
dictum implies, according to Hume, that our solution to this
particular puzzle must cohere with our solutions to other puzzles. The principle of analogy invoked in the argument from
design contains and requires the clause "other things being
equal." In this case, according to Hume, other things are *not*
equal. For we have the problem of evil to ponder.

In its traditional setting, the problem of evil was a problem of logical coherence for theism. Traditional Christian
theism typically involves at least the following four claims:
(1) God is ominipotent.
(2) God is omniscient.
(3) God is perfectly good.
(4) There is considerable evil in the world.
At a glance, this set appears incoherent. If there is evil in the
world, it would seem that an all-powerful, all-knowing, and
perfectly benevolent God would have the ability, the understanding, and the motivation to remove that evil. How, then,
can we explain the presence of evil without revising our conception of his might, his intellect, or his morals? One option for
the theologian is to say that *we* cannot explain the presence of
evil, that the puzzle is a mystery only God himself can fathom.
Another option is to explicate the four claims in question so as
to remove the appearance of incoherence. A third is to show
how dropping one or more of the claims might be consistent
with a position deserving the title "Christian."

For Hume, the problem of evil is really another problem
altogether.[45] The burden of proof has shifted. Theology now
seeks to defend itself in the court of internal evidence. Mira-

From Mystery to Paradox   123

cles fail as marks of revelation, for internal evidence always leans the other way. God's existence, treated now as a hypothesis, can garner only limited plausibility from the argument from design. The matter will have to be settled in light of all relevant considerations. But, Hume asks, does not reflection on the problem of evil render the existence of a fully personal God endowed with moral attributes antecedently improbable? This question does not ask whether an adequate theodicy can be worked out within traditional theological assumptions. Hume does not presuppose that claims (1) through (4), properly explicated, constitute an inconsistent set. The traditional question asked whether, given the presence of evil in the world, the existence of a God of the kind Christians affirm is *possible*. The fate of theology did not hang, in the traditional setting, on providing a persuasive answer. Hume asks whether, given the presence of evil in the world, the existence of a God endowed with any personal attributes at all — especially moral ones — is *probable*. The existence of such a God could be highly improbable without being strictly impossible. So traditional theodicy is beside the point. And if the presence of evil in the world renders the existence of a personal God antecedently improbable, the significance of arguments from design will wane, and the deistic strategy will fail.

The problem of evil is no longer a problem of figuring out what God is up to, given all the theology we already believe. In a context shaped by the new probability, it is a problem of figuring out what kind of God — *if any* — is plausible as an explanation of the origins of the universe as we find it. Given the existence of earthquakes, plagues, and the suffering of innocent children, the existence of a supremely perfect personal God seems unlikely. To postulate such a God in order to explain nature's internal evidence would require complications of theory reminiscent of traditional theodicy in its most elaborate forms. If God has moral attributes, they are probably evenly distributed between good and evil. More modest hypotheses that explain just as much would ascribe no moral attributes to God or (so Hume's readers inferred) postulate no God at all.

Thus ends Hume's critique of latitudinarian and deistic strategies. Descartes's arguments for God's existence he finds weaker still, dependent as they are on a highly questionable theory of ideas. Henceforth, religious thought will become increasingly preoccupied with attempts to separate theology from the domain of probable reasoning. Theism, attracted by the promise of the new probability, becomes Deism. Deism, subjected to the tests of its own standards of judgment, becomes thoroughgoing critique.

I have spelled out Hume's critique of Latitudinarianism and Deism in (perhaps tedious) detail mainly to establish two points. The first is that, *pace* MacIntyre, Hume is not merely giving novel twists to arguments that had been available for centuries. He is responding to the fresh problems posed by latitudinarian and deistic dialectical aims, and his response makes especially deft use of the new probability. Hume was not a great theorist of probability. The probability chapter of the first *Enquiry* would not have historical interest had Hume not written it. It betrays above all how clumsily new the new probability theory still was. Hume was anything but clumsy in *using* the new probability, however, as his writings on religion make clear.

The second point to be established is that, *pace* popular opinion, Hume's critique of religion is not primarily a product of his empiricism. It depends instead on features of the new probability that, while at times associated with empiricism, are perfectly compatible with its rejection. At no point has my restatement of Hume's arguments required a foundationalist premise. This is important, for it means that rejection of foundationalism might strengthen Hume's case against religion. The foundationalism that gives Hume problems with induction would make all beliefs founder equally, but in the absence of such foundationalism religious beliefs can be seen clearly to founder on their own.

The *Enquiry's* famous concluding paragraph surely presupposes empiricism:

> When we run over libraries, persuaded of these principles, what havoc must we make? If we take in our hand any volume; of divinity or school metaphysics, for instance; let us ask, *Does it contain any abstract reasoning concerning quantity or number?* No. *Does it contain any experimental reasoning concerning matter of fact and existence?* No. Commit it then to the flames: For it can contain nothing but sophistry and illusion.[46]

But notice that the conclusion of the section on miracles can easily be detached from empiricist assumptions. Faith requires a continuous subversion of *all* the principles of understanding, and gives the believer "a determination to believe what is most contrary to *custom and experience.*" Hume has throughout the essay, been applying the principle that the wise man proportions his belief to the evidence, and this he interprets under the category of custom. He need appeal to experience in this context only in the nontechnical sense, not in the radically private sense essential to empiricism. So Hume's discussion of miracles, the crucial step of his critique of religion, can be viewed as part of the tradition of Castellio and Chillingworth — the tradition of "sound human judgment," not that of foundationalist epistemology. These traditions intermingle in the writings of Locke and Hume, but it is most important to untangle the strands if proper appreciation of Hume's accomplishment is to be achieved.

Stand back for a moment and compare extremes — not the extremes of witch doctor and nuclear physicist, but rather Aquinas and Hume. Aquinas represents a mode of thought in which, as Skorupski says, apparently "paradoxical beliefs can be defused by a second-order, or philosophical reinterpretation of the relationship between meaningfulness and intelligibility." For Hume, in contrast, "the recognition of logical paradox among accepted beliefs" necessarily "generates attempts to replace the affected parts by new theories at the first-order level." Nothing illustrates this better than the issue of miracles. Questions about the probability of miracle reports handed on by authority were, for Aquinas, self-answering. But where probability no longer can be equated with what the authorities approve — because we lack agreed-upon means for settling conflicts among authorities and questions of interpretation — miracle reports take on a new status. Internal evidence makes miracles, and for that matter the supernatural mysteries of faith, seem intrinsically improbable. The connection between credibility and authority is no longer there to protect the anomalies once central to tradition from critical scrutiny and likely rejection.

If Proudfoot is right, this should help explain why Aquinas would be given to distinctively religious experience whereas Hume would not.[47] When faced with an anomalous instance, both Aquinas and Hume would probably experience emotional arousal. But Aquinas's cognitive context would in some cases heighten this state and then supply religious interpretations. The connection between probability and authority would defuse ordinarily operative objections to the incomprehensible, and a theory of meaningfulness and intelligibility would distinguish religiously mysterious speech from the ordinary perils of self-contradiction. Not all paradoxical speech would be permitted — only that which ties into the testimony of authorities in the required way. So for Aquinas only some anomalies would be handled religiously. Others would arouse emotion as well, but this would be taken as doubt rather than awe — the emotional state that initiates inquiry and possible theoretical revision. For Hume, *all* anomalies would fall into this class, since the connection between credibility and authority no longer protects *some* anomalies from criticism.

Not all anomalies would lead to rejection or immediate revision of theory, even for Hume. Kuhn has shown why: even the most critical scientist will hold onto an accepted theory in the face of acknowledged anomalies so long as competing theories seem even more problematical or less intelligible. Hume might be given to heightened emotional states when faced with an anomaly — states such as the despair, expressed in Hume's lament, that nature cannot be known or, more positively, the awe scientists sometimes speak of when frustrated in their attempts to explain. But neither Hume nor the critical scientist would be disposed to take a hard paradox or a miracle precisely *as true*, and this would, in effect, disenchant their experience of the world.

What is it, then that accounts for the emergence of the distinctively modern cultured despiser of religion, his critique of traditional theism, his sensibility? MacIntyre has distinguished three types of conceptual change:

> There is the type of case where a concept works very well, so long as certain questions are not asked about it, and it may be that for a long time in a given society there is no occasion for raising such questions. The concept of the divine right of kings will undergo a strain which reveals internal incoherences only when rival claimants to sovereignty appear, for it contains no answer to the question, which king has divine right? Then there is the type of case where incoherence . . . (is) to some extent manifest to the users of the concept. But the use of the concept is so intimately bound up with forms of description which cannot be dispensed with that any device for putting up with the incoherence is more tolerable than dispensing with the concept. A third type of case is that in which the point of a concept or

group of concepts lies in their bearing upon behavior. But changed patterns of social behavior deprive the concept of point. So that although there is no internal incoherence in the concept, the concept can no longer be embodied in life as it once was, and it is either put to new uses or it becomes redundant.[48]

MacIntyre suggests that the answer to our question will pertain to "the second and third types" just described.[19] My rendition of the story suggests a more complicated answer. For the problem of many authorities bears resemblance to the problem of divine right mentioned under MacIntyre's first type. I am suggesting that late medieval and early modern circumstances made the leading available solutions to the problem of authority seem incapable of restoring order to a divided Europe, and thus made a new, less distinctively religious, approach to the problem desirable. The Port-Royal *Logic* is one, especially influential, attempt to work out such an approach, making special reference to the notion of probability. The new notion of probability secularized a major area of thought and ushered in a distinctively modern kind of criticism. This does not mean that MacIntyre's second and third types are not part of the story, but only that the first warrants more attention than it has yet been given. My version of the story also brings out, I think, exactly how the relativity of refutability figures in.

7. Paradox Lost, Paradox Regained

The first crisis of modern theism was brought on by the problem of many authorities and culminated in the radical critique of religion Holbach and others were able to extract from Hume. The second was brought on by the question of what to do about Hume and culminated in the Christian critique of religion one can extract from Kierkegaard and Barth. The first crisis transformed the "mysteries" of traditional Christian faith into paradoxes, and then pushed them from the arena of serious discussion altogether, at least for a highly instructive moment or two. The second carried them back with a vengeance in all their rigidity, though not without altering significantly the social location of theology. All paradoxes possess what Quine once called "an initial air of absurdity." One softens a paradox, as I am using the expression, when one removes the initial air of absurdity by reinterpretation of terms, conceptual revision, or the introduction of relevant but previously overlooked information. A hard paradox is a proposition, set of propositions, or state of affairs the unintelligibility of which resists complete removal by any such means. We need to discover how such paradoxes came to be deemed essential to Christian faith even by its more critically insightful friends. This may also provide clues for understanding the declining cultural significance of debates about God.

The dialectical progression that leads from Kant and Schleiermacher to Hegel, through Hegel's followers to Marx and Kierkegaard, and finally into Barth, Bultmann, and Tillich takes Hume's accomplishment for granted, and asks simply what remains possible *after* Hume. Post-Humean theology, like modern philosophy, is essentially belated, but it was fathered in circumstances it would rather disown — under the rude charge of illegitimacy. Its central decision has always been whether to bear illegitimacy as a cross, the scandal of faith, or to explain the stigma away with special pleading. Either way, the question is *how*, not *whether*, to make a virtue of post-Humean necessity. The attempt to refute Hume on his own terms, to revive natural theology by meeting the challenge head on, had retreated into obscure corners of the academy by the end of the Victorian period.

Just as the problem of authority manifested itself in both social and intellectual dimensions, the problem of how to handle Hume's intellectual challenge was from the start intertwined with the general cultural problems posed by social differentiation. The new probability had been designed to sidestep theological problems created by the fragmentation of authority. Once unleashed from a narrowly delimited position between the traditional categories of demonstration and testimony, the new probability caused problems for theology. But by the time these problems became evident, the new probability had already been used to win greater independence for other domains of thought and practice — especially natural science and the law, each of which seemed central to the emerging culture and quickly became enshrined in powerful institutions. This development was soon to become more pronounced in the disciplinary differentiation of the university. The simultaneous emergence of Pietism combined with such factors to pose pointed questions about the place of religious thought and practice in a differentiated society.

We can see how all this related to Hume's challenge by turning to Kant, the most influential respondent to Hume's critique of religion and the great philosopher of differentiation. Stanley Cavell has written that modern philosophy and the modern arts share with theology a common difficulty, brought on by

> a moment in which history and its conventions can no longer be taken for granted; the time in which music and painting and poetry (like nations) have to define themselves against their pasts; the beginning of the moment in which each of the arts becomes its own subject, as if its immediate artistic task is to establish its own existence.[1]

For Kant, this crucial moment came when Hume awakened him from dogmatic slumber. His response was to try to do for all spheres of culture what they would soon have to do for themselves. As Richard Rorty has written,

Kant thought that there were three permanent data of philosophy: (1) Newtonian physics and the resulting conception of a unified science centering on mathematical descriptions of micro-structures; (2) the common moral consciousness of a North German Pietist; (3) the sense of delicacy, of playful freedom from the imperatives of scientific inquiry and moral duty, offered by the eighteenth-century aesthetic consciousness. The aim of philosophy was to preserve these cultural accomplishments by drawing the lines between them (preferably writing a separate book about each) and showing how they could be rendered compatible with one another and made "necessary." Philosophy . . . was a matter of drawing boundaries to keep scientific inquiry from interfering with morals, the aesthetic from interfering with the scientific, and so on.[2]

In taking on this project, Kant was reflecting the growing differentiation of his own culture as well as defending that culture against both (a) the imposition of an overarching unity that would restrict the autonomy of the various domains and (b) the elimination of any domain that deserves a place in the scheme of things.

Ernest Gellner has referred to Kant's "two fears": "The first fear is that the mechanical vision does *not* hold; the second fear is that it *does*. The first fear is for science, and the second for morality."[3] Both fears, of course, had been heightened for Kant by Hume — the first by Hume's empiricist skepticism about science, the second by Hume's writings on morality and religion. Kant set out to allay these fears by delimiting the respective spheres clearly, distinguishing their proper from their improper functions, and grounding each in universal structures of the human mind. The transcendental argumentation that was meant to provide this grounding had the added benefits of giving philosophy a role central to the culture (as a kind of cultural magistrate) and of giving it something suitably distinguishable and disciplined to do in the academy during a period of growing professionalization.[4]

So Kant "justified" science transcendentally, and thus described the newly disenchanted world of Newtonian science as universal and necessary,[5] while limiting the pretensions of science, and thus making room for moral responsibility and faith. He declared Hume right about our ignorance of things-in-themselves but wrong about the structures of mind that make knowledge of the world of experience possible, and right about the inability of theoretical reason to achieve knowledge of things divine but wrong about the essence of religion. Kant's response to Hume's critique of religion is a reflection, on the plane of philosophical sophistication, of the Pietist solution to the problem of faith and culture. Religion is not essentially a theoretical matter at all. Deism, like the "overly intellectual" Lutheranism against which the Pietism of Kant's upbringing rebelled, is both bad religion and bad science — the result of cultural trespassing. Deism deserves Hume's rebuke. The simple moral faith of a North German Pietist, with its stress on the contrite conscience and its avoidance of theoretical abstraction from the life of faith, does not.

Schleiermacher experienced Kant's work of separation as both a victory and a threat — a victory at the level of general strategy, but a threat to religion and theology in the execution of detail. Schleiermacher took it as his own task to establish the existence of religion and theology within the culture without permitting their reduction to morality, and this he attempted to do by working variations on the Kantian theme of differentiation. Religion deserves a sphere unto itself. It is a separate "third" over against the realms of theoretical and practical reason. It deserves its own full-scale transcendental analysis.

Schleiermacher too was a Pietist by upbringing and disposition. It is no accident, then, that piety was, for him, the essence of religion. What is piety? Piety is neither a knowing nor a doing. The phrase "knowledge of God" is, as Schleiermacher puts it in the wake of Kant's first *Critique*, "an old expression."[6] But, Kant notwithstanding, the pious man, *qua* pious, "knows nothing" about the object of Kantian ethics.[7]

> Only by keeping quite outside the range of both science and of practice can it maintain its proper sphere and character. Only when piety takes its place alongside of science and practice, as a necessary, an indispensable third, as their natural counterpart, not less in worth and splendor than either, will the common field be altogether occupied and human nature on this side complete.[8]

Religion, the essence of which is piety, must be separate but equal, and piety is a determination of *feeling*. This conclusion avoids the reduction of religion to morality, and thus forestalls the rejection of theism by those who find Kant's arguments for the postulates specious or superfluous, but it does raise a new kind of difficulty for theology, and it may make religion seem altogether too separate for either its own good or that of the culture as a whole.

Kant had already been faced with the difficulty of showing how the religion of pure rational faith could be related to historical Christianity in its concreteness without rendering the latter merely redundant. His response to this difficulty treats historical religions as "vehicles" of pure rational faith — vehicles ultimately to be overcome by moral progress but still suited to the needs of a fallible, sensuous humanity.[9] The seemingly theoretical claims of traditional theism are given allegorical interpretations intended to extract latent moral content. Schleiermacher agreed with Kant's conclusion that theology could not be both legitimate and theoretical, but he wanted more for theology than allegorical speech that could be explained away in terms of Kantian ethics. Hence his stress on feeling. Yet how might theology be related to feeling? Piety is a determination of feeling, but a feeling we express in speech as an experience *of* something, an experience of absolute dependence *on* the "Whence" of that very feeling. The word "God," according to Schleiermacher, originally means for us simply the "Whence" of our piety. Religious language *expresses* religious experience. This dictum should tell us how to interpret religious texts, like the Bible, and also how to proceed with theology. Just as the Bible must be interpreted historically as a human document giving expression to the experience of piety in an actual religious community, the theologian must begin and end with the experience of his own tradition and community in all its concreteness and phenomenological complexity.

In saying this, Schleiermacher opened the way to biblical criticism, the phenomenology of religion, and hermeneutics as these fields developed from the early nineteenth to the midtwentieth century.[10] He also opened the way to liberal theology, and thus to liberal theology's central problems. We have seen that Schleiermacher accepted Kant's criticisms of pseudoscientific theology, the theology which claims for itself theoretical knowledge of God. But does not going this far with Kant threaten to reduce the interest of theology? What makes theology more interesting than so many *oohs* and *aahs* or descriptions of heartburn if it is essentially expressive or descriptive of feelings? Even if we postpone the question of whether feeling and knowing can be distinguished as radically as Schleiermacher supposes, we shall need to ask how theology can retain interest without entering the cognitive sphere. It may be that Schleiermacher's theology *seems* interesting *only* because its essentially emotive character is masked by misleadingly propositional forms of expression. It is more likely, however, that Schleiermacher has simply smuggled extensive cognitive commitments past his own Kantian censor. Either way, his hopes for theology are jeopardized.

Notice how many apparently epistemic categories Schleiermacher actually uses to characterize piety and to elevate its importance above the realm of heartburn and tickles. The pious person is *conscious of* an utter causality, *aware of* the Infinite. He *feels that* he is absolutely dependent upon something, which he designates with the term "God." Now either explanatory claims are being made here or not. If not, we remain in the realm of heartburn and tickles. But if such claims are being made, the Kantian criticisms can be brought to bear. If religious experience is immediate or intuitive, in the sense of "not mediated by the concepts of the understanding," then it must surely be blind by Kantian standards. If it is blind, it is unclear how one theological utterance could be judged better than another as an expression of religious experience except perhaps with respect to emotive tone.

These and related difficulties have haunted the liberal theological tradition from the beginning. How can theology be rendered defensible without drastically diminishing those of its features that make people *want* to defend it? A closely related question, which brings out the social dimension of Schleiermacher's intellectual predicament, is this: How can theology be successfully separated from the arena of probable reasoning and "theoretical inference to the best explanation" without also being isolated from the culture upon which it would like to have an impact? How, in other words, can we accept the Pietist solution to the problem of faith and culture without sentencing religion to exile from the cultural center?

Kant had claimed an underlying unity for theoretical and practical reason and had used the aesthetic to mitigate the sense that he had given no account of human wholeness. But piety alone, in Schleiermacher's nonetheless paradoxical view, could be both a separate "third" and the tie that binds an otherwise fragmented individual or community together. How so?

Schleiermacher's answer tries to turn the connections between Pietism and Romanticism to the benefit of each. As a Moravian raised in the Pietist enthusiasm of a transitional social class and as one of the socially displaced young men drawn to the Schlegels and the Romantic salons of Berlin, he (like Schelling) was especially well situated to make the most of these connections. (Schelling's synthesis was more philosophical than theological, his Pietism of the more mystical Württemberger variety.) Schleiermacher used Romantic categories to temper the Pietist tendency toward cultural isolation. In giving Pietism appropriately Romantic ideological trappings, he sought to establish for it some measure of continuity with the principal vitalities of contemporary arts and letters. By stressing the communal dimension of Pietism, he mitigated the Romantic tendency toward individualism and tried to secure a spiritual unity for the differentiated spheres of the emerging national culture.

Hegel and his followers would hereafter always treat Pietism and Romanticism as two aspects of a single cultural development, best expressed in the thought of Schleiermacher and Schelling. Hegel applauded this development as the broader realization of Luther's discovery of the heart, but he found the Romantic glorification of intuition and feeling one-sided — and therefore to be transcended. Hegel prosecuted what amounted to a Kantian case against Schleiermacher, though of course not in the pursuit of ultimately Kantian ends. Experience that remains unmediated by concepts also remains blind, "the night in which all cows are black." Intuitive experience of the absolute must not simply be expressed in imagistic representations but must also be raised into cognitive reflection. Only such reflection, as achieved in Hegelian philosophy, can overcome the bifurcation and division to which late-eighteenth-century German culture and Kantian philosophy had reduced everything. Only such reflection can give the truth of an underlying unity its proper *form* of expression.

As a young man, Hegel was completely convinced that, as he put it in his first published pamphlet, "bifurcation is the source of the need for philosophy." He became increasingly convinced that the overcoming of bifurcation in his own culture would have to be achieved concretely before it could be given convincing philosophical expression. In the dimension of political economy this was Hegel's problem of the state, in the dimension of spirituality his problem of public religion. Hegel's experimental "lives" of Jesus, which display most clearly the movement of his early thinking, finally reject the religion of Kantian morality as a symptom of modern alienation in favor of the unity of the Hellenic ethos as an ideal. Yet how can such unity be achieved again now that the immediacy of Greek *Sittlichkeit* has been lost? Hegel was too sensitive to the specificity of historical development to suppose that the Greek ethos could simply be transplanted to modern Germany. What, then, about Christianity? Can it, even after the demise of medieval Christendom and the emergence of "enlightened" thought, meet contemporary needs, "not only as a private religion but also as a general public religion"?[11]

Hegel reached maturity finally ready to answer this question firmly and affirmatively.[12] In doing so, he took Christianity with full seriousness as both a developing social-historical entity and a rich doctrinal system. For Hegel, the culmination of the development of Christianity is the complete integration of Pietist subjectivity with the secular this-worldliness of contemporary culture — an integration that "actualizes" the union, expressed imagistically in the incarnation, of the divine and the human. It is this bourgeois-Christian world, as Karl Löwith has called it, to which Hegel's mature system gives philosophical expression. In Emil Fackenheim's words, "the actual existence of one specific historical world is the cardinal condition without which, by its own admission and insistence, the Hegelian philosophy cannot reach its ultimate goal."[13]

> What attests to the finality and indestructibility of the modern bourgeois, Protestant world? As regards its religious aspect, it is the faith of a community which bears witness to the indwelling Kingdom of God, which is eternal. As regards its secular aspect, it is the varied manifestations of free modern rationality. These range from modern natural science through modern morality to the modern state, and they are all free or rational because ideally infinite: present and future obstacles are all potential conquests. But the two testimonies — religious and secular — are inadequate so long as they are mutually hostile or indifferent. They become adequate only when they point to each other, i.e., when they make the modern bourgeois, Protestant world *one* world. The Christian salvation has descended from a medieval Catholic heaven into a modern Protestant heart on earth; this remains a worldless pietism unless

this heart demands free worldly action as its authentic secular expression.[14]

The attempt to transcend a merely separate Pietism and to secure a truly spiritual cohesion for modern culture is for Hegel a sign of the arrival of the cultural preconditions for philosophy's absolute achievement — the *comprehension* of what, for Schleiermacher's intuitionism, must remain blind to itself. From a strictly religious point of view, Schleiermacher's problem is that he cannot finally do justice to Christianity as a doctrinal system. Hegelian philosophy comprehends and transcends this-worldly Protestantism by giving Christian doctrine, as the highest expression of religious consciousness, its properly philosophical form, thereby recognizing and affirming its *cognitive content* as well as its emotive inwardness.

It is here that the paradoxes of Christian faith re-enter our story. Deists had discarded the hard paradoxes as patently improbable; Kant had reduced them to moral allegories fit for the purposes of educating a fallible, sensuous humanity but ultimately to be overcome in pure rational faith; Schleiermacher had subjected them to the equally reductive hermeneutic of emotive expressivity. But Hegel was prepared to treat them as the essential truths of religious consciousness. Religious consciousness attempts to say in symbols and stories what ordinary consciousness cannot say in more direct fashion. Judged by the standards of the understanding, religious language seems to violate our basic norms of intelligibility. Deists took the violation seriously and responded with disbelief. Kant and Schleiermacher explained the violation away by softening the paradoxes with reductive interpretations. Hegel took such responses as evidence of the limitations of ordinary understanding. Religious paradoxes should not be explained away in terms of ordinary language. Their whole point is to represent (*vorstellen*) what ordinary consciousness cannot express directly — the underlying unities that escape the essentially rigid and divisive categories to which the understanding reduces everything. The most paradoxical of all truths — the unity of subject and object, conscience and community, human and divine — must be preserved but transcended. These very truths (and not softened versions thereof) must be given comprehensible form. This is what the new logic and conceptuality of Hegel's mature system are meant to provide: an interpretation of the hard paradoxes that, far from reducing them to the categories of the understanding or mistaking their higher truth for ordinary falsehood, raises them up to the comprehensive intelligibility of reason.

One problem with Hegel's comprehensive system, of course, was comprehending it. And, as his critique of Kant shows, Hegel was perfectly prepared to treat his opponents' difficulties on this score as symptoms of entrapment in the workings of the understanding (as contrasted with the higher faculty of reason): Kant had failed to achieve a correct view of the capacities of reason (*Vernunft*) largely because he philosophized from the vantage point of the understanding (*Verstand*). Hegel had to take more seriously, however, those problems connected with the empirical implications of his doctrines, for it follows from his own pronouncements that the bourgeois-Christian world must be and increasingly become the unitary culture his philosophy brings to self-consciousness in thought. If the system presupposes a history of a certain sort, a history that has now culminated in a culture that unites possibilities once viewed as strictly opposed, then evidence of an inability to transcend fragmentation in life would have severe consequences for thought. Radical fragmentation of the bourgeois-Christian world would, by Hegelian lights, disconnect the system — and above all its philosophies of religion and of right — from its world. The system would become what Hegel most definitely did not want it to become — a mere idealism, unfaithful to the reality of life.

Karl Barth was right to speak of Hegel as the philosopher of self-confidence. Without the evidence that confirms the self-confidence of supreme cultural achievement, Hegelian philosophy leaves the reality of this world for merely abstract thought. But, contrary to legend, Hegel was not always sure that this self-confidence could be sustained in the face of contemporary evidence, and he was perfectly aware of what disconfirming evidence in the political and religious life of his people would mean for the fate of his thought. Fackenheim points to remarks in *Philosophy of Right* and *Philosophy of History* in which Hegel voices his fear that unity has been achieved in thought but *not* in life. Fackenheim continues:

> Most startling, and indeed for all its restraint altogether shattering, is the end of the *Philosophy of Religion*. This is a mournful litany on contemporary Christian decadence. Faith — for which "the very gates of hell cannot prevail against the

Kingdom of God" — may reject the "discordant note (of) the spiritual community . . . passing away." Philosophy cannot reject it; for it sees faith itself in a state of decay. "The discordant note is actual in real life. Religious unity has vanished from modern life, as much as it did in Imperial Rome . . . when the Divine was profaned." Hence political life — which requires a religious basis and inspiration — is "inactive and without confidence," so much so that all artificial attempts to revive it are foredoomed to failure.

   . . . Philosophy, itself a form of spiritual life, can heal fragmentation in the sphere of thought; it cannot otherwise heal it. In life, the discordant note remains. And — so Hegel concludes — philosophic thought has no choice but to become a "separate sanctuary," inhabited by philosophers who are an "isolated order of priests." They cannot "mix with the world, but must leave to the world the task of settling how it might find its way out of its present state of disruption."[15]

It is as if Hegel foresaw both the complete disintegration of the bourgeois-Christian world and the resultant fragmentation of his philosophy into the philosophical idealism of the Hegelian Right and the post-philosophical worldliness of the Hegelian Left.

   As James Massey has shown, the events of 1837 gave rise to a new sense that liberal Hegelian hopes for German culture may have run aground in the backwaters of reaction. Arnold Ruge's conflicts with Heinrich Leo and C. W. Hengstenberg, which led to the first of many lost professorships for the young Hegelians, provoked a reassessment of the historical significance of religion in general and of Pietism in particular. The Hegelian Left quickly came to identify Pietism with the forces of reaction, and defined its essential tendency as withdrawal from the world. According to Ruge, Romanticism and Pietism — however progressive at their moment of birth in rebellion against overly formal rationalism and a heartless religious orthodoxy — must now be opposed as regressive. Those features of Christianity that have contributed to the possibility of a genuinely unified culture are now so thoroughly integrated with the secular world that they can no longer be singled out as distinctively religious. That part of the original Pietist impulse still distinguishable from the culture as a whole, a kind of monkish withdrawal alien to the spirit of modernity, we may now renounce as an obstacle to future human development, the mere residue of a earlier struggle for freedom.[16]

Feuerbach would soon draw out the consequences of this reassessment for theological reflection. If Pietism in its mature (and therefore essential) form is a regressive social force, so too will theological trappings in philosophy become manifestly regressive once the higher standpoint of reason has been achieved. Philosophy retains the truth that humanity is divine, but (Hegel notwithstanding) only a radically anthropological reading of this truth can overcome the alienation of man from himself. History is not the process by which God overcomes his alienation from himself by uniting with humanity but rather the process by which man overcomes his alienation from himself by reclaiming for himself the attributes of the divine. So long as the divinity of humanity is interpreted theologically, the complete immanence of spirit has not yet been achieved. If God is human nature objectified in wishful and imaginative representations, he can be nothing *more* than that without prolonging *human* self-alienation. A humanity perfectly at one with itself will be post-religious. Theology brought down to earth will be Feuerbachian humanism.

Beyond Feuerbach lay a challenge to religion which, because it could take Hume's accomplishment for granted, was all the more radical. Kant and Schleiermacher had unwittingly set the stage for what Paul Ricoeur has called the hermeneutics of suspicion, as practiced by Marx, Nietzsche, and Freud. The strategy of separation, far from protecting religious life and thought from criticism, had produced a new brand of critic. Henceforth, defenders of theism had to face a kind of diagnosis more searching than Hume had undertaken in his *Natural History*.

Hegel, it seems in retrospect, had been right to treat the strategy of separation as overly successful. Only by restoring to Christian theism its cognitive dimension and by taking seriously precisely those paradoxical doctrines that make it seem distinctive to secular thought could it retain a role of *any* centrality in modern culture. But what Bishop Atterbury had said of Deism could also be said of Hegel's system: it was an intrinsically unstable position. After his death, Hegel's followers lost no time dividing on the issue of what his reformulations of paradoxes might mean. Their interpretations slid away from what Fackenheim calls the Hegelian middle — either toward an abstract idealism or away from metaphysics altogether. No one could occupy the middle ground Hegel had tried to stake out. Hegel, it would seem, had attempted the impossible. Neither philosophical thought nor practical activity could be both completely secular *and* completely religious. Religion could not be both distinguishable *and* thoroughly integrated.

Hegel knew that his philosophy would seem unintelligible if the culture itself was not capable of uniting opposed forces. From his own point of view, then, the appearance of Marx and Kierkegaard in the 1840s could be explained only by the disintegration of the bourgeois-Christian world. Löwith's is, therefore, the most telling commentary on Hegel. A latter-day owl of Minerva takes flight at the twilight of Christendom, and surveys the pieces even Hegel could not put back together again. Between them, according to Löwith, Marx and Kierkegaard pose the "exclusive choices" of post-Hegelian Christianity — Marx by diagnosing the Pietist spirit as withdrawal from the suffering of a spiritless (but nonetheless actual) world, Kierkegaard by diagnosing the public religion of the official culture as essentially irreligious. Christianity either becomes an opiate or loses its soul.

This was the Hegelian conclusion to draw from the disappointment of Hegel's hopes for bourgeois-Christian society. It was not, however, the conclusion mainstream bourgeois-Christian thought drew for itself in the nineteenth century. Hegel's most careful and insightful readers — those who, like Marx and Kierkegaard, took him most seriously — were better prepared than others were to find the century's "culture Protestantism" disappointing. Albrecht Ritschl was able to return to Kant in the 1870s — and, by way of Kant, to the Reformation and the New Testament — without a sense that something had gone wrong at a very profound level in his society. The Kingdom of God, so central to Ritschl's theology and so potentially radical a doctrine, was for him largely an affirmation of the present. Original sin was a doctrine to be discarded. Ritschl lacked not only Hegel's sensitivity to the tragic disunities of modern life but also his own master's sense of the depth of human evil.

It is interesting to note that Ritschl took pains — the pains it took to write the three volumes of his *Geschichte des Pietismus*[17] — to oppose Pietism publicly and vehemently. He was, in this one respect, an heir to Hegelianism, and carried on the decidedly "unKantian" tradition that identifies Pietism with monastic withdrawal and mystical tendencies. Unlike Hegel, he did not want to subsume Pietism into a higher synthesis. He wanted simply to get back, behind the mysticism implicit in Schleiermacher and explicit in Schelling, to Kant. Ritschl preached a public religion of private virtue — a Hegelian culture of a sort, though without the dialectical tension or metaphysical bent. It was to this end that he used Kant's moral religion: as a way to relieve pressures at the level of theory while praising Protestant culture as a way of life.

Looking back on his own youth Karl Barth would later say, "To the prevailing tendency of about 1910 among the younger followers of Albrecht Ritschl I attached myself with passable conviction."[18] This conviction did not, as anyone even remotely familiar with modern theology knows, survive the events of the next dozen years. It took the First World War to bring the discordant voices of the previous century to center stage, where Barth made them speak as a single chorus — echoing, however faintly and indirectly, the gospel itself. The war had created an audience hospitable to attacks on liberalism. At first Barth simply addressed this audience with his own disillusionment. As he put it, in the darkness of the church steeple he reached for a rope to keep himself from falling, and found himself surrounded and the entire countryside awakened by the clanging of bells. But Barth made his case so forcefully and with such brilliance that the dialectical setting of theological discussion was completely transformed. Barth transformed the dialectical setting mainly by giving an implicit account of it that others had trouble evading.

Barth was fully prepared to say that there is no way around Schleiermacher and Kant to the revival of natural theology. Hume was right about Deism. But, Barth added, the alternative of liberal theology is also closed. One cannot begin with Schleiermacher's principles without ending in something like Feuerbach's conclusions. If theology, thanks to Kant's so-called Copernican revolution, takes as its point of departure the phenomena of human religious experience (as in Schleiermacher) or the phenomena of the moral life (as in Kant and Ritschl), it will inevitably come to grief in the diagnosis of merely human projection. Moreover, Marx and Kierkegaard were right, each in his own way, about "Christian" religiosity. Most important, these conclusions follow from St. Paul as much as they do from Hume or Marx. Human religion — in-

cluding the public religion of Christendom, the private religion
of Pietist enthusiasm, and the intellectual religion of natural
or liberal theology — is, quite simply, all too human. If
Christian religion is, like all religion, *human* striving after God,
then the gospel condemns it in the name of God far more forcefully than secular critics could ever condemn it in the name of
human reason and freedom. Justification is by faith alone, and
faith is God's gift to give.

The theological significance of Barth's critique of religion
rested first of all in his attempt to bring out the epistemological
meaning of the doctrine of justification by faith. Barth had in
effect returned, by way of Kierkegaard, to the conclusion of
Hume's "Of Miracles," though of course without the ironic
inflection:

> . . . we may conclude, that the *Christian Religion* not only was
> at first attended with miracles, but even at this day cannot be
> believed by any reasonable person without one. Mere reason is
> insufficient to convince us of its veracity: And whoever
> is moved by *Faith* to assent to it, is conscious of a continued
> miracle in his own person. . . .[19]

Faith creates a crisis in our very being. It is not something to
which *we* move in order to resolve problems or fill lacks. Theology is not a striving for faith — except insofar as it is merely
religious. Faith grounds itself in God's word. It does not need
grounding from us. Attempts to place faith on firm grounding
or to reach faith from a basis of human reason or experience are
clearly an affront to God's otherness and bound to erode faith's
essential content. Natural and liberal theologies tend to sweep
aside or soften the hard paradox of God's revelation in Christ
from which faith must proceed. Faith, with God as its object,
cannot help but be paradoxical.

Feuerbach and Kierkegaard could agree with Hegel that
the hard paradoxes of faith are essential to genuine Christianity, but neither could find any reason for believing
that Hegel had absorbed firmly paradoxical content into a
higher synthesis. For Feuerbach, the divinity of humanity
therefore became a figure of speech; a less symbolic reading of
the paradox would be as unintelligible as the barely stated
paradox itself. For Kierkegaard, the union of divine and human
in Jesus Christ remained absurd; only a misreading of the paradox could absorb it into the intelligibility of a higher synthesis.
But Hegel's accomplishment had made clear to both that when

Christianity ceases to be a paradox, it ceases to be itself. Kierkegaard's recognition of this Hegelian truth was one of the morals to the story of nineteenth-century thought with which Barth confronted academic theology.

Kierkegaard argued, in the voice of Johannes Climacus, that the "trick that speculative philosophy contrives to perform" with the word *aufheben* is like talking "with one's mouth full of hot mush."[20] In Hegel's system, the concepts of Christianity have "been emasculated and the words have been made to mean anything and everything."[21] This insistence on the absolute rigidity of the paradoxes of faith requires no documentation; it is the most familiar aspect of Kierkegaard's authorship. But it is still striking to find Kierkegaard, in his little book *On Authority and Revelation*, linking as a Proudfoot might the hardness of the paradox to the possibility of distinctively Christian emotion. "For a Christian awakening what is required, on the one hand, is being grasped in a Christian sense and, on the other hand, conceptual and terminological firmness and definiteness."[22] Here we have the full — and now unmitigated — recovery of paradox.

Christianity, if it is to be true to itself, will have to make ontological claims. But it cannot *defend* them in secular or philosophical terms. Theology cannot be apologetics. This is the conclusion that stands behind both Kierkegaard's indirect communication and Barth's *Dogmatics*. Each had to discover something nonapologetic to do with his authorship. The problem was further complicated for Barth by the fact that he was not Kierkegaard. Because *theology* "could not actually be the 'theology of crisis' for longer than a moment,"[23] Barth had to find something nonapologetic for theology to be as an intellectual discipline, while also avoiding Schleiermacher's (and Protestant Scholasticism's) reduction of theology to *Glaubenslehre*. The second turning point in Barth s work — the point at which he moved beyond his critical negation of liberalism and discovered his constructive vocation as a dogmatic theologian — was his book on Anselm.[24] For here, without turning away from his earlier claims (except to admit their one-sidedness), Barth portrayed theology as "faith in search of understanding" — a positive project, both cognitive and "rational," but one that proceeds from God's word rather than striving toward faith. The revelation of God in Jesus Christ is the *sole* condition of whatever knowledge (if that is the right expression) we might have of him. "Knowledge" is not the right expression if it implies that *we* justify the theological claims of dogmatic theology. But we can *be* justified in making these claims — justified by God's word. Barth's project is not epistemologically motivated. His early use of neo-Kantian and idealistic vocabulary was meant to undercut epistemological orientation in theology, though the vocabulary itself was still epistemological. After 1931, Barth dropped this vocabulary, turned his attention from Schleiermacher, and set himself the task of concentrating first and foremost on the *object* of faith.[25] We cannot reason our way to faith, but actual faith does create a context of reasons within which theology as a rational endeavor can be undertaken.

Theology may be a rational endeavor for Barth, and he certainly does not revel in the paradoxical as many "Kierkegaardians" and "Barthians" have, but he does seek to return theology to its "proper basis" in the divine authority of God's word. He cannot say, as Aquinas could, that divine authority makes revealed truths — however incomprehensible in the final analysis — the most highly probable of all truths. For probability in Barth's context is not a matter of what the authorities approve. Faith causes us to believe (and, after that, to seek appropriately partial and modest understanding of) what seems supremely improbable to the natural light of the human intellect. Even in faith understanding never fully penetrates the mystery. Faith remains a paradox despite the fact that in this mystery it *is* God who is revealed. "He that is hidden reveals himself in hiddenness."[26]

Barth, accepting God's word as his starting point, did not proceed by developing independent arguments on behalf of faith or by elaborating a system in terms of which God's revelation in Christ might be explicated. As Frei has put it,

> Barth was about the business of conceptual description: He took the classical themes of communal Christian language moulded by the Bible, tradition and constant usage in worship, practice, instruction and controversy, and he restated or redescribed them, rather than evoking arguments on their behalf. It was of the utmost importance to him that his communal language, especially its biblical *fons et origo* — which . . . he saw as indirectly one with the Word of God — had an integrity of its own: It was irreducible. But in that case its lengthy, even leisurely unfolding was equally indispensable.[27]

Barth does, in the course of this "leisurely unfolding" in the *Dogmatics*, engage in what Frei calls "*ad hoc* apologetics," though only "to throw into relief particular features of [the temporal world of eternal grace] by distancing them from or approximating them to other descriptions of the same or other linguistic worlds. In such cases, and in very few others, he engages in argument, usually of a highly dialectical kind."[28] While Barth certainly uses philosophy, and insists on the necessity of so doing, he is careful to use it eclectically and never more than instrumentally. The irreducible language of Christian communal existence must maintain control over *what* is said in Christian theology and over *how* the theologian says it.[29]

It would be hard to overestimate the importance of Barth's authorship, taken as a whole, in twentieth-century theology. Not only did the second edition of *Der Römerbrief* force the dominant traditions of theological reflection to pass muster before judges as various as Marx, Kierkegaard, and St. Paul, but the constructive work of the 1930s and thereafter held out a severely demanding model of what theology should become after the critical verdict has been rendered. This model was, in the first place, difficult to understand — partly because of the effect of Brunner's misinterpretations (which might be compared to Russell's distortions of Wittgenstein), and partly because the actual shape of Barth's project could be discerned fully only *after* many of its volumes had appeared. Frei rightly argues that the lengthiness of the prose is essential to the project. But how many have read more than a volume or two?

So the first reason this paradigm was demanding was that few theologians felt secure in saying what it consisted in and were therefore unsure how to imitate it. Those who felt secure were, for the most part, those who rejected Barth on Brunner's interpretation. A deeper reason, however, was that the model is intrinsically difficult to imitate, even (perhaps *especially*) if it is understood. For Barth alone seemed to possess the patience, energy, and brilliance needed to carry even a part of the project to completion. Many of his most insightful and dedicated readers have been reduced to silence, dwarfed by the majesty of his production. This man has inspired much uneasy modesty.

The model is also severely demanding for the simple reason that it abandons apologetics so completely. Barth opposed Kant's strategy of separation and its later variants, largely because he sought to restore to theology its dogmatic dimension, but he also carried the dialectical isolation of theological discourse from the rest of culture to an extreme. This is not to say, of course, that Barth in any sense withdrew, as a citizen or a churchman, from the political and economic controversies of his time. But Barth's unwillingness to argue, his acceptance of paradox, and his insistence on the irreducibility of God's word undermine the preconditions for genuine debate with secular thought.

It is above all for this reason that even those most deeply influenced by *Der Römerbrief* have typically sought to evade the conclusions Barth drew either early or late concerning the future of theology. Their problem has been how to evade these conclusions without falling back into the positions Barth had already successfully criticized. This brings us back to MacIntyre's dilemma for modern theology. Common to such theologians as Tillich and Bultmann, MacIntyre writes,

> is the project of distinguishing the kernel of Christian theism, which they believe can and must be detached from the outmoded husk. . . . But each of these theologians requires that his own restatement of Christian theism shall both distinguish the theistic kernel from the theistic husk and be intelligible to contemporary educated, secular-minded men. I maintain, however, that these aims are essentially incompatible with each other; that any presentation of theism which is able to secure a hearing from a secular audience has undergone a transformation that has evacuated it entirely of its theistic content. Conversely, any presentation which retains such theistic content will be unable to secure the place in contemporary culture which those theologians desire for it. I am thus advancing not merely the weaker contention that all their attempts so far have failed but the stronger contention that any attempt of this kind must inevitably fail.[30]

Bultmann's reinterpretation of Christian theism becomes hard to distinguish from Heidegger's existentialism. The theism in which Tillich believed seems suspiciously akin to Feuerbach's atheism. Both Bultmann and Tillich, of course, make claims that resist reduction to Heideggerian and Feuerbachian speech, but these claims are not made intelligible at all and stand in an uneasy relationship to the idiom of reinterpretation. So what remains distinctively Christian in these theologies remains irreducibly paradoxical — a more natural point of departure for Barth's project than for demythologization or talk of ultimate concern. To leave the paradoxical features out, either by returning to Deism or by divorcing theology from the realm of ontological claims, is to make theistic vocabulary superfluous. "It is no accident," MacIntyre rightly concludes, "that Karl Barth is the greatest of modern theologians. . . ."[31]

Theologians determine their relationship to the culture, now as in Tertullian's day, largely by saying what they say about paradox. Kierkegaard was right in thinking that the recovery of paradox moves genuinely Christian thought and experience to the periphery of the culture. Distinctively Christian thought and experience may still be possible in an age largely shaped by social differentiation and the new probability, but only at the margins of public life and in the recesses of private existence.[32] This should help us see why the debate about God has shifted to the periphery of the culture. For a Barth, girded with a radical distinction between religion and faith for which he refuses to argue, simply accepts the cultured despiser as substantially correct about human religion and then leaves the final word about faith to God. Theologians who seek another kind of interaction with the cultured despiser, on the other hand, offer him "less and less in which to disbelieve."[33] MacIntyre is therefore right to say that "the lack of confrontation is due not only to the directions in which secular knowledge is advancing but to the directions in which theism is retreating."[34]

Theology since Barth is a sad story. The radical theologies of the 1960s served finally as the *reductio ad absurdum* of the premises with which Bultmann and Tillich tried to save theology from Barth's *Dogmatics*. Those theologians who continue to seek a way between the horns, and thus to remain within the secular academy without abandoning the community of faith, have often been reduced to seemingly endless methodological foreplay. This foreplay, when it leads anywhere, typically leads toward disguised versions of liberalism. But the pathos of liberalism, as Van Harvey has shown case by case over the last two decades, is alienation from both the community of faith and the secular academy — a nearly complete loss of audience being the least painful major consequence.[35]

Harvey has used the problem of faith and history, in particular, to show how theologians — despite their attempts to reformulate Christian theism in terms acceptable to a secular academic audience — continue to skirt the issues implicit in Hume's dictum that a wise man proportions his belief to the evidence (as defined by the new probability and as manifested institutionally in the modern academic disciplines). It is hard to imagine a Christian, Jewish, or Islamic theologian abandoning the historical claims central to his own tradition without also alienating himself from his own community of faith. But the task of making the traditional claims seem probable has become increasingly difficult in the period defined by Port-Royal, D. F. Strauss, and Ernst Troeltsch. Yet the only alternatives to accepting this task involve either "giving the atheist less and less in which to disbelieve" or a direct (nonapologetic) appeal to the authority of revelation. The problem is that revelation, according to the major Western traditions, is itself a historical event.[36]

It is symptomatic of the state of academic theology that essentially critical essays like Harvey's are among the most enduring theological accomplishments of recent years. Contemporary theology, like an empty pile in solitaire, is waiting for a new king to come along and get things moving again. It could be that Barth was the last. Barth's point, of course, was that theology, by its own best lights, should have been waiting for a king of another sort.

8. Explicating Rationality

My reformulation of MacIntyre's narrative can now be abridged as follows. The fate of modern theism is the story of a traditional mode of thought and practice frustrated in its search for an acceptable response to a modern situation. But this does not mean that something called the "modern mentality" one day suddenly confronted traditional beliefs with abstract Popperian canons of refutability. Rather, traditional thought generated its own problems, centering in the problem of many authorities, and these problems could be resolved only by loosening the ancient connection between authority and credibility. That is, the dialectical impasses of the Reformation, which consisted in two incompatible kinds of argument *from* authority, could be bypassed only if means for arguing *to* conclusions about *which* authorities should be recognized were first given self-conscious formulation. But the self-conscious formulation of such means, the new notions of probability and internal evidence, served in effect to secularize a major domain of discourse. To adopt these means was to remove from discourse about authority and credibility the *presupposition* that a specific sort of god exists. For it was the traditional connections between authority and credibility that had given belief in a specific sort of god its former presuppositional status. When theism lost this status, it at first seemed plausible to treat theism as a collection of hypotheses to be vindicated or convicted in light of the *internal* evidence. This deistic option, however, immediately transformed the "supernatural mysteries" of traditional faith into paradoxes one had to either explain away or reject. Moreover, the hypotheses that remained after this transformation had been carried out seemed neither clearly evident nor religiously satisfying.

149

The problem of evidence could be pushed aside, of course, if theism were taken not as a collection of hypotheses but rather as something essentially nontheoretical. Yet to take this tack was to diminish the content of theism as much as any Deist had and, therefore, to undermine the rationale of using traditional theological vocabulary and of demanding for that vocabulary the serious attention of the host culture. On the other hand, to retain elements of traditional theism despite the difficulty of defending them as credible, however satisfying religiously, was to accept isolation from the center of the culture on which theism would like to have an impact.

The contrast between traditional and modern thought implicit in this version of the story does bear on the treatment of anomaly, though without invoking a priori criteria of a kind that would tells us, for any imaginable case, when anomalies should be tolerated and when they should be turned against theory. I have tried to follow MacIntyre's injunction to "view the demands for justification in highly particular contexts of a historical kind," and this procedure reinforces Skorupski's conclusion that

> The traditional thinker is, precisely, traditional: this is not directly a matter of being unwilling to reject one's own theories, but of unwillingness to reject traditionally handed-down ones — of "piety for what actually, allegedly, or presumably has always existed."[1]

The traditional thinker is not, however, pre- or nonrational, as Skorupski's Weberian terminology might suggest. He has his reasons, and these are — in a certain historical context — good reasons. They happen to be reasons in which appeals to authority have a priority the thinkers of the seventeenth century were prepared to withdraw. Traditional reasons ceased to be good reasons when, under specific historical conditions, they led to a dialectical impasse from which the culture could extricate itself only by inventing reasons of another sort.

So perhaps there is, as a character in Tom Stoppard's *Jumpers* suggests, "a calendar date — a *moment* — when the onus of proof passed from the atheist to the believer, when, quite suddenly, secretly, the noes had it." If so, it was not a matter of majority rule. (In that sense the noes have probably never had it.) But there may be some sense in saying that, when Arnauld and Nicole wrote the final chapters of their *Logic*, and despite their explicitly theological convictions and intentions, the onus of proof passed, quite suddenly, secretly, from the atheist to the believer. This is not to say, of course, that something was in fact proved one way or the other. It is only to say that the debate was, from that point on, profoundly different in character. And before long the secret was out. The rules had changed.

Criteria, MacIntyre has said, have a history. But can this be the case? If the criteria of rationality can be relative to historical context, then why is the fideist wrong to view them as relative to a specific, narrowly circumscribed, conceptual scheme? Has not my historicist avoidance of the quest for universal criteria simply begged all the crucial questions? In the present chapter, I shall try to show that we do not need universal criteria of rationality to save ourselves from the arguments of fideists and the other perils of relativism. Steven Lukes's argument for the necessity of universal criteria, which is often treated as the basic alternative to fideism and relativism, seems the appropriate place to begin.

Lukes argues that there are universal criteria of rationality as well as context-dependent ones, and that the former include the laws of identity and noncontradiction plus the notion of truth as correspondence to reality.[2] If we can attribute a language to someone, his speech must be the kind of thing we could translate into our language.

> It follows that if S has a language, it must, minimally, possess criteria of truth (as correspondence to reality) and logic, which we share with it and which simply *are* criteria of rationality. The only alternative conclusion is Elsdon Best's . . . which seeks to state the (self-contradictory) proposition that S's thought (and language) operate according to quite different criteria and that it is literally incomprehensible to us. But if the members of S really did not have our criteria of truth and logic, we would have no grounds for attributing to them language, thought or beliefs and would *a fortiori* be unable to make any statements about these.[3]

Obviously, we can attribute a language to the fideist and we can translate it. That means, according to Lukes, that we can use the laws of logic and the criteria of truth (as correspondence to reality) in judging the fideist's rationality. In so doing, we are simply judging him by criteria that must be applicable if the attribution of language is correct. If he seems, as many fideists do, to violate the law of noncontradiction or, at least, some proscription of nonsense deriving from that law, we shall presumably be bound to judge him irrational.

This is not the place for a full-scale critique of Lukes's argument. My main aim will be to show not that he is mistaken, but rather that the battle against relativism can be waged perfectly well even if he is. I do wish, however, to indicate briefly some of the things that make me think his conclusions have not been established. Most generally: Lukes does not say enough to clarify which criteria he has in mind, how he supposes they operate, or why he thinks his argument proves their "universal" or "fundamental" status.

Take, for example, the claim about "correspondence to reality." Such claims are notoriously ambiguous, yet Lukes neglects to single out the sense he prefers. At times he seems to be insisting only that all language users "share a reality which is independent of how it is conceived," but he will have trouble finding live opponents for that thesis.[3] While Lukes thinks he has a live opponent for his thesis in Thomas Kuhn, the textual evidence he cites in support of his interpretation of Kuhn is not convincing. He quotes Kuhn to the effect that we "may be *tempted* to exclaim that when paradigms change, the world changes with them," that "we may *want* to say that after a revolution scientists are responding to a different world," and then adds:

> From wanting to say it, Kuhn gradually induces himself to say it. Thus he writes that at "the very least, as a result of discovering oxygen, Lavoisier saw nature differently" and "in the absence of some recourse to that hypothetical fixed nature that he 'saw differently,' the principle of economy will *urge* us to say that after discovering oxygen Lavoisier worked in a different world." Then, more boldly, he expresses his conviction that "we must learn to *make sense* of statements that *at least resemble* these"; and finally, he claims that in "*a sense that I am unable to explicate further*, the proponents of competing paradigms practice their trades in different worlds."[4]

I have italicized those of Kuhn's words which Lukes's reading seems to gloss over. Kuhn seems to have gone out of his way to put distance between himself and the rhetorical expressions he is here discussing. He speaks of what we are *tempted* to say, of what we might *want* to say. Does he gradually induce himself to say it? Not without reasonably careful qualification, so far as we can tell from the evidence Lukes cites. There is a perfectly clear and noncontroversial sense in which Lavoisier saw nature differently — a sense that presupposes Lavoisier saw the *same thing* before and after the revolution, however differently he *saw* it. Kuhn's point then becomes clear: that we lack theory-independent *recourse* to what Lavoisier saw first in one way, then in another. When Kuhn proceeds to mention the idea that after the revolution Lavoisier worked in a different world, this is explicitly labeled as something the desire to save words will *urge* us to say. If we are then enjoined to *make sense* of statements *like* these, the implication is clearly that precisely *these* statements do not yet fully make sense. The proponents of competing paradigms are finally said to practice their trades in different worlds, but *only* in a sense previously explicated — namely, that scientists (like the rest of us) lack theory-independent recourse to "that hypothetical fixed nature." Lukes asserts, rightly (to be sure), that "The influence, however deep, of theories upon men's perceptions and understanding is one thing; the claim that there are no theory-independent objects of perception and understanding is another."[5] But who would disagree? Certainly not Kuhn.

The issue Kuhn seems to be raising has to do with how "correspondence to reality" could ever function nontrivially as a *criterion* of rationality. Yet it is this question that Lukes begs. To say that something is a criterion of rationality or of truth is to imply that it is the kind of thing one could appeal to in a dispute over what should be counted as rational or as true, but to say that a theory corresponds to reality seems to add nothing to the notion that it is true and therefore ought to be accepted. What we want to be told is how to tell the true from the false, the justified from the unjustified. That is what we expect from criteria of truth and rational acceptance. For "correspondence" to become a criterion in this sense, we would have to characterize the "reality" to which correspondence is sought. But the characterization we choose will place us within the logical space of one or another theory of the way things are. What Lukes seems to want, however, is a theory-independent criterion for judging which theory gets it right. The problem is that "reality" cannot be theory-independent without ceasing to be a criterion. We are perfectly free to use "reality" to signify "the purely vacuous notion of the ineffable cause of sense and goal of the intellect,"[6] but we would be foolish to suppose that any notion this vacuous could help us award the title of truth.

A less vacuous notion of "reality," on the other hand, would be theory-dependent and therefore relative in a way that might encourage just the worries Lukes is trying to undercut.

Equally serious problems arise when we turn to the other "universal criteria" Lukes proposes — the laws of identity and noncontradiction. These laws belong to logic. The idea here seems to be that universal logical laws impose constraints on all reasoning. To violate these constraints is to be convicted of irrationality by criteria that are not dependent upon any particular cognitive context. Presumably, the law of noncontradiction, for example, constrains us to accept only consistent sets of beliefs. But is this so? I am not sure. I do grant without hesitation that inconsistency is often — that is, in some contexts — a mark of irrationality. If it were *always* a mark of irrationality, perhaps there would be no harm in referring to the law of noncontradiction as a criterion of rationality. Lukes, however, makes no attempt to demonstrate this. He neither tells us how laws of logic are supposed to function as criteria of rationality, nor how any particular logical law should be construed. To see why this omission might be problematical, consider the following question: is there a law of logic that enjoins us, on pain of irrationality, never to accept a logically inconsistent set of beliefs? The answer may seem both simple and obvious. Yet the simple and obvious answer might not be the right one. What answer we should give depends upon how we choose to handle a complicated and confusing collection of issues, ranging from the familiar paradoxes of logical theory to the bizarre ideas of unorthodox quantum mechanics. We need not ponder such issues for very long to accomplish the present purpose of posing problems for Lukes.

I believe that at least some of my beliefs about Hegel are false. Unfortunately, I do not know which ones are false; otherwise I would make the appropriate changes. But as things stand now, it could not be the case that *all* of my beliefs are true. If all my beliefs about Hegel are in fact true, then my belief about those beliefs is false; and vice versa. Strictly speaking, then, my belief about my beliefs is logically inconsistent with my beliefs about Hegel (taken as a whole). Yet we naturally — at least within our community — count the belief that we are fallible in the pursuit of truth as a healthy corrective to irrational complacency. The more difficult the topic, the more reasonable the belief that some of our beliefs about that topic are false. Hegel is very hard to understand. We are sometimes wrong about him at just those points where we feel most certain that we have him right. So although I have good reason for each of my current beliefs about Hegel, I also have a good reason to believe that at least one of these is false. It is (at the moment) *more* rational for me to accept both my beliefs about Hegel and my belief about my beliefs than it would be for me to give up either the former or the latter in the hope of restoring consistency. I could always eliminate the risk of inconsistency by believing little or nothing, and that is what I would do if consistency were an absolutely overriding requirement of rationality. But it seems rational, in the present case at least, to risk or tolerate inconsistency of a limited kind — namely, among beliefs of different Russellian "types," or among beliefs accepted more or less guardedly, or among beliefs in different "assertion zones" — in order thereby to engross more truth.[7]

Suppose there is no law of logic that enjoins us, on pain of irrationality, never to accept a logically inconsistent set of beliefs. It does not follow from this conclusion that there is nothing worth calling the law of noncontradiction or that no formulation of this law is in some sense universal. It follows only that if there is such a law, its connection to the criteria of rationality is not as plain or immediate as Lukes seems to think. Lukes is free to argue, of course, that the case I have just presented is unconvincing, that the conclusion has not been justified. Perhaps I have misdescribed my beliefs by failing to make explicit the degree of credibility I attach to each. Or perhaps I am wrong to conclude that my current set of beliefs is the best available alternative.[8] My point here is simply that cases like the one just introduced will have to be settled before the relationship between laws of logic and criteria of rationality becomes clear.

Even if the present case proves misleading or insignificant, many factors remain to be considered. It seems at least plausible to argue that consistency is merely one virtue among the many an ideal system of beliefs would have — an important virtue, to be sure, but not one to be pursued at all costs. Arguing thus would put us in good company (with the likes of Peirce and Wittgenstein); it might also drive a wedge between logical laws and the principles of rational acceptance (ours or anybody else's). If we do accept an epistemic principle implying strictures against inconsistency in beliefs held, its scope of proper application might well be limited by other epistemic principles we accept. No one has shown that these other principles must be universally accepted if translation is to be possible. In the absence of such a demonstration, it remains unclear how the law of noncontradiction might in any strong sense be a universal criterion of rationality. To know whether someone who holds strictly inconsistent beliefs should be charged with irrationality, we might have to know much more about his epistemic principles than Lukes lets on.

William James argued many years ago that believing truth and shunning error are both ideals of the rational agent, but ideals which often give conflicting advice and which therefore need to be weighed carefully case by case.[9] Nicholas Rescher and Robert Brandom have recently argued at some length that the ideal of believing truth often outweighs that of shunning error so as to permit localized inconsistencies.[10] They go on from this argument to propose carefully limited formulations of basic logical laws and an unorthodox semantics designed to block the possibility of logical anarchy without excluding inconsistency altogether. Whether we accept this proposal or not, it does at least underline the importance of determining not only *how* the law of noncontradiction relates to the criteria of rationality, but also *which* law of noncontradiction (or version thereof) is under consideration. Yet Lukes says as little about the latter issue as he does about the former.

The term "logic" may be a source of confusion in its own right. Some writers, such as P. F. Strawson and Steven Toulmin,[11] use the term to cover the theory of inference or the "ethics of belief," while others, like Gilbert Harman, confine it to the theory of logical implication. In the present context, where the relationship between laws of logic and criteria of rationality is at issue, it seems wise to keep the distinction clear by following Harman's choice of terms. "There are neither inductive arguments nor deductive inferences," he writes. "There are only deductive arguments and inductive inferences."[12]

> Deductive logic is a theory of logical implication. . . . It is concerned with "arguments" and "proofs," but in technical senses of these words. An argument in this sense consists of a set of "premises" and a "conclusion." The argument is "valid" if the premises logically imply the conclusion. A proof in the technical sense consists of a number of steps of argument whose

conclusions are logically implied by "axioms," which are specified in advance, together with any previous conclusions, each
step being in accordance with a set of rules of logical implication, also specified in advance.[13]

If a given conclusion follows logically from premises already
accepted, that is a *reason* for accepting the conclusion as true.
But there may be other, more compelling reasons for rejecting
the same conclusion. In that event, one or more premises may
have to be rejected in the name of consistency. Inference involves weighing the reasons for and against the various alternatives in light of our epistemic principles and deciding which
alternative to accept. Logic can tell us when we have an inconsistent set of beliefs, but it cannot tell us when the
inconsistency should be tolerated or how to remove it. Logic
can tell us what our beliefs logically imply, but not whether
we should accept these implications while standing pat on
premises.

We can distinguish two kinds of moves in the language
game of thought: testing and revision moves. A testing move
attempts to locate sources of incoherence in one's total view —
perhaps by rehearsing a deductive argument to test a collection
of beliefs for consistency. A revision move makes some substantive change in one's total view — for example, by adding
to, subtracting from, or rearranging some aspect of physical
theory. Deductive logic comes into play when we test our
total view for coherence. An inference is the decision to accept
or reject a revision in the total view. In these terms it is misleading to speak of deductive inference. That would be to confuse testing and revision moves. I can "deduce" a conclusion
from a set of beliefs I already hold by running through the
steps of a deductive argument while testing for validity. But
that would not be an inference, for it would not commit me to
acceptance of the conclusion thus derived. I am always free to
turn the argument on its head to cast doubt on premises.

The idea that there is such a thing as deductive inference
derives whatever plausibility it has from what Frederick Will
calls the "standard" kind of case to which philosophical logicians devote attention:

> The prevailing view of inference, in which young philosophers
> are commonly indoctrinated from their earliest introduction in
> logic, is distorted by a fixation upon a certain kind of standard
> case. . . . The standard case is one in which the context of the

inference is such that the steplike pattern, *A, B, . . .N; therefore Q,* fits very well. But this pattern fits very well because the context of the inference is so stable that there is no question about the identity and significance of the proposed premises and conclusion, so that the only question of substance remaining is whether from the fixed premises the fixed conclusions can be derived by fairly fixed means.[14]

Preoccupation with this sort of case is encouraged by the logician's interest in formal deductive systems operating in accordance with axioms and laws that are, as Harman puts it, "specified in advance." We tend to lose sight of the fact that the enforced stability of the formal deductive system simply leaves the questions of ordinary inference to one side. By "ordinary" inference I mean that in which axioms and laws are not specified in advance as they would be in a formal deductive system. Ordinary inference, in this sense, often occurs in a context that lacks the stability of the formal deductive system. The identity and significance of proposed premises and conclusions may be in doubt. In ordinary contexts we often need to know not only whether a particular conclusion follows from a given set of premises, but also whether these premises should themselves be accepted, rejected, or reinterpreted. What should be allowed to remain fixed, in such contexts, is itself often the primary question of substance our norms of inference are expected to answer. Lukes needs to show either that there is a stronger connection between the formal logician's laws and the norms of ordinary inference than we might think or that "logic" in the sense favored by Strawson and Toulmin includes a norm, worthy of being called the "law of noncontradiction," that must be universally shared by all language users.

It is not even clear, according to some philosophers, that the laws of orthodox logic (in the sense proper to the theory of logical implication), including the law of noncontraction as usually interpreted, must be universal. We may grant, Harman argues,

> that a person who denies our basic logical principles thereby indicates that he misunderstands what he says or means something different by his words from what we would mean. This does not imply that we cannot conceive of someone giving up our basic logical principles nor does it imply that we cannot conceive of these principles failing to hold. At best it implies

that these principles cannot be false, that one cannot give them up simply by denying them. . . . Perhaps the law of the excluded middle (for all P: P or not-P) fails to hold, even though it is not false. A person who accepts a logic withóut this law may mean something different by "not" from what we mean; but his language may contain no principle we can identify with our law. According to such a person, our law of the excluded middle fails to have a truth value: he rejects our notion of "not."[15]

Harman goes on to draw similar conclusions about the law of noncontradiction. In the first place, a logic lacking our law of the excluded middle would shift the sense of "not," and this would in turn affect the law of noncontradiction. Moreover, in a logic like Strawson's, "in which failure of reference deprives a sentence of a truth value, the principle of noncontradiction does not hold, since if P contains a referring term that does not refer, so will *not both P and not-P*."[16] This is not to argue that some deviant logic should be preferred to contemporary orthodoxy, but only that the matter cannot be settled a priori. The problem with deviant logics tends to be that they ask us to give up deeply entrenched principles without sufficient compensation.[17] Lukes has not shown, however, that there are no possible circumstances under which such a logic ought to be adopted. Nor has he shown, in particular, that we could not identify and learn the language of a community using one. A translation of such a language might require extensive meta-linguistic commentary to be made useful or convincing, since any mapping of its sentences onto ours will be clumsy at best. No doubt we would be moved to ascribe a language involving a deviant logic only after growing dissatisfied with an even clumsier translation bound to more orthodox assumptions. But if we could identify and (roughly) translate the deviant language, it is unclear how any particular logical law could be universal or fundamental in Lukes's sense.

We have now spent several pages noticing obstacles in Lukes's path. I have not shown, or tried to show, that any of these obstacles is insuperable, though I doubt that any attempt to establish a particular criterion of rationality as universal or fundamental could succeed. My basic reason for remaining suspicious of Lukes's conclusions is simply that projects of this sort inevitably take on all the problems and perplexities associated with foundationalist and transcendental philosophy. It seems unlikely that Lukes will succeed where so many others have failed. Let us assume that he cannot. Are we then driven to accept a conceptual relativism of the kind Lukes ascribes to Peter Winch? Must we conclude, as Lukes asks at one point, that for any group of persons "the truth of their beliefs and the validity of their reasoning (are) simply up to them, a function of the norms to which they conform"?[18] An affirmative answer would imply the impossibility of responsible criticism. Is rationality itself always relative to norms implicit in a given community's (perhaps completely idiosyncratic) conceptual scheme? An affirmative answer would imply the impossibility of cross-cultural understanding. These unwanted results make Lukes and others quest after universal criteria — the essence of rationality.

Fortunately, these results do not in fact follow from denial of Lukes's theory or rejection of his quest. There is after all an important grain of truth in Lukes's reasoning, and this has been captured in an argument of Donald Davidson's.[19] Lukes is right in treating the idea of an untranslatable language with suspicion. It is unclear, to begin with, why something that cannot in principle be translated should be called a language. If we can identify foreign behavior or marks as linguistic, we should be able, by adjusting hypotheses about foreign attitudes, to map foreign linguistic units onto our own. The mapping may be clumsy. Short sentences may have to be mapped onto very long ones. We may have to supply a lot of commentary as context for the sentences on our side of the mapping. But if even a clumsy mapping conjoined to a cumbersome commentary will not do, this would show only that there is little reason to treat the behavior or marks in question as linguistic.

Lukes is also right in supposing that translation from one language into another must assume substantial agreement between speakers of the two languages. This agreement will involve beliefs and plans, epistemic principles, and logical laws. As Quine has argued for some time, substantial agreement at these levels must be assumed before translation can begin. Substantial agreement need not, however, involve total agreement. And the postulation of differences here and there can improve a translation significantly by smoothing out the proposed mapping. But there are limits to the extent of disagreement any system of translation can tolerate. Beyond a certain point, it always becomes more plausible to treat apparent disagreement as merely verbal and to adjust sentence-mapping accordingly. That substantial agreement between any two speakers must be assumed is a methodological requirement of translation. If, therefore, *any* two speakers must be assumed to be substantially agreed, provided only that we want a plausible theory of translation, the very idea of alternative conceptual schemes is clearly called into question. It follows that conceptual relativism, which presupposes this idea, is implausible. It does not follow, however, that there are *universally* shared criteria of rationality.

Davidson's view is, roughly, that it is hard to see, at least from the vantage point of a thoroughgoing holism, how we could ever have evidence for the existence of an alternative conceptual scheme. If translation always involves a trade-off between belief-ascription and sentence-mapping, then we shall never be able to distinguish clearly between cases of truly radical disagreement, of the sort that might justify talk about alternative conceptual schemes, and cases of mistaken translation. Given the methodological limitations inherent in translation, it will always be more plausible to assume major areas of agreement than to assume the existence of alternative schemes. We cannot identify alternative schemes by first identifying untranslatable languages, for translatability can always be salvaged by adjusting belief-ascription accordingly. No other means of identification has fared any better. The distinction between conceptual scheme and uninterpreted content cannot, it seems, be made out clearly. Nor, therefore, can the metaphors Lukes and others have used to combat relativism and idealism: correspondence to reality, organization of experience, and so forth. The metaphors are designed to connect scheme with "uninterpreted" content, thus providing means independent of any given scheme for establishing which scheme deserves the title of truth. But the metaphors presuppose the distinction, which cannot itself be made coherent. It is, as Davidson says, the third and last dogma of empiricism.

There is more than one way to express disagreement with the relativism Lukes ascribes to Winch. One can deny its central thesis, as Lukes does. Or one can deny something both that thesis and its denial presuppose, as Davidson does. The presupposition to deny is the distinction between scheme and content. If that distinction cannot be made out, then the relativist's thesis that there are many schemes but no independent way to judge their adequacy suffers presupposition failure. Lukes can be read as saying that there is only one scheme or as saying that all schemes have the basic criteria of rationality in common. But if Davidson is right:

> It would be wrong to summarize by saying we have shown communication is possible between people who have different schemes. . . . For we have found no intelligible basis on which it can be said that schemes are different. It would be equally wrong to announce the glorious news that all mankind — all speakers of language, at least — share a common scheme and ontology. For if we cannot intelligibly say that schemes are different, neither can we intelligibly say that they are one.[20]

To eschew the distinction between scheme and content is not to decide the debate between Lukes and Winch in favor of one or the other party; it is to undercut the debate by dissolving its topic.

It simply does not follow from reflection on the methodological constraints on translation that there must be universal criteria of rationality. It follows only that any two language users must be united by massive agreement.[21] Exactly what the common ground consists in might well vary from pair to pair. Davidson shows that reflection along Lukes's lines disposes of conceptual relativism without either supporting or relying upon transcendental justification. Just as there is no way to rule out a priori that any given belief now held might be placed in jeopardy as inquiry proceeds, it is conceivable that we shall discover disagreement between ourselves and another linguistic community with respect to any given belief — including logical principles. Yet just as we could never place more than a relatively limited number of beliefs in question at once, whatever disagreement separates two linguistic communities will have to be relatively local — however otherwise startling.

We all agree that we sometimes disagree. Relativists go on from this truism to imagine instances of global disagreement. They then proceed to offer special explanations, involving the postulation of alternative conceptual schemes, to account for these instances. But if Davidson is correct, then all such instances must be merely imaginary. The point is methodological, like Hume's about miracles. After Hume, many of us stopped worrying about the bare "possibility" of miracles, convinced we could never have evidence sufficient for believing in one. Davidson proposes a similar nonchalance concerning the dangers of global disagreement and the existence of alternative schemes. The point is not that talk of alternative schemes is, by the lights of a verificationist theory of meaning, nonsensical. It is rather that we lack any good reason for supposing that alternative schemes exist. The evidence that makes some people postulate alternative schemes is always accounted for at least as well by more modest hypotheses. Just as we do not need to be verificationists to side with Hume on the evidential status of miracle reports, we do not need to be verificationists to side with Davidson on the evidential status of conceptual schemes. An alternative conceptual scheme can never be proved so as to be the foundation of a system of philosophy.

Disagreement can be intelligibly postulated only if widespread agreement is assumed from the start. Lukes wrongly concludes from this that there must be some beliefs and principles from which we can derive universal criteria of rationality and about which we could never significantly or reasonably disagree. Such beliefs and principles would *always* be in position as a fulcrum for critical leverage and as a schematism for understanding. The possibility of responsible criticism and cross-cultural understanding does not depend, however, on the existence of an invariant set of such beliefs and principles. All we need to make criticism and understanding of another culture possible and reasonable is a shared background of entrenched assumption. Davidson shows that to assume, in any given case, that such a background is lacking is also to accept an implausible translation of the language in question. So there will always be enough beliefs and principles in place to provide criteria for criticism and understanding, even though we cannot settle on universal criteria in advance of inquiry into all the cases.

Sometimes two cultures, or two scientists, have great difficulty understanding each other. Some cases of disagreement strike us as especially difficult to resolve without resorting to coercion. Instances like these make us want to speak, with Kuhn and Feyerabend, of incommensurability. There is no harm in speaking thus, provided we stay clear of conceptual schemes. If you and I differ with respect to a number of central tenets of physical theory, we will also use at least some central theoretical terms differently. This will both hinder our attempts to translate each other's remarks and diminish the background of shared assumption to which we could appeal in rational persuasion. We may speak of this as an instance of incommensurability, for it clearly differs from cases where disagreement does not invade relatively central tenets, thereby complicating translation and debate. Kuhn's point has never been that successful translation and rational criticism are impossible between incommensurable theories. He *has* argued that under some circumstances we cannot find "a set of rules which will tell us how rational agreement can be reached on what would settle the issue on every point where statements seem to conflict."[22] And he *has* argued that mutual understanding can be difficult under such circumstances. To say this much and no more is not to commit oneself to conceptual relativism, though it is to put oneself at odds with transcendental philosophy and to give up the a priori quest for universal criteria of rationality. Disagreement can be difficult to resolve, and it can lead to misunderstanding or befuddlement, but there is nothing philosophically deep about even the more extreme cases — nothing, at least, involving conceptual schemes,

If Kuhn did not exist, his critics would have had to invent him. As it is, they have only had to read him as he would rather not be read, stressing the romantic rhetoric while ignoring or explaining away his surprise and irritation at being charged with relativism. If Kuhn's surprise and irritation can be taken at face value, it follows that his mistake (if it can be called that) was to be "tempted" by the romantic rhetoric in the first place. Charitable reinterpretation of his use of terms like "world-view" and "world" gives us an anti-empiricist philosopher of science and a mild-mannered historian but neither an irrationalist nor a conceptual relativist. Kuhn's doubts about the interest of the notion of truth, which have so troubled MacIntyre and others, can then be read (with Davidson's help) as elements of a more general suspicion of conceptual schemes and the metaphors commonly associated with them.[23] On this reading, it would be not the ordinary but certain distinctively philosophical uses of "true" and "real" to which Kuhn objects — in particular, "truth" as a nonvacuous relation between conceptual scheme and uninterpreted content, "reality" as the uninterpreted content to which any conceptual scheme ought to correspond. Kuhn has never denied that we ought to utter true sentences, that "Snow is white" is true if and only if snow is white, or that science can tell us about the real world. He simply affirms, with

Davidson, that "Neither a fixed stock of meanings, nor a theory-neutral reality, can provide . . . a ground for comparison of conceptual schemes."[24]

I am not interested in defending one or another reading of Kuhn. Where he ultimately lands in the assembly of possible positions is less important than where he should. Where he should land becomes clearer as neglected possibilities come into view. Transcendental philosophy and conceptual relativism are not his (or our) only alternatives. Conceptual relativists, if there are any, rightly insist that transcendental philosophy (and "realistic" philosophy of science) cannot be made to work. But to express this opposition by proclaiming conceptual relativism is to leave one foot in the position under attack — an awkward posture, to say the least. Better to dissolve the thesis on which both relativists and their targets take their stands.

If Davidson helps us split the difference between the bogey of relativism and the quest for transcendental perspective, he also deflates the need for a theory of rationality. Worries over relativism make us wish rationality had an essence we might discover a priori and enshrine in a theory. But if the worries are themselves incoherent, we have a reason (over and above more general scruples about a priori quests after essences) for abandoning the quest for this particular essence. Yet if we ask whether a specific historical figure is rational, what are we asking for if not a theory of rationality and its application to a case?

Recall Quine on explication and elimination (as discussed in chapters 1 and 4 above). Without striving after essences or offering conceptual analyses, we can substitute a clearer question for the puzzling one in the hope of serving our purposes better and improving conversation. I fear my proposal will seem bland, but perhaps a bland question will make for better conversation than one that tempts us to mention conceptual schemes. When inquiring into the rationality of historical figures, I am really asking only whether they had good reasons for believing and behaving as they did. Larry Laudan writes that

> At its core, rationality — whether we are speaking about rational action or rational belief — consists in doing (or believing) things because we have good reasons for doing so. That does not solve the problem, of course, but only restates it. The restatement, however, is a useful one, for it makes clear that if

we are going to determine whether a given action or belief is (or was) rational, we must ask whether there are (or were) sound reasons for it.[25]

Laudan need not concern himself with whether his explication preserves the "core" of rationality. It gives us a better question, and that is what we need. To determine, for example, whether Aquinas had good reasons for accepting the articles of faith, we shall need to know what reasons were "available" to him.[26] We shall need also to judge whether among these were reasons sufficiently "good" to warrant acceptance of the beliefs in question.

Not that we can postpone the normative question until historical description is complete. Translation itself involves the attempt to avoid ascribing irrationality if possible. One translation is deemed better than another, other things being equal, if it enables us to "make more sense" of the beliefs (intentions, hopes, and so on) it forces us to ascribe. This suggests a "broadening" of the principle of charity usually associated with Quine's discussions of translation. The translator must be charitable to his subjects not only, as Quine and Davidson maintain, by maximizing the areas in which we agree with them but also, as Kuhn and Hacking argue, by doing his best to make their beliefs and actions seem reasonable. Kuhn has recently reported two lessons to be learned from his own struggles to understand old texts:

> First, there are many ways to read a text, and the one most accessible to a modern are often inappropriate when applied to the past. Second, that plasticity of texts does not place all ways of reading on a par, for some of them (ultimately, one hopes, only one) possess a plausibility and coherence absent from others. Trying to transmit such lessons to students, I offer them a maxim: When reading the works of an important thinker, look first for the apparent absurdities in the text and ask yourself how a sensible person could have written them. When you find an answer, I continue, when those passages make sense, then you may find that more central passages, ones you previously thought you understood, have changed their meaning.[27]

There are limitations to this maxim, of course, for we sometimes can make sense of a text (in context) only by supposing that apparent absurdities in the text are real. But that is a more extravagant hypothesis than supposing the reverse. We are therefore right to begin with Kuhn's maxim, retreating to the postulation of real absurdities only when our broadened policy of charity plainly fails.

We have already encountered more than one instance of this procedure. Consider Hacking on Paracelsus. In Paracelsus the distinction between natural and conventional signs is missing. We tend to supply it without thinking or perhaps because we think it uncharitable to suppose Paracelsus could make no such distinction. Paracelsus says that God authored nature, that the firmament is a book to be deciphered. We take this for a quaint metaphor. Paracelsus makes no mention of statistical frequencies, degrees of credibility short of certainty, or of probable opinion backed up by anything but testimony. We assume all this must be unspoken presupposition, there in the background, perfectly clear to any reasonable adult. Then we puzzle over a surplus of absurdities in Paracelsus's words and deeds. But Hacking follows Kuhn's maxim, trying to imagine how a remotely sensible person might be responsible for such apparent absurdities. He takes with full seriousness what is actually inscribed in Paracelsan texts, avoids assuming in advance that a phrase *we* could not intend literally is a mere figure of speech, and keeps an eye out for what is *missing* from the texts themselves. He gives us a more plausible Paracelsus. Hacking sometimes speaks of his practice as a "reversal" of the procedure of charity. I would rather say that he *is* being charitable — though by rejecting the principle of charity in its excessively narrow formulation. It is no charity to modernize, to smooth out real differences between one period and another.

So the translator's own normative judgments about the "goodness" of reasons will enter in from the start. This may sound like an imposition of foreign standards, an inevitable source of distortion. But Davidson shows that any plausible translation would involve the assumption of overarching consensus. The translator and his subject must, then, have enough in common, at the level of beliefs held and at the level of epistemic principles accepted, to justify the relevant normative judgments. It would, of course, be unfair to render these judgments while making essential use of reasons unavailable to the subjects in question. As Harman writes,

> . . . in order to see whether certain reasons or reasoning might

explain a particular person's beliefs or actions we must try to imagine ourselves in his position, with his antecedent beliefs, desires, moral principles, and so forth, to see whether we can imagine what sorts of conclusions we might draw by reasoning from that position. This appeal to the sympathetic imagination is necessary, because we cannot appeal to explicit principles of the theory of reasoning to tell us what is possible and what is not.[28]

Back to Collingwood. Rationality, in the sense of Laudan's explication, is, obviously, relative in one significant respect. That is, the rationality of a given person's beliefs or actions is relative to the reasons or reasoning available to that person. And the availability of reasons and reasoning varies with historical and social context. Provided we stay clear of conceptual schemes, this relativity can be accepted as both commonsensical and philosophically innocuous. If this be relativism, relativism need not be vicious.

We have already tried to re-enact the reasoning available to Aquinas. I want now to reaffirm my claim that this reasoning justifies his acceptance of the "supernatural mysteries" of faith. The crucial point is that Aquinas accepted — and, unlike those who came several centuries later, had no compelling reason to abandon — epistemic principles that made the "supernatural mysteries" seem highly credible. The link between credibility and authority still firmly in place, Aquinas could accept on authority even the most "paradoxical" beliefs without violating any available norm of probable opinion. Authority makes opinions as probable as they could be. *Divine* authority confers objective certainty. Even a doctrine the very coherence of which must be taken on faith is perfectly acceptable by standards Aquinas had no compellingly good reason to revise or reject.

Aquinas accepted epistemic principles that, in effect, limit the scope of strictures against incomprehensible speech. In order to utter or assent to analogues of the truths properly known only in God's *scientia*, we must accept what in our language and from our point of view remains incomprehensible and mysterious.[29] But Aquinas's acceptance of such talk does not differ completely from our willingness to attribute truth or high probability to the apparently nonsensical utterances of contemporary theoretical physicists. We accept their statements on authority, even though we do not know exactly what they are saying or how it is that such sentences could be true. We sometimes utter apparent nonsense in the conviction that we thus speak analogues of truths that do not seem nonsensical in the properly theoretical context we know little about.

The difference, of course, is that Aquinas lacked the means for asking with any subtlety why one authority should be accepted as divine. The new probability equips us to defend our ascriptions of authority as Aquinas could not defend his. This does not mean that Aquinas was not rational in Laudan's sense, for he clearly made the most of the reasoning available to him. After Port-Royal, however, Aquinas's reasoning is no longer available to us. Once the connection between authority and credibility has been loosened, the "supernatural mysteries" are no longer shielded from criticism. They come to seem antecedently improbable, which in turn weakens the status of the relevant authorities. When I accept the authority of a theoretical physicist, I have independently probable reason for believing that he exists and that he can successfully defend his weird utterances in terms of the new probability. But to defend his own ascriptions of authority Aquinas had to assume both the existence of the authorities in question and their status as authorities: this is what led to the dialectical impasse of the Reformation. The fragmentation of authority made appeals to authority dialectically useless, and therefore made the innovations worked out at Port-Royal especially attractive. In the wake of these innovations, it became reasonable to ask what might be said in favor of God's *existence* if we do not assume from the beginning that certain documents and persons possess divine authority. Once this question had been asked, the "supernatural mysteries" of faith were bound to appear in a new light, as paradoxes of theory, potential obstacles to belief. In MacIntyre's phrase, it became "too late" to be medieval.[30]

Fideists sometimes defend the rationality of contemporary faith against the likes of MacIntyre by appealing to standards of judgment supposedly peculiar to faith.[31] MacIntyre's conclusion is then pushed to one side as the application of inappropriate standards, a kind of intellectual imperialism. This kind of apologetics, however, requires precisely the distinction Davidson's argument dismantles. If there were such things as conceptual schemes, they would probably make nice havens for fideists. As it is, believers will have to justify their judgments more or less as the rest of us do. If they want to avoid the consequences of Port-Royal, they will have to give reasons of the ordinary variety for favoring the old probability over the new, and it has never been made clear what such reasons might be. The problem with accepting the consequences of Port-Royal, as we have seen, is an unpleasant dilemma. To defend theism in terms of the new probability is in all likelihood a hopeless task, but to give up the claims to which probable reasoning is relevant is to empty theism of its distinctive content.

It is interesting to note in this context Barth's reluctance to engage in apologetics. Barth realizes that he cannot maintain the integrity of theology without appealing directly to the authority of God's word. In the absence of the old connection between probability and authority, he bypasses probability altogether — yet without giving up the traditional ontological claims or smuggling them into theology in symbolic dress. He accepts God's word as authoritative not because he has good reason but simply because he believes he can do nothing else. (He cannot help himself.) An apologist would give us reason at precisely this point. Barth does not. Theology is, for Barth, a "rational" endeavor in the sense that faith seeks an understanding for which revelation supplies a context of reasons. But Barth does not, any more than a good historian or sociologist would, try to explain his acceptance of God's word as authoritative in terms of available reasons. He refers instead to a nonepistemic category — grace. His explanations differ in content but *not* in kind from the explanations we devise whenever beliefs and actions cannot be explained by reference to available reasons. This may help explain why Barth can wholeheartedly accept, while fideist apologists cannot even seriously consider, social-scientific theories of religion.

Barth implicitly acknowledges, then, what MacIntyre explicitly affirms: that we "need to discriminate between rational and irrational beliefs in order to explain the origin and maintenance of those beliefs."[32] The point is not that historical or sociological explanation necessarily presupposes an a priori theory of rationality but simply that reference to an agent's reasons can go an important part of the way toward explaining his beliefs and actions only if the reasons are good ones. We have seen that to judge available reasons "good" (or "not good enough") we need not establish criteria a priori. But explanations are the sorts of things that resolve puzzles, and we have one kind of puzzle when an agent believes or acts as he does for good reasons, another kind when he does not. What kind of explanation we give depends on the kind of puzzle we want resolved. Where reasons are good, whatever puzzle we have about the relevant beliefs and actions will typically involve why these reasons — and not some others — were available to the agent. Where, on the other hand, the reasons, beliefs, and actions in question fail to hang together in the normal way, we have an additional puzzle. What allowed the incoherence to be tolerated? Did something block the incoherence from view? What nonepistemic factors entered in?

Some sociologists of knowledge fear that to make the normative assessment of reasons crucial to explanation in this way reduces their field to the "sociology of error."[33] This fear derives, however, from a misunderstanding. MacIntyre, for example, does not deny that historical and sociological explanations should be brought to bear on our puzzles about *which* reasons are available to which agents. He simply wants to argue that historians and social scientists should and do have *more* to say about cases where reasons, beliefs, and actions do not cohere. Coherence is the standard case that allows us to take reasoning seriously in the explanation of belief and behavior. Incoherence requires additional explanation.

Legitimate suspicion of a priori theorizing (and of the nineteenth century's armchair conclusions about savage minds) has led many students of culture to avoid ascribing irrationality at any cost — either by saving the subject's rationality with reductively symbolic interpretations of his initially bizarre sentences or by eschewing talk of rationality and irrationality altogether. Yet reductively symbolic interpretations of foreign beliefs, while sometimes justified, more often seem to take foreigners and the reasons actually available to them with insufficient seriousness. And we have already seen that judgments of rationality and irrationality, at least in the sense of Laudan's explication, inevitably enter in even at the level of translation. It is a priori theorizing about rationality, not the case-by-case assessment of available reasons, that we can safely avoid. Indeed, there is much to be gained by avoiding it. We are bound to go wrong if we approach other cultures with a set of "transcendentally justified" criteria of rationality in hand, for we shall then be unprepared to consider the possibility of differences that would affect the availability of reasons in unexpected ways. We would then be *forced*, prematurely, either to attribute irrationality to our subjects or to rescue them from this fate by reducing their apparently literal sentences to symbolic speech, whereas these alternatives should be adopted only as last resorts. Only, that is, when the search for explanations in terms of available reasons fails should we retreat to ascriptions of irrationality or reductively symbolic interpretations.

It is not easy, in practice, to know when we have our translations, ascriptions of belief, judgments of rationality, and nonepistemic explanations in order. For the "broader" principle of charity we use in understanding other cultures (and each other) asks us both to maximize areas of agreement and to ascribe rationality when we can. But these desiderata often point in opposite directions in a given instance. To make the beliefs and actions of Aquinas and Paracelsus explicable in terms of available reasons, we have had to posit disagreement at unexpected points. We had to say, for example, that Aquinas does not share our notion of probability and that Paracelsus lacks our distinction between natural and conventional signs. Positing disagreement at such points is a cost warranted only by the significant advantages that accrue. Many modern interpreters of Aquinas soften his sentences with supposedly charitable interpretations, even though this involves ignoring or explaining away a great deal of what he says explicitly. It is tempting to make Paracelsus seem even more foolish than he was by taking his equation of natural and conventional signs as mere analogy.

But we can take both men at their word without deeming them irrational if we consider their reasons in context. Modernizing their reasons at the outset does them no favor. The mistake is to bypass reasons available to them that are not available to us — reasons therefore likely to remain inaccessible to twentieth-century a priori reflection or to insufficiently self-conscious investigation. What constitutes charity in a given case involves careful weighing of cost against advantage. Davidson's argument shows that we cannot posit too much disagreement without sacrificing the adequacy of translation. But we can posit disagreement here and there in the interest of explaining beliefs and actions economically. Only if this procedure fails should we undertake the still more treacherous tactics of reductive interpretation and explanation. Such tactics are often necessary, but their overuse has given reductionism a bad name.

I have tried to show that the reasons available to Aquinas differ from those available to Hume and that the evolution of this difference has contributed heavily to the secularization of thought. Can we say anything more general about the contrast between traditional and modern? It would drastically oversimplify, of course, to say that the Port-Royal *Logic* marks *the* transition to modern thought, that the 1660s are the pivot on which history turns, that several slim chapters could account for so much. There are many other significant episodes in the history of secularization, many enlightening stories that would take us intelligibly from medieval to modern thought without passing through Port-Royal, and many relevant facts (especially about the societies we call traditional) about which I know nothing. I think we now know enough, however, to conclude that any adequate distinction between traditional and modern modes of thought will highlight differences in the status of authority. This suggests that Weber was right to distinguish types of society according to types of legitimation and types of legitimation according to the role played by the notion of authority in each, however harshly we may want to judge his formulations of the distinctions or the historiography that results from his use of them.[34]

The relative priority of appeals to authority in traditional thought may help us account not only for Aquinas's acceptance of the more mysterious articles of Christian faith but also for the ethnographic phenomena that so concerned Lévy-Bruhl and has since troubled his critics. Lévy-Bruhl studied primitives whose sentences struck him as utterly paradoxical. His problem was how to explain his subjects' acceptance of such sentences as true. His solution, at one point in his career, was to view savage minds as "pre-logical." It is not fully clear what Lévy-Bruhl meant by this. He seems to have meant at least that savage minds, if they operate according to principles at all, must employ principles very unlike those of our own logic. If this is what Lévy-Bruhl meant, he must have been wrong. Even the most savage mind, if it possesses a language, must have *something like* our logical principles — this is what makes the term "pre-logical" a misnomer. But the primitive, like the medieval theologian, might possess epistemic principles that could be used to justify acceptance of beliefs we would feel bound to reject as utterly paradoxical. Perhaps both exist, in an important sense, *before* the fall of authority. Where probability consists in what the authorities approve, a host of "mysteries" tends to remain untouched by criticism.

This does not mean, however, that all traditional thought gives either authority or mystery pride of place in the scheme of things. It is worth recalling in this context that traditional conceptions of probable opinion keep close company with epistemic notions, like Aquinas's *scientia*, which are not essentially authoritarian and which could (at least before Ockham) easily be stressed at the former's expense. We must therefore be careful not to draw the contrast between traditional and modern thought too sharply — as if we were dealing with alternative conceptual schemes. The priority of authority in traditional thought is relative, not absolute. Traditional thought is itself anything but a unitary phenomenon. We can justify speaking of it as a discernible type only by taking our orientation from specific, limited comparisons. And we must be careful not to generalize too quickly from our cases. We are struck by the sixteenth century's appeals to authority, but we must keep in mind that before the erosion of *scientia* traditional thinkers had less need for appeals to authority. In addition, and more important, when they did appeal to authority, they were appealing to a rich and relatively coherent tradition — a luxury no sixteenth-century thinker knew.

Moreover, there is another possibility to ponder. I do not know enough about Lévy-Bruhl's subjects to speak about them with any confidence, but it may even be the case, for all I know, that they stand, as it were, before the *emergence* of authority. This would mean that the distinction between traditional and modern modes of thought is not exhaustive. Perhaps the epistemic principles that would explain Lévy-Bruhl's paradoxes have nothing to do with terms we should translate by our word "authority." Here we must be mindful that "authority" descends from the Latin *auctoritas*. It may be that our references to "traditional thought" should be confined to an intellectual universe defined by the transmission of Latin ideas. Aquinas might qualify, while Homer and Nuer tribesmen might not. These are, however, questions for another day, and for someone with skills I lack.

Nonetheless, it seems safe to say that modern thought was born in a crisis of authority, and owes its secular character largely to a series of bold attempts to circumvent the dialectical impasse imposed by that crisis. One such attempt came at Port-Royal. Another, as we shall see, came when the Huguenots, hoping to recruit revolutionaries from beyond the confines of Protestantism, began to stress political rights over religious obligations in their defenses of revolution.[35] The problems of a divided Europe could not be adequately addressed so long as arguments *from* authority held precedence over arguments *to* it. But arguing to conclusions about authority without either moving in a circle or bringing conversation to a halt with appeals to inner persuasion involved fashioning forms of discourse from which theistic presuppositions had largely been removed. Modernity managed to contain the violent effects of religious disagreement only by creating nonreligious means for discussing and deciding matters of public importance. It is no accident that religious commitment has come to seem a dispensable or marginal aspect of modern life. The irony is that all the religious intensity of the sixteenth and seventeenth centuries could produce such a result.

Those of us who are not theists may be tempted, even after we have disavowed the Enlightenment's antitraditionalist rhetoric of radically autonomous reason, to treat this result, in a spirit of self-congratulation, as the triumph of reason over superstition. We might then simply congratulate ourselves twice — once for falling heir to the Enlightenment's great accomplishment and once for recasting that legacy in a language free from delusions of radical autonomy. But to leave the matter at that would be delusory in its own right. We have not yet told the whole story, and what remains to be told makes an attitude of self-congratulation seem smug and onesided. In real life, comedy and tragedy come together, inextricably intertwined. To narrate the tragic dimension of our story is necessarily to abandon the ironic detachment that views the fate of theism as involving no real loss for those of us who are not theists. It is with this in mind that I turn now to morality and its relation to the fate of theism in modern culture. I shall begin once again, however, with the relatively abstract formulae of unhistorical philosophy, gradually working my way, by a series of stages, into the dense conceptual strata lying beneath. Our next concern, therefore, must be the language of moral philosophy in the age of analysis. For this is the language in which questions about morality's relation to religion have, in recent years, been posed — by theologians as well as professional philosophers. Here we have the third, and last, site I have chosen for my archaeology.

PART III

Morality after Authority

9. Beyond Metaethics

When philosophers believed in conceptual analysis, they called moral philosophy "metaethics." The point of the barbarism was to sharpen the distinction between properly philosophical discourse about ethics and such genres as moralizing and ethical historiography. Some conceptual analysts thought that metaethics might have implications for moralists, but there was general agreement that it could and should be pursued in perfect ethical neutrality. And while many metaethicists drew upon the history of ethics for illustrative examples or sought out parallels between their own analyses and the positions of their philosophical ancestors, the data of moral change were happily left to the professional historians to ponder. Nowadays, with the idiom of conceptual analysis in disrepute, moral philosophers are moralizing again. They are also, as it turns out, more interested in the history of ethics than they used to be — not merely for the sake of illustrative examples or ancestral parallels but in the name of philosophical insight. In this chapter, I hope to illumine (and reinforce) the movement *beyond* metaethics *toward* the perspective of a genealogy of morals.

Old ideas rarely die, they just fade away. When ideas die, it is usually by abuse or neglect at a tender age. Any idea that lives long enough to be old can often avoid the finality of death by lingering in an afterimage, like minimal foundationalism or liberal theology. Metaethics has not lived long enough to be old, but it does seem to be fading away — dissolving into the genres from which it was supposed to be distinguished sharply — rather than suffering sudden death. It may already be too late for mourning. It is not too late, however, to inspect the afterimage in the work of distinguished contemporary philosophers. One of these, in many ways the most interesting, is William Frankena.

Consider, for example, Frankena's essay, "Is Morality Logically Dependent on Religion?,"[1] which will not only provide a point of comparison when we turn to other views on roughly the same topic, but will also reveal arguments and themes characteristic of Frankena's contributions to metaethics. Readers familiar with Stanley Fish's book of literary criticism, *Self-Consuming Artifacts*, will notice that my reading of Frankena parallels the interpretation of Bacon's *Essays* given there.[2] Bacon's *Essays*, according to Fish, are self-regulating, as opposed to either self-consuming or self-satisfying, artifacts. Self-consuming artifacts disappear before one's eyes. They announce a topic, and begin a refinement of reflection seemingly designed to produce an insight statable as a thesis about that topic; but the refined turn of thought turns in upon itself, giving us not the expected thesis but a new topic. The new topic is typically the inadequacy of the reader's assumptions, which the author at first seemed to share. Self-satisfying artifacts, in contrast, are always what they seem to be. They leave assumptions in place, and move more or less straightforwardly to the satisfaction of the expectations they arouse at the outset. Self-regulating artifacts, like the self-consuming kind, frustrate the satisfaction of the expectations they arouse and undermine assumptions they initially seem to take for granted. But they do not seek to dismantle the very mode of thought they make manifest or to dissolve the genre to which they contribute. Instead, they simply guard against hasty or muddled conclusions, and in so doing hold out the possibility of future satisfaction while exerting pressure in the direction of further inquiry. This pressure reinforces the mode of thought and genre in question.

Most writings in contemporary philosophy, like most scientific papers, are self-satisfying. Yet the self-regulating artifact has been anything but uncommon in twentieth-century philosophy, especially among authors influenced by preoccupation with ordinary language. The reason, I suspect, is that the self-regulating style lends itself to the expression and cultivation of virtues often taken to be definitive of "the philosophical mentality" by philosophers themselves. In his discussion of Bacon's "Of Love," Fish lists three of the essay's major intended effects upon the reader:

(1) a felt knowledge of the attraction generalities have for the mind and therefore a "caution" against a too easy acceptance of

them in the future; (2) an awareness of the unresolved complexity of the matter under discussion; (3) an open and inquiring mind, one that is dissatisfied with the state of knowledge at the present time. In short, the demands of the prose have left the reader in a state of "healthy perplexity," neither content with the notion he had been inclined to accept at the beginning of the experience, nor quite ready to put forward a more accurate notion of his own.[3]

The reader is meant to have become, in the experience of reading, "observant, methodical, cautious, skeptical, and yet, in long-range terms, optimistic."[4] These are the virtues of professionalized philosophy, the soul of conceptual analysis.

The danger of the self-regulating style, from the author's point of view at least, is oversuccess in the frustration of the reader's expectations and in the challenging of entrenched assumptions. For an essay that sets out to be merely self-regulating, by raising doubts more radical than had been anticipated, can consume itself, and thus destroy the reader's long-range optimism about further inquiry along the suggested lines. The reformer, despite himself, foments revolution. This is exactly what happens, I think, in Frankena's most interesting work, including the essay at hand. Whatever his intentions, Frankena's methodically discursive operations double back upon themselves, undermining the impression that there is much to be gained by pursuing the mode of thought and analytical genre characteristic of metaethics. The progression is reminiscent of Hegelian dialectic. Metaethics, taken far enough in the work of an honest and rigorous thinker, consumes itself and becomes the seed of something new.

The essay begins with a paragraph designed, like most leads, to capture our interest.

One of the central issues in our cultural crisis, on any view, is that of the relation of morality to religion. That morality is dependent on religion is widely maintained by theologians arguing for the need of a return to religion, by moralists seeking to promote virtue, civic or personal, by educators advocating the teaching of religion in the public schools, and, of course, by many laymen and parents, not to mention politicians trying to impose an oath on teachers and other state employees, and political theorists trying to re-establish democracy and Western culture on their "true basis." And, indeed, if morality (and hence politics) is dependent on religion, then we must look to religion as a basis for any answer to any personal or social problem of any importance; but, if not, we may answer at least some of these problems on an "independent bottom," as people used to say; for example, on the basis of history, science, and practical experience. If morality is dependent on religion, then we cannot hope to solve our problems, or resolve our differences of opinion about them, unless and in so far as we can achieve agreement and certainty in religion (not a lively hope); but, if it is not entirely dependent on religion, then we can expect to solve at least some of them by the use of empirical and historical inquiries of a publicly available and testable kind (inquiries that are improving in quality and scope).[5]

If we want insight into "one of the central issues in our cultural crisis," we would seem to have good reason to read further. And if we want to disarm "politicians trying to impose an oath" or to avoid importing all the doubt and disagreement associated with religious controversy into the moral and political spheres, we would seem to have good reason for desiring a negative answer to the title question. This paragraph appeals directly to the concerns of a responsible citizenry, connects these concerns to the essay's nominal topic, and prepares us for an argument in the support of the negative thesis.

The next paragraph, however, signals complications even in its first word.

Nevertheless, although the thesis that morality is dependent on religion is of such crucial importance, and is so often asserted, assumed, or clung to, it is rarely, if ever, very carefully formulated or argued for by those who believe it.[6]

The implication is that we need, above all, precisely those virtues elevated in the self-regulating style. The thesis that morality is dependent on religion, we are told, "is both vague and ambiguous." Frankena proposes to initiate a refinement of reflection "by discussing with some care" one of this thesis's many forms — "the claim that morality is *logically* dependent on religion." The plot thickens, but the topic narrows. Causal, historical, motivational, and psychological forms of dependence are explicitly excluded from consideration. Only logical dependence remains.

But has the topic merely been delimited, or has it also been changed? What evidence do we have that logical dependence is at issue in our "cultural crisis"? Frankena complains that proponents of the view that morality is dependent on religion "generally do not make clear" what they have in mind, though "they do often seem to say or at least suggest that morality is logically dependent on religion or theology." We are then ushered quickly past two quotations from Reinhold Niebuhr's *An Interpretation of Christian Ethics:*

> Thus, Reinhold Niebuhr writes that the ethic of Jesus "proceeds logically from the presuppositions of prophetic religion," and that "The justification for these demands (of the ethic of Jesus) is put in purely religious and not in socio-moral terms. We are to forgive because God forgives; we are to love our enemies because God is impartial in his love." Hence he seems to be thinking that these demands depend on prophetic religion, not just causally or motivationally, but also logically. This is the question I wish to discuss, though not merely with respect to Niebuhr or to the ethics of Jesus.[7]

Note, however, that Niebuhr has confined himself to discussing the ethics of Jesus and has said nothing whatsoever about logical *dependence* in the passages cited. Surely there are significant logical relations between the presuppositions of prophetic religion and the demands of the ethic of Jesus. And surely Niebuhr is right in saying that the justification of this ethic, at least as given in the biblical passages he is examining, must be phrased in religious terms. What this has to do with Frankena's topic remains unclear. For all Niebuhr has said here, neither morality as such nor the ethic of Jesus in particular requires logical derivation from purely religious premises for its justification. In the footnote to his quotations from Niebuhr, Frankena cites one passage each from Joseph Fletcher and Karl Barth, but neither passage (if read in context) shows that theologians have proposed the thesis of morality's logical dependence. Fletcher, in fact, seems explicitly to deny the thesis.[8]

I raise these points only because the transition from a "central issue in our cultural crisis" to the analytic philosopher's own version of the problem is executed so quickly. The apparent smoothness of this transition is essential to the essay's self-regulating form, for Frankena will eventually undermine the assumption he is now encouraging — namely, that logical dependence is in some important respect the most fitting kind of dependence to consider. Before moving any further, however, he introduces additional complications. The thesis of logical dependence has not yet been clarified enough to be assessed. Frankena therefore illustrates what he means

by "religious" and "ethical" terms and judgments by giving
examples of each. He then specifies four claims relevant to the
thesis of logical dependence:

1. The term and concepts of ethics are to be defined by reference
   to (derived from or analyzed into) those of religion. . . .
2. The judgments of ethics can be logically inferred, deduced,
   or derived from those of theology.
3. Ethical judgments can be justified by being derived logically
   from theological ones.
4. Ethical judgments can be justified only by being logically
   inferred from theological ones, that is, they depend logically
   on religious beliefs for their justification.[9]

Of these, (4) is singled out as "the most crucial claim."

It now becomes clear that the issue to be addressed is the
justification of moral knowledge. The thesis asserted in claim
(4) is thus placed squarely within the context of a distinctively
philosophical debate — one that proceeds on the assumption
that epistemic justification essentially involves logical derivation from what we already know. It is this conception of justification that makes talk of *logical* dependence seem the "natural"
way to phrase questions about the relation between religion and
morality. Frankena seems here to be presupposing the truth of
foundationalism, even though he will eventually call foundationalist assumptions into question. So let us assume for the
moment, as Frankena seems to assume, that a successful
justification of moral knowledge would first establish a firm
foundation of some kind and then show how ethical judgments
can be connected logically to that.

It follows that if moral knowledge depends for its justification on religious knowledge, we must show both that the
relevant religious beliefs are justified and that they imply
(without presupposing) moral judgments. Otherwise we would
be encouraging moral skepticism. The difficulty of securing a
foundation of religious judgments is itself enough to raise
serious doubts. This suggests that claim (3), on which the truth
of (4) obviously depends, is uncertain. "In fact," writes
Frankena, "the conviction that this is so is part of what moti-
vates me in writing this paper."[10] Anyone familiar with modern
religious controversy has good reason to wonder whether
"there is anything to be gained by insisting that all ethical
principles are or must be logically grounded on religious beliefs." But Frankena concentrates on what Will would call the

"construction" difficulty — the theological version of the problem of "is" and "ought."

Consider, for example, the following argument schema:

(P) x is against God's will; *hence*
(C) it is not the case that, morally speaking, one ought to do x.

Does P logically imply C? If so, there would be no problem in justifying C provided the truth of P were known. Yet no one would claim that the argument from P to C is *formally* valid as it stands. If C follows from P, it is not simply by virtue of logical form. Some appeal must be made, then, to the *content* of the propositions in question. Unless there is some sort of conceptual connection between God's will and the requirements or morality, the proposed justification of moral knowledge cannot succeed. We began with claim (4), and saw that it depends on the truth of (3). The foundationalist assumption implicit in (3) and (4) highlights claim (2). But formal considerations do not by themselves establish the wanted connections between religious and ethical judgments, as we can see by taking up any plausible example (like the argument from P to C). We are thus brought back to claim (1) and the issue of the analysis or definition of ethical terms. Frankena helps us see how the central issues of metaethics — namely, epistemic justification, the "logic" of moral discourse, and the definition of ethical terms — all hang together as an interlocking set. It is especially important to notice that foundationalist assumptions serve as warrant for the transition from the basic issue of moral epistemology to the subsidiary issues of logical and conceptual analysis.

We are now ready to attend to Frankena's treatment of the conceptual issue implicit in claim (1). Is there a conceptual connection — of the kind we could state in a definition or an analytic truth — between, say, God's will and moral requirement? There are several problems here. First of all, a defense of claim (1), if it is to prove useful in an eventual defense of (3) and (4), will have to remove the impression that the problem of justifying moral judgments has simply been pushed one step into the background and thereby obscured. For if the asserted conceptual connection does hold, the religious propositions of the proposed foundation would themselves seem to be at least partly ethical. The question becomes how these partly ethical propositions might be justified if not by appeal to explicitly moral judgments. Circularity threatens. We are thus confronted with the problems usually associated with Plato's *Euthyphro*. For if the asserted conceptual connection holds, but the propositions of the proposed foundation are purely religious (that is, not ethical in the least), then the use of ethical language adds nothing. It would follow that the vocabulary of normative assessment is rather more impoverished than it is usually assumed to be. It seems to follow in particular that theists lack the conceptual means for distinguishing God from an all-powerful tyrant.

Frankena mentions these problems, which are the usual stuff of philosophical and theological discussions of the relation between religion and morality, but does so only in passing. He is more interested in a further difficulty. We can approach this difficulty by asking how claims about conceptual analyses or definitional truths might be assessed. How do we find out about conceptual connections? Appeals to "immediately given" meanings would of course be dialectically useless in this context, because whatever disagreement we encounter over the question of *what* implies what will turn up again in the reported intuitions of meanings. But avoiding the impasse brought on by appeals to intuited immediacy involves placing a premium on the actual use of words and sentences. Suppose, then, that a theologian proposes theological definitions of various ethical terms. Frankena writes,

> Whatever they are, if they are not merely arbitrary, they must be offered either as reportive elucidations of what we *do* mean by these terms or as recommendations about what we *should* mean by them. I am inclined to think . . . that theological definitions will not do simply as reports of what we do mean. But, even if they did correctly report what we do mean, one could still ask if we should go on using them in this sense. *A fortiori*, if they are proposals about our future use of ethical terms, we may ask for reasons why we should adopt them. Either way, it seems to me that accepting the definition offered as a basis for our future speech, thought, and action is tantamount to accepting a moral principle. I do not mean that a definition is a moral principle. What I mean is that, when one accepts a definition of any term that can be called ethical, one has already in effect accepted an ethical standard.[11]

As Frankena has put it elsewhere, "Appealing to a definition in support of a principle is not a solution to the problem of justification, for the definition needs to be justified, and justifying it (as a proposal for future use) involves the same problems that justifying a principle does."[12]

If meanings were immediately given and absolutely fixed, it might make sense to use knowledge of meanings in the justification of moral principles. Frankena's bewilderment over how a definition could be used to support a principle is but one effect of erosion in the assumptions about language that once sustained analytic philosophy. Quine's attack on analyticity, Wittgenstein's meditations on meaning and use, and Sellars's critique of the "myth of the given" all make the appeal to meanings seem redundant. For if we find out about meanings not by bringing the immediately given into focus before the eye of the mind, but rather by attending to the publicly available evidence of actual linguistic behavior, then meaning and use must be closely related. "Meaning," if we choose to go on using the term for philosophical purposes at all, can be nothing more than (in Putnam's phrase) "a coarse grid laid over use." Changes in belief, by virtue of affecting use, cannot be sharply distinguished from changes in meaning — especially if the beliefs in question express adherence to deeply entrenched, lawlike sentences, such as moral principles. So an attempt to defend such principles by appealing to the very "conceptual connections" they establish would be circular. Meanings reflect beliefs. They cannot tell us which beliefs to accept.

This line of reasoning, Frankena concludes, surely clinches the case against claim (1). And if (1) cannot be established, neither can (2), (3), or (4). The author seems to be preparing us for the straightforward conclusion that moral knowledge, if there is any, cannot depend for its justification on a foundation of purely religious propositions. But we are instead swept beyond this conclusion to a broader, more startling one as the announced topic recedes from view. For the point about definitions undermines *all* forms of "definism" — theological and nontheological alike. *No* definition could suffice to bridge the gap between "is" and "ought." "I doubt," Frankena suddenly announces, "that basic ethical judgments are self-evident and that they can be proved logically by derivation from other propositions, whether these are religious ones or not."[13] Furthermore, neither inductive logic nor some "third" logic can be used to justify basic ethical judgments. The means of justification seem to have been exhausted. Moral skepticism seems the inevitable result.

Now, however, Frankena informs us that moral skepticism

follows only if we assume, with foundationalism. that justification consists either in self-evidence or in logical proof (deductive, inductive, or whatever). This is, of course, precisely the assumption Frankena seemed to be encouraging at the outset in his smooth transition to talk of *logical* dependence and in his formulation of claims (1)-(4). But his point, we finally discover, has been to call this assumption into question. He does this not with an argument but with a quotation from Mill's *Utilitarianism*, one Frankena has alluded to or transcribed several times in his published writings.[14] After denying, much as Frankena does, that a basic ethical principle can be strictly proved, Mill adds,

> We are not, however, to infer that its acceptance or rejection must depend on blind impulse, or arbitrary choice. There is a larger meaning of the word "proof," in which this question is as amenable to it as any other of the disputed questions of philosophy. The subject is within the cognizance of the rational faculty; and neither does that faculty deal with it solely in the way of intuition. Considerations may be presented capable of determining the intellect either to give or withhold its assent. . . .

The quotation comes only three paragraphs from the end of the essay, and is introduced simply in the hope of "pointing out a direction for further inquiry." These are Frankena's words, but they are also Bacon's — drawn as they are from the basic vocabulary of the self-regulating style. A new topic has emerged — namely, the inadequacy of standard assumptions about justification — and we are cautioned against premature conclusions. Only further inquiry along the lines Mill's sentences suggest, but undertaken in a careful and rigorous spirit, will achieve more than merely tentative conclusions.

Frankena does not hesitate to announce tentative conclusions, provided they are billed explicitly as tentative. He suggests that religious beliefs may in fact justify moral principles, in a suitably broad sense of the term "justify," at least if the religious beliefs themselves are presumed true. "It does not follow, however, that they are *necessary* to justify those ethical principles even in this larger sense, for it may be that certain non-religious considerations are also capable of determining the intellect to give them its assent."[15] It is unclear how one could show that even a single moral principle depends for its justification on religious propositions without rebutting *every possi-*

ble attempt at nonreligious justification of that principle — an apparently interminable task. So a claim of epistemic dependence would be intrinsically difficult to defend decisively, whether justification conforms to foundationalist assumptions or not. The essay ends as follows:

> If (theologians) admit that such a larger kind of objective and rational justification of ethics is possible, but insist that it requires religious premises, though not in a logical sense of "requires," they might be right for all I have shown here. Indeed, I believe that this is the line to be taken by theologians who wish to hold that religion is required to justify the principles of morality (and not merely to motivate people to act according to them). I myself think that even this weaker claim about the dependence of morality on religion is at best true only if it is carefully qualified. But that is another story.[16]

Even in bringing his essay to a close, Frankena is telling us to be skeptical, to aim for careful qualification of theses, and to await patiently the outcome of additional inquiry along more or less standard lines. Any reader who remembers after all this that the essay's first sentence speaks of "our cultural crisis" deserves congratulations.

We have found much evidence of the self-regulating style. Frankena does not stop playing tricks with nominal topics until, in the essay's final section, we are brought up short by an overturned assumption and a tantalizing suggestion of unconsidered possibilities. Our own tendencies to accept generalities, to underestimate complexities, and to be too easily satisfied with accepted conclusions finally emerge as the real topic. Like Bacon, Frankena is anything but heavy-handed in all this. The "machinery of the surface argument is maintained even when the alert reader's attention has been drawn away to other concerns."[17] But the effect of piling qualification upon qualification is, in the end, to create tension between what Fish would call the "inner" and "outer" forms of the essay.

> What we have, then, are two discursive structures in a single space, and to the extent they pull against each other or point in different directions, the reader's experience of them is strenuous and, what is more important, inconclusive. Not that one cancels the other out; rather, neither finally carries the day, with the result that the reader remains suspended between the conclusions each of them is separately urging, and ends by asking a question instead of assenting to an argument.[18]

Nothing in the "outer" form, the surface rhetoric of the essay, signals that we are first exchanging one of "the central issues in our cultural crisis" for the topic of the title question and then, more important still, exchanging the latter for open-ended inquiry into a kind of epistemic dependence that may have nothing to do with logic at all. These transitions are not heralded. They are, to the contrary, made to seem as coherent as possible. But the "inner" movement of the essay is disrupting the sense of coherence at every step. The "outer" form simply urges a negative answer to the title question, while the "inner" simultaneously encourages a kind of skepticism with respect to all answers to all questions. The resulting tension is meant to dissolve both our interest in the answered question and our sense that interesting questions can be answered well without pursuing additional inquiry in the manner of the professional analyst.

The essay clearly sets out to be self-regulating. But does it, however accidentally, consume itself? Does it, by virtue of the doubts it raises, threaten to destroy the reader's long-range optimism about further inquiry along the suggested lines? I can clarify my reasons for believing that it does by returning to Frankena's point about definitions. His point, you will recall, was that one could not legitimately appeal to definitions of ethical terms in order to justify moral principles, for accepting a definition of an ethical term "as a basis for our future speech, thought, and action is tantamount to accepting a moral principle" and therefore requires the same sort of justification. In saying this Frankena has implicitly, though rightly, rejected theories of language that would make definitions seem like a source of independent leverage for the problem of justification. If meanings were immediately given, definitions would not require the same sort of justification a moral principle does, and might indeed prove useful in determining which moral principles to accept. If matters of meaning and matters of substance were as clearly separable as defenders of the analytic-synthetic distinction thought, accepting a definition would not in fact be tantamount to accepting a principle, and might therefore provide independent epistemic leverage. So Frankena's conclusion makes sense only if we ascribe to him some form of holism in the theory of language. And I would certainly not advise him to retreat from holism to the discredited doctrines of immediacy and analyticity. But what becomes of metaethics when holism is taken seriously?

Frankena continues to use the term "metaethics" as if it referred to a distinguishable subject matter or genre. The force of his point about definitions does, however, push him toward a distinction between two kinds of metaethics — *descriptive* and *normative*. He writes:

> Let me explain the phrase "normative metaethics." By a *normative* inquiry, I mean one that aims at and results in conclusions to the effect that something is desirable, good, bad, right, wrong, or ought to be done. By a *metaethical* inquiry, I mean one that asks about the meaning and justification of such conclusions. Now, a metaethical inquiry may and usually does take a descriptive, elucidatory, or reportive form, that is, it may seek simply to lay bare what we actually mean when we judge that something is good or right or what our actual logic is for justifying such judgments. But it may also be normative, telling us what our meanings and our logic should be; and then it may be either *conservative*, bidding us to go on using our normative terms and justifying our normative judgments as we have, or *revisionary*, proposing that we reconstruct our meanings or our logic, more or less radically.[19]

Frankena then uses his distinction between descriptive and normative metaethics to criticize metaethics as it has usually been practiced — as, for example, in R. M. Hare's use of the "open question" argument. Consider this passage from Hare:

> . . . if "right" meant the same as "in accordance with the will of God," then, "whatever is in accordance with the will of God is right" would mean the same as "whatever is in accordance with the will of God is in accordance with the will of God"; but according to our actual use of the words, it seems to mean more than this mere tautology.[20]

If this argument is good, Frankena contends, its force is merely descriptive. It does not show that theological *proposals* about how our words *should* be used are incorrect. "In order to operate in the field of normative metaethics," Frankena continues, Hare's argument must be rephrased:

> If we take "right" as meaning the same as "in accordance with the will of God," then we must take "whatever is in accordance with the will of God is right" as meaning the same as "whatever is in accordance with the will of God is in accordance with the will of God," but surely this is not a desirable use of words.[21]

But this version "simply begs the question." The lesson to be learned from such cases is that "No metaethical Ought can be logically inferred from any metaethical Is alone."

Something very interesting has happened here. Frankena persists in taking the topics of "meaning and justification" as the distinguishing marks of metaethics. But from what is metaethics being distinguished? Metaethics now consists in two parts, one purely descriptive and the other normative. Yet how is descriptive metaethics to be distinguished from ethical historiography? And how is normative metaethics to be distinguished from ordinary moralizing? Metaethics seems to have disappered in all but name.

Descriptive metaethics seeks "simply to lay bare what we actually mean when we judge that something is good or right or what our actual logic is for justifying such judgments." If we were willing to embrace the immediately given or analytic truth, the task of descriptive metaethics would be distinguishable from a historian's, but there would also be no reason for distinguishing descriptive from normative metaethics. If, on the other hand, meanings are intersections in the web of belief, as holists hold (and as Frankena seems bound to hold), then descriptive metaethics can be nothing but the history of ethical belief and moral reasoning. Whether we speak of analyzing meanings or of doing history will then be a matter of merely autobiographical interest — provided we attend to the historical details in either case. To speak of oneself as a descriptive metaethicist may be a way to signal one's intellectual upbringing. It may also, however, be a way to do history in bad faith — that is, without taking on the historian's obligation to specify about *whom* he is talking. If we want "to lay bare what *we* actually mean when we judge that something is good or right," we had better clarify the group to which we refer. That would be to begin the task of locating ourselves in a history of moral change.[22]

Normative metaethics tells us what "our meanings" ought to be. But, once again, if accepting a proposed definition of an ethical term is "tantamount to accepting a moral principle," then telling us what our meanings ought to be is tantamount to telling us what principles to accept. And doing normative metaethics is tantamount to moralizing (in the nonpejorative sense). Talk of meanings and metaethics here seems a pointless detour and an invitation to confusion. Perhaps if we wish to sound less like the preacher and more like the professional philosopher, we can call our moralizing "normative metaethics," but we shall be moralizing nonetheless.

Frankena, as Fish might say, has given us one distinction too many. His point about definitions, itself an effect of holism in the theory of language, breaks metaethics in two. Each of the shards quickly dissolves into a genre from which metaethics had initially been distinguished. Metaethics has faded away. When this has happened it becomes unclear why we should be preoccupied with meanings at all. Frankena himself helps us see why "meaning and justification" once seemed a matched pair. For if justification is largely a matter of logical derivation from certified foundations, and merely formal considerations clearly do not by themselves secure the wanted logical connections, then conceptual content (or meaning) must be crucial. Yet Frankena shows that this way of posing the problem of justification leads either toward implausible theories of language or toward skepticism. When the foundationalist linkage of justification and logical derivation is loosened, however, so too is the connection between justification and meaning. Preoccupation with meanings loses its point.

Moreover, the very holism that lies behind Frankena's point about definitions also undermines the impression that there is a general philosophical problem of ethical justification to worry about (or to claim as the special subject matter of one's field). Frankena obviously believes that the principles we accept in large part determine the meanings of the terms we use. But if he is right about this, no sharp distinction between descriptive and evaluative language can be drawn, and we can therefore never be faced with the problem of bridging the "gap" between "is" and "ought." No such gap exists. So Frankena is not consistent with his better insights when he says that we bridge the gap with our "moral concern," "sympathy," or "commitment to the moral point of view."[23] If we do in fact use moral language meaningfully, even in the formulation of our ethical doubts and difficulties, we must *already* accept moral principles in which connections between so-called descriptive and evaluative terms are established. Ethical reasoning, like any other form of reasoning, always begins in a position defined by currently accepted principles, beliefs, hopes, and plans, and moves from that position toward the resolution of outstanding problems.

This is simply to repeat my contention that holism in the theory of language leads *away from* epistemologically oriented philosophy, as expressed in the notion that there is a *general* problem of justification to be solved (in ethics or anywhere else), *toward* historically oriented philosophy, as expressed in the view that all problems of justification are radically situated in specific historical contexts. If we take Frankena's implicit holism seriously, we shall also have reason to take his quotation from Mill as the acid in which metaethics consumes itself. For if holism is correct, the "larger kind" of justification Mill is reaching for will not be the kind of thing we need a general philosophical theory of. Metaethics does not survive as moral epistemology; it gives way to historical investigation. Historical investigation alone seems likely to tell us the specific things we need to know about our ethical and cognitive context in order to pose and address our normative problems well. If we ever achieve a general theory of justification that is worth having, it will probably be a sociological theory of the kind that emerges from extensive historical and anthropological research. This is not, of course, what Frankena has in mind when he holds out the promise of "further inquiry." Hence my conviction that he has been more successful than he intended to be in raising doubts about the state of contemporary metaethical reflection.

Frankena is right when he says that morality's putative independence from religion is more complicated than it seems. But increasingly rigorous argumentation and careful analysis will not by themselves tell us what we need to know. How, then, does morality's relation to religion look when we follow the holism and historicism implicit in Frankena's work to their conclusion?

Holism helps us see, in the first place, that theologians do not necessarily commit a "logical fallacy" when they allow their theological beliefs to inform their moral conclusions. The idea that they do derives from foundationalist epistemology and its puzzle about how to bridge the gap between moral conclusions and purely factual premises of any kind — be they natural or supernatural. If theologians have tried to bridge such a gap, they have surely committed fallacies, but these would be the product of foundationalist and not strictly theological convictions. According to holism, no such gap could exist, because the very idea of "purely factual" premises whose meaning can be determined in isolation from the rest of discourse is itself mistaken. The meaning of both factual and moral terms is determined in part by the roles such terms play in moral principles we already accept. There is no "pure" basis on which to begin a project of reconstruction. The theological ethicist does what we all do when we engage in moral reasoning: he stands within a system of conjecture and assumption in terms of which his sentences get their meaning, and he moves toward the resolution of outstanding problems by making adjustments in this inheritance as they seem appropriate. We call him "theological" because his moral principles can be rightly understood only as part of a system in which theological propositions play an important role, not because his ethics derives from a theological foundation.

Kantians have long argued against the possibility of theological foundations for ethics by contending that theism itself presupposes a moral vocabulary which can be independently understood.[24] There is more than a grain of truth in the argument, but its conclusion should not be conflated with the thesis that morality is logically autonomous. The idea is to show that a purely theological foundation would be too weak to accomplish some of the jobs theists want done, such as distinguishing God from Satan in ways that make the former but not the latter seem worthy of worship. These tasks are theologically important; many theologians deem them essential to the project of articulating a coherent theology. But it seems one has to have moral judgments already in place to have any chance of success, and this means that a purely theological foundation will be hard to come by without sacrificing features that would make it religiously attractive.

This line of argument will fail to have the desired effect, of course, upon any theologian actually willing to accept a version of theism lacking these features. The argument, even if successful, simply raises the cost of advocating theological foundations for ethics.[25] Furthermore, it may be possible to diminish this cost by distinguishing sharply between moral and nonmoral value judgments, allowing the latter but not the former into the theological foundation.[26] But such complications will be beside the point if we possess strong arguments against the idea of epistemological foundations itself, for in that case theological foundations would not constitute a special instance requiring its own separate critique.

It is crucial that the Kantian argument works, if it does work, only against a variety of *foundationalism*. The argument does not undermine theological ethics *per se*. Nor does it show that morality is autonomous in the sense of "providing its own foundation" without help from a context of supporting "factual" judgments. What force the argument has derives from the fact, recognized more clearly in holism, that the constraints foundationalists (of the more than "minimal" variety) place on their "basic" propositions impoverish the proposed foundations to the point of uselessness. Kantians point out one respect in which a purely theological foundation would be weak. The deeper problem is how to assign meanings to "basic" propositions at all, and this problem remains even for basic propositions thought to be purely moral (such that morality would have its own, completely autonomous, foundation). Like so many Kantian arguments, the present one is transformed and preserved in holism as the more general truth that proposed foundations tend in fact to be "parasitic" upon propositions they are designed to support, just as the skeptic's radical doubts are "parasitic" upon what he sets out to deny.[27]

Moral judgments, like judgments of any kind, cease to be intelligible when deprived of a rich context of judgments in which terms of various sorts are "mixed." There is thus a clear sense, according to holism, in which morality could not be radically autonomous and still make sense. It does not follow that the supporting cast *must* include theological judgments. Moral judgments *per se* have not been shown to depend upon theology for their justification. On the other hand, the removal of theological beliefs from the context within which moral judgments are interpreted would, if holism is correct, change (perhaps significantly) the *kind* of morality one could justify. It would do this by shifting the meaning of the judgments which would be candidates for justification. So some kinds of morality might indeed depend upon theology for their justification. Which kinds? The theological ones — namely, those in which the meaning of moral terms is partly determined by the role such terms play in judgments that also include theological vocabulary.

Being a theist does not by itself commit someone to the view that morality has or requires a theological foundation. Nonfoundationalists who are also believers would not worry themselves with theological foundations for moral knowledge because they would not bother with foundations for knowledge at all. Similarly, belief in God does not necessarily entail acceptance of a particular theory of moral language. Yet those who speak of theological "metaethics" typically have in mind a species of the descriptivist theory of moral language. All *descriptivists*, as I understand the term, view moral expressions as reducible in meaning to descriptive expressions. Some descriptivists are naturalists: they view moral statements as elliptical statements about natural facts. A theological descriptivist would simply replace natural with supernatural facts in the proposed reduction. The meaning of moral expressions, on this view, can be stated fully in strictly nonmoral theological terms.

The trouble with descriptivist theories of moral language, be they theological or naturalistic, is precisely their reductive character. Standard antidescriptivist theories, be they emotivist or prescriptivist, are equally reductive, though in other directions. That is, they propose to reduce the meaning of moral expressions to that of expressions of some other sort, where this sort is not descriptive. Emotivists focus on expressions or reports of emotions, prescriptivists on commands, imperatives, and the giving of advice. Each of these various species of reductionism continues to thrive, where interest has been maintained at all, mainly on an unending supply of counterexamples to its opponents' attempts at reduction.

The debate proceeds more or less as follows. A descriptivist proposes a definition of a moral term — say, that "morally wrong" means "against God's commands." A critic then argues (following G. E. Moore) that if the definition were correct, it would not make sense to ask whether an act that is against God's commands is in fact morally wrong. But, according to the critic's intuitions, this is clearly an open question. If God commanded me to murder my son, it at least makes sense to ask whether, morally speaking, disobedience would be wrong. The critic then suggests that a similar "open question" argument can be brought against any naturalistic or supernaturalistic definition of moral terms. So the meaning of moral expressions must be found elsewhere. But what, the descriptivist asks in return, could be the point of using evaluative terms that lack determinate criteria of descriptive application? Why, moreover, should the critic's intuitions about the "openness" of certain questions be accepted as final? We seem able to give relatively determinate descriptive criteria for the application of words like "courageous" and "rude." Why not "morally wrong" as well? Perhaps the critic is simply mistaken about which questions really are open. A die-hard descriptivist will profess intuitions that go the other way.

From the vantage point of holism, the debate seems pointless. If meaning and substance cannot be separated clearly and sharply, it should not be surprising that persons with conflicting moral beliefs will have conflicting intuitions about the meanings of moral terms. These differences will, in turn, make different questions seem "open" or "closed." Appealing to intuitions about meanings and open questions does nothing to resolve the debate simply because the differing intuitions reflect correspondingly different beliefs at the level of substance.

Holism explains the ease with which the two sides have produced counterexamples as an inevitable consequence of a debate between two kinds of reductionism. It splits the difference between descriptivists and their most vocal critics by opposing the reductive intent both share. It affirms a close relation between meaning and belief, and therefore between the meaning of moral expressions and moral principles that are in fact accepted in the linguistic community in question. But it sees no point in reducing the meaning of any moral expression to its use in any single moral principle. What would be the point of such a reduction?

The original parties to the debate thought the point was perfectly plain. Descriptivists saw themselves as holding the line against moral skepticism, and thought they required for this purpose a theory of meaning allowing for "necessary connections" between descriptive and evaluative terms such that what counts as a moral reason is, as Philippa Foot put it, "always determined" and not a matter of radically subjective choice.[28] "Necessary connections" could then be used to bridge the gap between "is" and "ought." Evaluative sentences could be reduced to descriptive statements and assessed accordingly as objective matters of fact. Prescriptivists found the supposedly "necessary" connections specious, however, and used Moore's "open question" to reinforce the intuition that any such connection can be placed in jeopardy. This tended to show, they argued, that what counts as a moral reason is not determinate after all, that the gap between "is" and "ought" cannot be bridged, that the proposed reductions cannot be carried out. Prescriptivists then drew the moral that ethical judgments, if they "rest" on anything, must be founded on "decisions of principle." The corollary to this subjectivist conclusion was a theory that assimilated the meaning of moral expressions to that of imperatives, as opposed to that of the declarative, statement-making discourse which would be more obviously relevant to cognition. The perils of irrationalism were to be held at bay, though not very convincingly, by a meagre constraint of consistency and R. M. Hare's thesis that moral sentences logically *imply* sentences of universal form.[29]

Descriptivists and prescriptivists alike were, then, foundationalists, differing mainly on whether the "necessary connections" could be found that would link moral conclusions to an objectively factual base, and also on whether "universalizability" was enough to stave off the fanatics if "necessary connections" could not be found. Descriptivists used their form of reductionism to secure the wanted connections between fact and value. Prescriptivists used theirs to explain the difficulty of bridging the gap. A thoroughgoing holist, however, can agree with the prescriptivist claim that any moral principle can be placed in jeopardy, while also maintaining with descriptivism that what counts as a moral reason is never a matter of merely subjective choice. He can say that Hare was right to resist Foot's belief in necessary connections, just as she was right to resist his implicit skepticism. If we reject foundationalism, then the failure to supply necessary connections does not deprive moral reasoning of something any full-fledged cognitive endeavor ought to have. We thus lack the motive for hoping that a form of reductionism will come to the rescue. There is then much less point in opposing one kind of reductionism with another.[30]

Foundationalism makes one wish a form of reductionism were true. But the failure of the various reductionisms to account for each other's counterexamples is evidence of a weakness inherent in reductionism. And if reductionism falls, foundationalism falls as well. Yet, as we have seen, when foundationalism falls, the associated skeptical worries cease, and the cycle of opposing theories is broken. By the holist's lights, therefore, much of the debate over the autonomy of morals is simply misplaced.

Consider, however, the following possibilities. Holism

holds that a radically autonomous morality, precisely by virtue of its detachment from the rest of discourse, would be unintelligible. Similarly, if the theological reductionist were right about the meaning of "good," according to holism, moral language would be severely impoverished. We have seen that holism also requires that, with respect to any descriptive claim about the meaning or use of language, we must try to be as specific as we can concerning precisely what language is to be investigated. Is it not possible that the proponents of radical autonomy and theological reduction are both right, but in reference to different, relatively local, linguistic phenomena? This raises the further possibility that much disagreement among conceptual analysts might well be explained away. For the descriptivists and their critics may be analyzing concepts belonging, so to speak, to different languages (or different strata within the same language). If so, then the problem of the analysis of moral concepts has been misleadingly formed, and the history of analyses becomes revelatory in a new way. The analyses take on significance not simply as failed attempts to account for the supposedly global and unitary phenomenon, moral language, but also as possibly insightful descriptions of the use of moral language at a given time and place. They might then be the makings of a story that culminates in a depiction of our moral situation, the "cultural crisis" to which Frankena draws our attention but about which he has so little to say.

Might not theological reductionism in ethical theory reflect a stage in the disintegration of a formerly rich and coherent discursive practice? Could it not be that, as a matter of fact, moral judgments have since lost their holistic connections with the broader linguistic context which once made morality intelligible, and, further, that these lost connections have not since been replaced in such a way that genuine intelligibility could be restored? Morality would, in that event, be autonomous. It would also, according to holism, be in desperate straits as a form of life. If such a story is true, then the issue of autonomy cannot simply be dismissed as a philosopher's mistake, and historical insight will be the key to understanding its real character. That such a story *may be* true is, by itself, enough to underline the significance of history for ethical understanding.

10. Toward a Genealogy of Morals

As the distinction between matters of meaning and matters of substance dissolves, "conceptual analysis" seems more and more like a straightforwardly *historical* task, to be undertaken along with all the *responsibilities* of the historian. But what these responsibilities might be is by no means a self-answering question. Perhaps the next step on our way toward a genealogy of morals should be one of methodological preparation. We are certainly not lacking in detailed advice about how to proceed. Much of this advice is now coming from students of religious ethics, some of whom busy themselves exploiting one or another strand of a broadly neo-Kantian methodological tradition, apparently in the hope of overcoming the more strictly theological assumptions of their teachers and setting comparative ethics on the road to science. In this chapter I intend to subject some of this advice to critical scrutiny. Two books in particular will receive attention — *Comparative Religious Ethics*, by David Little and Sumner B. Twiss, and *Religious Reason*, by Ronald Green.[1] My reason for discussing these books is straightforward: if they are right about how the history of morality (and its relation to religion) should be approached, then the suggestions I shall be making in chapter 11 must be surely be wrong. Students of religion would be disappointed if I did not rise to the challenge. Philosophers, I hope, will be interested to see how the influence of philosophical assumptions has spread in neighboring disciplines. My conclusion will be that, because of the extent and shape of this influence, neither book's proposals are likely to issue in the kind of historical insight we need — the kind that would help us place the philosophical tradition itself (and especially its assumptions about the *logical autonomy* of morality) in perspective.

201

Comparative Religious Ethics is an attempt to renew and purify a program of research. Readers familiar with David Little's early work, *Religion, Order and Law,*[2] will not be surprised to learn that the program in question is Max Weber's. That book was a reformulation, in the tradition of Parsons and Bellah, of Weber's work on the Protestant Ethic. The new book revives Weberian interest in the entire breadth of religious and ethical traditions. Little and Twiss take Weber's program and send it through a series of "purifying" transformations, transformations executed with the help of "conceptual and methodological orientation" derived from a specific philosophical tradition at a specific stage in its development.

The irony of *Comparative Religious Ethics* is its air of novelty. The subtitle announces "a new method," but readers familiar with the philosophy of science will find the method's central distinctions suspiciously familiar. What will cure the ills of our field? *Conceptual analysis* of basic theoretical terms, sharp distinctions between descriptive endeavors and *explanatory* or *normative* projects, and a theory of justification pinned to a contrast between *validation* and *vindication.* This answer derives mainly from logical empiricism circa 1950. All the associated distinctions have been under attack in the philosophy of science for twenty-five years. It is no longer clear why such distinctions should be accepted or, for that matter, why we should share the empiricist preoccupation with method in the first place. Philosophers as various as Paul Feyerabend and Hans-Georg Gadamer have for some time now been urging relaxation of precisely those concerns Little and Twiss want to intensify.[3] In short, the career of methodological philosophy since the mid-century constitutes a prima facie case against the proposals — and perhaps even the genre — Little and Twiss put forward.

What saves their book from the dogmatism and rigidity most of us now associate with positivism is that Little and Twiss borrow from a stage of empiricism in which leaders of the movement were blurring the old positivist distinctions — the stage during which Hempel lost his optimism about the problem of theoretical terms and during which Feigl, Carnap, and Reichenbach gave pragmatism a new foothold in the theory of scientific knowledge. Pragmatism re-entered American philosophy on little cat feet, first with this one tentative paw but then suddenly on all fours — a calming fog of blurred distinctions. If the twilight of logical empiricism, viewed in perspective, is also the hazy dawn of a new pragmatism, then the real question for Little and Twiss is why we should settle for anything less than the "more thorough pragmatism" Quine foresaw as early as 1951 in "Two Dogmas of Empiricism."[4]

Consider first the problem of defining theoretical terms. If we propose to study religious ethics, we ought to begin, according to Little and Twiss, by clarifying what such basic terms as "religion" and "ethics," as well as such related terms as "law," mean. We need to know at the outset what we are setting out to study. Otherwise our inquiry will remain hopelessly confused throughout. "The sort of definitions we seek," write Little and Twiss, "are equivalent to Rudolf Carnap's and Carl Hempel's notion of *explication* or *rational reconstruction*."[5] We are referred to Hempel's *Fundamentals of Concept Formation in Empirical Science* for details.[6]

Little and Twiss refer to their definitional activity as an exercise in "conceptual analysis."[7] But it is interesting to note that Hempel, by the time he had written *Fundamentals*, had already been disturbed by Quine's attack on the distinction between the analytic and the synthetic:

> Now, I think it is often useful to make a distinction between questions of meaning and questions of fact; but I have doubts about the possibility of finding precise criteria which would explicate the distinction. . . . Reasons for this view may be found in White . . . and Quine. . . . This issue, however, is still the object of considerable controversy, and my remarks in the text are therefore deliberately sketchy.[8]

Hempel still refers to "meaning analysis" and "analytic definition," but explication is something else again:

> Meaning analysis, or analytic definition, in the purely descriptive sense considered so far has to be distinguished from another procedure, which is likewise adumbrated in the vague traditional notion of real definition. This procedure is often called logical analysis or rational reconstruction, but we will refer to it, following Carnap's proposal, as *explication*. Explication is concerned with expressions whose meaning in conversational language or even in scientific discourse is more or less vague . . . and aims at giving those expressions a new and precisely determined meaning, so as to render them more suitable for clear and rigorous discourse on the subject matter at hand.[9]

This notion of explication creates middle ground between the formerly sharply distinguished categories of conceptual analysis and empirical inquiry. A given attempt at explication is to "be adjudged more or less adequate according to the extent to which it attains its objectives."[10] The ideal of analytic definition has, in effect, fallen out. Before long, of course, Quine and others were eschewing such phrases as "conceptual analysis" altogether. The great merit of this passage from Hempel and of the quite similar passages in which Quine discusses explication is that they direct our attention to "the particular functions of the unclear expression that make it worth troubling about" and, hence, to "the extent to which it attains its objectives." This is to emphasize the dialectical relationship between theory, definition, and the aims of inquiry.

Little and Twiss chide Weber for writing that "To define 'religion,' to say what it *is*, is not possible at the start of a presentation. . . . Definitions can be attempted, if at all, only at the conclusion of the study."[11] Needless to say, we need some idea of what is to be studied and what is not in order to get empirical work under way. But is Weber disputing this article of common sense? Hardly. He is claiming simply that theoretical definitions are products of empirical inquiry. Such definitions attempt to characterize scientifically what sort of thing the object of study is. As a summary statement of a theory based on at least some investigation, such a definition *is* impossible at the outset. The ancient astronomers *did* have to know that stars are those skyward nocturnal bits of light — the sort of knowledge aptly stated in a *nominal* definition. They did *not* need to know what kind of thing stars are. An adequate theoretical characterization of stars first became possible many years later — a definitional advance that was the product of empirical work. Where should our theoretical definitions be presented? If Quine is right about conceptual analysis, Weber's procedure would seem to be in order. We should present our definitions where the criteria for their assessment will be clearest — along with all the messy empirical details.

Little and Twiss do of course draw heavily upon their considerable ethnographic and historical learning when discussing and defending their definitions, and this is all for the better. The problem is that the notion of conceptual analysis, which they hold out as an ideal, so often leads to excessive rigidity in empirical work. This is the problem Weber probably had in mind and the one MacIntyre nicely identifies in the opening pages of *A Short History of Ethics:*

> It is all too easy for philosophical analysis, divorced from historical inquiry, to insulate itself from correction. In ethics it can happen in the following way. A certain unsystematically selected class of moral concepts and judgments is made the subject of attention. From the study of these it is concluded that specifically moral discourse possesses certain characteristics. When counterexamples are adduced to show that this is not always so, these counterexamples are dismissed as irrelevant, because not examples of moral discourse; and they are shown to be nonmoral by exhibiting their lack of the necessary characteristics. From this kind of circularity we can be saved only by an adequate historical view of the varieties of moral and evaluative discourse. This is why it would be dangerous, and not just pointless, to begin these studies with a definition which would carefully delimit the field of inquiry.[12]

This leads me to believe that heeding Quine's warnings about "conceptual analysis" — and thereby emphasizing rather than playing down the dialectical relation between theory and the meaning of theoretical terms — is the best way to prepare for historical inquiry.

If we do stress the dialectical relation between theory and definition, it immediately becomes clear that definitional decisions are not as clear-cut as Little and Twiss suggest when they invoke theoretical neutrality and appeal to deceptively straightforward canons for good definitions. But if there are rules for good definitions, they must correspond to the virtues of good theories. Most of us will agree that an ideal theory is interesting, comprehensive, simple, clear, testable, in line with other beliefs we accept, and so forth. The difficulty we meet when choosing among competing theories, however, is that the several virtues stand in tension with each other. And so the definitional canons stand in tension with each other as well. Just as a gain in generality often complicates a theory, the rule that a definition ought not to conflict with a natural language user's prereflective understanding of the term often conflicts with the aim of cross-cultural applicability. Part of the problem is etymological. Words like "religion" and "morality" have roots in Western culture. Any prereflective understanding of the terms will betray a cultural bias. Ethnocentricity can be

tempered by broadening definitions. But broadening a definition often threatens to make a theory less and less interesting.
The more comprehensive a theory, the less its objects have in
common. A good theoretical definition, like the good theory of
which it is a part, achieves the best blend of virtues possible,
given the subject matter and the current stage of inquiry.
When Little and Twiss dismiss proposed definitions with a
wave of the hand, and justify the dismissal by appealing to *one*
of their rules for good definitions, they oversimplify.

Where did the "problem of theoretical terms" Hempel
addressed in 1952 come from? It was generated by two dogmas
of empiricism: the distinction between analytic and synthetic,
and the distinction between theory and observation. Full-
fledged empiricism required that the meaning of theoretical
terms be specified either in analytic definitions or through
reduction to observation sentences. Both alternatives led to
paradoxical results, and this forced empiricists to "liberalize"
their position to the point that it has become indistinguishable
from pragmatism. By the time he wrote "On the 'Standard
Conception' of Scientific Theories" in 1970, Hempel was able
to say simply that the problem of theoretical terms "does not
exist." "We come to understand new terms, we learn how to use
them properly, in many ways besides definition: from instances
of their use in particular contexts, from paraphrases that can
make no claim to being definitions, and so forth."[13] In the
absence of the distinctions that once made theoretical terms
seem problematical, we can perhaps afford to relax.

What, then, of the distinctions between description, on the
one hand, and explanation and normative assertion, on the
other? It seems that the view of language which results when
we eliminate sharp distinctions between the analytic and the
synthetic and between theory and observation also makes it
hard to keep descriptive discourse distinct from explanatory
or normative discourse.[14] Yet Little and Twiss want us to confine ourselves as comparative ethicists to description, leaving
explanatory and normative aims to others (or at least to ourselves in another, equally delimited, role). Even if the distinctions could be worked out, however, it is unclear why we should
want to enforce them. What would it be to have merely descriptive intent? It is a platitude that an infinite number of *accurate*
descriptions can be given of any object or event. We need a
sense of which descriptions will prove fruitful or useful. Other-

wise descriptions will have no more value than mere cataloguing, our histories will be chronicles without narrative. Where will our sense of fruitfulness and utility come from if not our explanatory and normative aims? Without substantive aims to motivate description we cannot generate criteria of descriptive success.

The same can be said for definitions. Recall Quine and Hempel on explication, drawing attention to the "functions of the unclear expression that make it worth troubling about" and to our "objectives" in using expressions. Without reasonably clear and explicit normative or explanatory aims (or both), how are we to figure out which functions of an unclear expression are worth troubling about? Once we have abstracted, as Little and Twiss profess to have done, from substantive objectives for inquiry, we would seem to *need* a doctrine of analysis as the "exposing" of hidden meanings — just to save ourselves from the appearance of arbitrary terminological choice. Thus Little and Twiss, when faced with the possibility that they have opened themselves "to the charge of arbitrariness," respond by saying "that boundaries must be drawn somewhere."[15] They want to shift the burden of proof, since they have at least given *some* reasons for their definitions and these definitions "have a strong ring of plausibility to them." But we are left in the dark about the purposes of inquiry.

The appropriate question is not *whether* we ought to allow normative and explanatory aims into our descriptive work, but rather *which* aims we ought to have and how we can avoid having such aims unduly prejudice our findings. Without such aims in view, we shall lack criteria for assessing whatever descriptions and definitions we produce. If Little and Twiss hear a "strong ring of plausibility" in their own definitions, but have trouble saying why, it is probably because they *have* normative and explanatory aims after all — aims sufficiently close to consciousness to make the definitions ring but too successfully repressed to make the reasons evident.

Hempel's *Fundamentals* is not the only document from the twilight of logical empiricism to hold sway with Little and Twiss. Another, also first published in 1952, is Feigl's essay on "Validation and Vindication,"[16] which provides the frame of their theory of justification. Just as Hempel was, at the same time, softening some of the dogmas written into the old manifestos of positivism, Feigl, Reichenbach and others were allowing a little holistic pragmatism into the empiricist theory of justification. Feigl and Reichenbach were working on the so-called problem of induction — the problem, that is, of how to account for inference from a finite number of observation statements to theories containing lawlike principles. If justification is strictly deductive and the use of observational vocabulary involves no implicit commitment to lawlike principles — as full-fledged empiricism would hold — then we could never justify the inductive leap to acceptance of a scientific theory. By virtue of containing lawlike principles with implications for an infinite number of possible instances (including future ones), a theory will always contain more than our necessarily finite observational evidence could deductively justify.

Convinced that inductive procedures *must* be sound, and finally defeated in the attempt to make such procedures *seem* sound in empiricist terms, Feigl and Reichenbach made a concession to pragmatism. They suggested that justification could still be viewed as largely deductive but that inductive procedures would have to be "vindicated" as preferable to the alternatives, given our purposes. In accepting induction we have nothing to lose, and, probably, a great deal to gain. So, like Pascal, we make our wager, confident that our policy is justified by our aims and a clear view of the options. "Validation" was Feigl's term for the standard case of deductive reason-giving. "Vindication" was his term for the Pascalian kind of reasoning that might pragmatically justify induction. Reichenbach had argued along these lines, already suggested by C. S. Peirce, as early as 1938. He and Feigl worked out the details in 1949 and 1950.[17] In 1952 Feigl expanded the analysis to cover justification in ethics.

The distinction between validation and vindication did not fare very well in the theory of scientific knowledge. Once again the question was why we should not follow Quine toward a more thorough pragmatism. He charged in "Two Dogmas" that the more limited pragmatism "leaves off at the imagined boundary between the analytic and the synthetic." "Each man," he continued, "is given a scientific heritage plus a continuing barrage of sensory stimulation; and the considerations which guide him in warping his scientific heritage to fit his continuing sensory promptings are, where rational, pragmatic."[18] If the distinction between theory and observation blurs in accordance with holistic scruples, it becomes unclear what problem Feigl's approach is supposed to solve. For if the observational vocabulary gets its meaning in large part thanks to theoretical context, then we are never faced with the problem of moving from theory-independent observation to lawlike principles in the first place. Hence, as Wilfrid Sellars put it, "there is no such thing as a problem of induction."[19] The problem of induction, like the problem of theoretical terms, dissolves.

Moreover, it is unclear why justification should *ever* be viewed as strictly deductive. We have seen that a deductive argument from premises we accept never *compels* acceptance of its conclusion. Unwanted conclusions cast doubt on the premises from which they follow, leaving open whether the argument in question constitutes a *reductio ad absurdum*. So if we accept a deductive argument from plausible premises as a "justification" for accepting its conclusion, we (at least implicitly) make a pragmatic choice between alternative systems of belief even here.[20] The moral to be drawn is that Feigl's distinction does not go far enough in the direction of pragmatism. A more thorough pragmatism would accept deduction as one tool among the many we use in the continuing process of testing and revising our beliefs and intentions, and leave it at that. The only theory of justification we need in the absence of such problems as Hume's puzzle over induction is the kind produced by historical and ethnographic insight into how people change their minds. Such insight does not depend on a priori analysis of the concept of justification.

In ethics the distinction between validation and vindication is intended to answer skeptical questions about the justification of basic moral principles. If justification is basically deductive, then specific moral judgments can be justified by derivation from basic principles. But how can basic principles be justified? Not, according to Little and Twiss, by derivation from nonmoral judgments, for moral judgments and principles are logically "autonomous."[21] And surely not by appeal to further moral principles, for the question is how to justify the "basic" ones and justification cannot be circular. How then? By pragmatic reasoning: vindication. But, once again, Quinean arguments call into question the crucial dichotomy — this time, the separation of "is" and "ought" — and reveal the pragmatic dimension of all reasoning.

Validation is a regress toward basic norms. We need

"basic" norms to halt the regress short of infinity. "These reasons," write Little and Twiss, "would be arranged in an appellate pattern, moving from the specific to the more general."[22] Justification here moves in one direction: from the specific to the general. For this reason, Little and Twiss conclude, "all codes of conduct can be reduced to a basic norm, or set of norms."[23] The study of religious ethics thus comes down largely to a process of reduction. But does ethical reasoning actually work this way? Does it move from specific judgments to general principles and only then become pragmatic and holistic? It would seem not. And if it does not, the proposed reduction will not work. The term "basic" will lose its intended sense.

To bring this out we need only reflect for a moment on the use of hypothetical cases in ethical theory. Hypothetical cases are usually introduced in order to generate strongly held and widely shared judgments of a highly specific kind. These judgments are then used to test relatively general moral principles and rules. A strongly held and widely shared specific judgment will, if incompatible with what we deduce from the principles and rules, call them into question. This may lead to revision or rejection of the principles and rules. Which is more *basic*: the judgment expressed in an intuition about the specific case or the one enshrined in our moral principle? The only notion of "basicness" worth having here seems to be a matter of entrenchment and acceptance. Of two incompatible judgments, the more deeply entrenched and generally accepted one will be more difficult to give up. This, however, has little to do with the continuum running from specificity to generality. In contemporary ethics, at least, the relation between "giveup-ability" and generality tends to be exactly the reverse of what Little and Twiss would have us think. Otherwise, hypothetical cases would not prove so useful. J. B. Schneewind argues the point as follows:

> Moral philosophers, whatever their theoretical programmes, have in practice always recognised that allegedly basic moral principles depend no less on fairly specific moral propositions than on the other sorts of grounds that have been offered for them; a principle that led to the conclusion that truth-telling was usually wrong, and torturing children normally permissible would be rejected, no matter what kind of proof it might have. But if general principles may sometimes depend on particular

moral judgments, and particular judgments sometimes on general principles, then there is no impersonal, necessary order of dependence within the realm of moral knowledge, and we are not compelled to conclude that there must be classical first principles.[24]

If Schneewind is right about classical first principles and the contextual character of epistemic dependence, then the attempt to reduce moral codes to basic principles is misleading at best. We can presumably approach the ethical discourse of any community, or the ethical language of any text, intent upon subsuming the specific judgments under the general principles. But what will this teach us about practical reasoning in the community or text under investigation?

Little and Twiss follow John Ladd in speaking of several "modes of validation."[25] These are: (a) the mode of direct deduction, "in which particular practical judgments are simply deduced in standard syllogistic fashion from the assumed basic norm"; (b) the mode of interpretation, "a somewhat vaguer way of validating practical judgments" in which "the content of the basic norm is openended, and subject to discretionary interpretation in the application of the norm to concrete situations"; and (c) the mode of selection, which "is pluralistic in assuming a set of basic norms, among which some choices must be made in specific cases."[26] Interestingly enough, they leave out Ladd's fourth type, "extreme particularism," which they deem "peculiar in that it does not presuppose any basic norm at all, but determines the moral thing to do anew in each set of circumstances."[27] It seems peculiar, of course, only because it does not fit the model required by the distinction between validation and vindication. Ladd, who also accepts Feigl's model, reluctantly introduced "extreme particularism" because he could find no other way to account for the practice of philosophers like H. A. Prichard.

"Extreme particularism," I think, is best construed simply as an instance in which the pragmatic dimension of practical reasoning is more explicit than usual. The other so-called modes of validation merely highlight one or another move always open to us in the process of testing and revising our moral views. Deductive arguments test for consistency and explore for possibly unwanted implications. When general principles conflict, we have to interpret, weigh, revise, or reject them as we see fit. Deduction, interpretation, and selection are not "modes of validation" found in some but not all communities. They are tools of reasoning — always available, not always needed or obvious. "Extreme particularism" is the kind of reasoning we employ — not without the help of deduction and interpretation — when general principles seem highly dubious but intuitions about specific cases do not.

Ladd once rejected "deductivism" as "an artificial logical construction not corresponding to any 'natural' ethics." He changed his mind when his "study of the Navaho ethical code" convinced him "that it is a perfectly genuine mode of validation."[28] And he treats this outcome as "a good example of the influence of anthropological knowledge on philosophical inquiry!" Ladd should not have changed his mind. A valid deductive argument can count as a reason for its conclusion, provided the premises are themselves sound and independent reasons against acceptance of the conclusion are not compelling. This does not show that inference is itself sometimes strictly deductive.[29] If Ladd's Navaho informant seemed to engage in strictly deductive inference, that is only because the premises in question seemed sound and other considerations did not intrude. Pragmatic and holistic dimensions of reasoning thus remained implicit.

Ladd's puzzle issues from an interesting coincidence — the structural similarity between the questioning of informants in the field and Socratic probing in philosophy. The anthropologist, like Socrates, often begins with a relatively specific judgment and asks why it should be accepted. The answer is then greeted with the same question, and so on, until the informant utters such sentences as "Because everyone believes that" or "It's ineffable" or "It's self-evident" or (if he is a Wittgensteinian) "That's a silly question." A sufficiently skillful (and imprudent) questioner could probably induce the puzzlement and skepticism Socrates induced in his audience, for questioning of this kind suggests the dilemma of circularity and infinite regress to which much Western epistemology is a response. Socratic questions made epistemologists think that justification must be deductive and that it must proceed from "basic" principles, which stop the infinite regress by providing evidence for themselves. It is no accident that questions of the same form make anthropologists think that their informants reason deductively from basic principles. If Wittgenstein and the pragmatists were right in diagnosing deductivism in philosophy, then Ladd was wrong to change his mind. The questioning of informants can itself produce "an artifical logical construction not corresponding to any 'natural' ethics."

If Little and Twiss, like Ladd, give us "artificial logical constructions," then the problem is not just paucity of historical information. Anthropologists often settle for something less than historical narrative because the data out of which a narrative might be constructed are unavailable. (It would be misleading to conclude, on the basis of the limited ethnographic evidence, that preliterate societies are "history-less.") But Little and Twiss apply their method not only to the Navaho but also to Matthew's Gospel and Theravada Buddhism, where more genuinely historical studies can be expected. Yet in each case, the picture is relatively static. The problem lies in the method itself.

This should come as no surprise. We have already seen that Feigl's model cannot account for the way in which someone could change his mind about a so-called basic moral principle for *moral* reasons. In fact, the model has trouble bringing *change* into focus at all. This was a major count against the model when it was abandoned in the philosophy of science: it could account for the kind of reasoning found in scientific textbooks, but it could not account for the kind found in the vicinity of the great scientific revolutions. This deficiency was, for a time, papered over with a distinction between context of discovery and context of justification. As the more thorough pragmatism took hold, however, so did more genuinely historical treatments of scientific revolution,[30] and the distinction between discovery and justification dissolved. The model did not work where it was most likely to work — as an account of science. It would be surprising if it *did* work for morality.

What would a more genuinely historical approach to religion and morality look like? Probably rather like some of the work Little and Twiss find lacking in rigor. What seems like insufficient dedication to rigor on the part of historians may well be an altogether healthy willingness to make contact with all the messy details of historical change. The role a given judgment plays in the theoretical and practical life of a community cannot be displayed simply by applying the procedures Little and Twiss gather under the heading "conceptual analy-

sis." For this role is largely a function of the judgment's relation to traditions, both living and dead, and problems, both
lasting and ephemeral, that impinge on a community at a point
in time. And this relation, complicated and temporal as it is,
can be displayed fully only in all its historical specificity and
only in the dimension of narrative.

Just as logical empiricists gave better accounts of textbooks than of Galileo, Little and Twiss should have more
success with some applications of their method than with
others. They should do better, for example, with systematic
treatises motivated by Socratic doubts than with texts written
for liturgical recitation without a thought given to systematic
elaboration in the Cartesian style. This points up the need, in
any genuinely historical study of ethical texts, for careful
attention to genre. Matthew's Gospel clearly contains action-
guiding language, but is it, in whole or in part, an attempt at
justification? The answer to this question is not at all clear if
we accept Feigl's model of justification.

If, on the other hand, we avoid preoccupation with justification *per se* and instead try to understand the document as
part of a continuing process of testing and revision of beliefs
and plans and hopes in response to impinging traditions and
problems, we need not treat Matthew's genre reductively. We
can instead, following Hans Frei,[31] take the narrative structure
of the Gospel more seriously than ever. We can also separate
our questions about the text itself from questions about the
use of the text by subsequent Christians. Bits of Matthew's
Gospel no doubt entered into more systematic attempts at
justification as time went on, but that leaves open the question
of how to characterize the genre of the text itself. The answer
to this question should help determine what sort of approach
to the text should be taken. Actually, the chapter on Matthew
is the best and most historical one in the book, probably because Little and Twiss *know* the historical background in this
case in great detail and included it as a matter of course.
Matthew *is* portrayed as responding to the rabbinic tradition,
for example. Even here, however, the model succeeds in keeping many relevant historical details near the edges of
the picture.

If all this is true, if the weakness of the model has already
been discovered the hard way in the philosophy of science, then
what explains the fact that this book will, in all likelihood, be

received as a major contribution to the study of religious ethics? It is true that, despite my criticisms, I can still find much of value in *Comparative Religious Ethics*. The authors' practice is obviously more dialectical than most of their methodological pronouncements let on. Yet my hunch is that the book's happy reception among religious ethicists will *hang on its connection with empiricism*, not on something else. Why, then, are the empiricist distinctions and the associated preoccupation with method still so seductive?

The answer to this question will become clear, I think, as soon as we determine what made logical empiricism seductive to philosophers in the first instance. An answer to this prior question has been suggested by Richard Rorty and Bruce Kuklick.[32] Logical empiricism was attractive, according to this view, in large part because it "invented something scientific and rigorous and difficult for philosophy to become" during a period of academic professionalization.[33] Might not *Comparative Religious Ethics* best be read as a response to the pressures of professionalization in the academic study of religion?

Notice the words "religious" and "comparative" where the words "Christian" and "theological" used to be.[34] Once upon a time, when academic departments of religion, constructed along the disciplinary lines of Protestant seminaries, were set up in some of our major secular colleges and universities, "Christian theological ethics" seemed like a fitting title for a subfield. In time, however, the secular setting was bound to have its effect. Jewish students wanted to know which principle in the liberal convention had been used to single out Christianity for special treatment. Atheists wanted to know if they had to accept theology to pass courses. "Christian theological ethics" made sense as a basic component of a curriculum designed for the professional training of ministers and theologians. But what kind of professionals will staff the corresponding subfield in secular departments of religion? They will need a suitably noncommittal title: "comparative religious ethicist." And, to have proper standing in an already professionalized academy, they will have to have "something scientific and rigorous and difficult" to do. How to train such people? Send them through a rite of passage in which they are taught preoccupation with method, encouraged to have merely descriptive intent, and equipped with a battery of technical distinctions. Or have them read *Comparative Religious Ethics*.

What could possibly do the job better than echoes of Hempel and Feigl?

It would be nice, of course, if those of us interested in comparative ethics could maintain our standing in the academy and some measure of intellectual respectability without giving up either the profoundly historical character of our topic or our reasons for being interested (be they theological or not). And this thought brings me back to Weber and to the deeply ambivalent normative attitude toward modern rationalism that gave rise to his explanatory aims and descriptive projects. Weber's own discussions of value-freedom and the vocation of the scientist can — especially if read backward, through logical empiricism — obscure the extent to which normative attitudes and explanatory purposes generate the criteria for assessing Weber's actual descriptive work and his use of theoretical terms. These attitudes and purposes are the very heart and soul of Weber's legacy. In reading Weber's references to the iron cage in which we live — or, for that matter, in reading Marx on alienation or Durkheim on anomie — we can discover more than enough reason for pursuing the comparative history of ethics, as well as criteria for assessing the fruit of that pursuit.

But we must be careful, in deciding how to appropriate the legacy of a figure like Weber, to place his contribution in its dialectical context and evaluate it accordingly. It goes without saying that Weber has a great deal to teach us. It is not clear, however, that the basic dualisms of Weber's methodological reflections, which he took over from Heinrich Rickert and the Baden neo-Kantians,[35] can any longer be taken as our starting point for historical and sociological inquiry. The use Little and Twiss make of distinctions from logical empiricism serves only to reinforce the very aspects of neo-Kantianism we should be treating with the most suspicion — the dualisms of theoretical and practical reason, of fact and value, of transcendental and empirical, of nomothetic and ideographic, and of real and ideal. It may seem ironic that logical empiricism is now being used to reformulate a methodology originally designed (in large part) to overcome the perils of positivism, but logical empiricism itself derived from a form of positivism that had already absorbed a great deal from the neo-Kantian tradition. The problem is that these traditions all share a commitment to the dualistic thinking that has dominated modern philosophy. I have been trying to show how thoroughly such thinking must be left behind if the likes of Quine and Davidson are taken to heart. If Quine is right about analyticity and Davidson is right about scheme and content, then professional philosophy is not the only intellectual enterprise that will require painstaking reappraisal. The standard methodological distinctions of social and historical thought will have to be re-examined as well. They may have trouble surviving.

Kantianism was revived in the second half of the nineteenth century not only to overcome the effects of an earlier positivism, but also to counteract a kind of historicism that tended to collapse into either radical relativism or speculative metaphysics. Kant's arguments proved as effective as they had always been against the metaphysicians. How then can relativism (and the associated evils of nationalism) be avoided? If one subtracts Hegel's metaphysics from his historicist variations on Kantian themes, relativism seems the inevitable result. For we are then left with a series of apparently independent conceptual schemes and no way to organize them into an evolutionary sequence that culminates in the achievement of absolute knowledge, the union of real and ideal. Faced with this problem, the neo-Kantians sought to revive some of the Kantian distinctions Hegel had tried to blur (the exception being that between phenomena and noumena). Little and Twiss are clearly heirs of this strategy.

It now seems, however, that Hegel was right to blur the Kantian distinctions. If speculative metaphysics of a kind Kant had already successfully dismantled seemed the only alternative to radical relativism once so many of the basic Kantian distinctions had been abandoned, that is only because Hegel and his fellow nineteenth-century historicists joined their opponents in *accepting* Kant's distinction between conceptual scheme and uninterpreted content. Hegel historicized the distinction, by suggesting the possibility of alternative conceptual schemes, yet he accepted it nonetheless. Hegel, like Kant, thought he needed to distinguish scheme from content in order to make his case against immediate cognition. The nineteenth-century opponents of immediate cognition argued that the merely immediate could not be cognitive, for cognition requires both intuitions and concepts, content and scheme. But to say this was to grant that *something* is immediately given and then to quarrel over whether this something should

be counted epistemic. We can, however, dismantle the entire
controversy by giving up "the given" altogether. Moreover,
as we have seen in chapter 8, it is precisely the distinction
between scheme and content that leads to relativism. We can
therefore avoid both transcendental method and metaphysical
speculation without succumbing to relativism simply by
abandoning all the traditional dualisms, including that of
scheme and content.[36] This would leave us with a thoroughly
holistic historicism consistent with the best in American pragmatism.

   If we want to deepen our understanding of neo-
Kantianism and its impact on social and historical thought, we
should perhaps turn to a work explicitly devoted to the project
of reviving and refining the Kantian tradition, such as Green's
Religious Reason. Like Little and Twiss, Green divides his
book into two parts — the first relatively abstract and methodological, the second an attempt at historical application. Also
like Little and Twiss, Green views the application section as a
test of his method.[37] In Green's case, the three historical chapters treat materials from Judaism, Christianity, and the religions of India. The method, Green hastens to point out, is
not new. "In broad outline it has been suggested frequently
in the past, and in its specific form it was stated almost two
centuries ago with considerable precision by Immanuel
Kant."[38]

   Historical inquiry into morality and its relation to religion should begin, according to Green, with a transcendental
analysis of reason and its various "employments": theoretical,
prudential, moral, and religious.

> Part I of this book is devoted to an explanation of these terms
> and to a careful following of the progression of reason through
> its religious employment. But the essential point I want to
> stress here is that the progression toward religious belief and
> activity takes place within the operations of reason and is a part
> of the conceptual structure of every rational agent.[39]

We need a new book, not because Kant was wrong about some
important feature of this progression, but rather because recent
work in Kantian ethical theory — especially John Rawls's
A Theory of Justice[40] — puts us in a much better position to
understand and learn from Kant. Since "Kant's understanding
of religion proceeds from his ethical theory," and this ethical
theory has been widely misunderstood, "the understanding of

his philosophy of religion has suffered."[41] As a result, the hermeneutical power of Kant's *Religion within the Limits of Reason Alone* has been underestimated; its approach to moral and religious history has been insufficiently exploited. So Green accepts Kant's distinctions between the theoretical and the practical and between the prudent and the moral, reconstructs the "moral" in Rawlsian terms, and portrays religious reason as arising "because of an important conflict between prudential and moral reason." He then retraces the ground originally charted in Kant's *Religion* by undertaking his own series of historical investigations.

Green begins by asking whether there is a rational justification for the institution of morality. His answer is that "our very idea of morality holds it to be a rational phenomenon." Morality is, quite simply, that set of rules resulting from a "strictly rational method of selecting social principles." A society without morality would be one in which the principles guiding social life had not been chosen rationally. "Such a society would probably be characterized by persistent conflict, and whatever order prevailed would result only from fleeting coalitions of power and force."[43] Moral rules, Green writes,

> . . . would be of the sort to which all members of the society could freely agree. This idea of unanimous agreement by free consent really follows from the idea of a principled and rational means of social settlement. For if agreement were less than unanimous, then for some members of the society the so-called moral rules would be merely a ratification of the existing power relations of the society, and the same would be true if some members' agreement was secured by coercion.[44]

But how can unanimous agreement be achieved if the interests and powers of individuals vary greatly? Only, it seems, if we impose strict constraints of impartiality on the choice of social principles. These constraints are properly explicated, Green believes, in Rawls's discussion of the "original position." In selecting social principles from the vantage point of Rawls's original position, individuals pass behind a "veil of ignorance," which

> . . . has the effect of depriving each participant of knowledge of all those particular features of his situation which distinguish him from the other participants. . . . Each is prevented, for example, from knowing his sex, race, physical strength, or intellectual capacity. Each is also prevented from knowing the

special circumstances of his birth, whether he was born into favorable or unfavorable social circumstances. And finally, each is prevented from knowing the special ends or values he wishes to pursue, what Rawls calls, his special "plan of the good."[45]

Deprived of such knowledge, Green argues, societal members could reach "unanimous agreement by free consent" in selecting social rules. Decision behind the veil of ignorance would therefore be rational. The vantage point of the original position *is* the moral point of view, part of the conceptual structure of every rational agent. The question of whether the institution of morality can be rationally justified is, it follows, self-answering.

In chapter 11, I shall try to show that Rawls's mode of thought — and, more generally, the modern preoccupation with the autonomy of morality — is the product of highly specific historical circumstances. But we can start to see how Green's use of Rawls might arouse suspicion by posing a question: "What language is spoken behind the veil of ignorance?" Green does not pose this question himself, but he seems bound to answer as David Richards does. In discussing the veil of ignorance, Richards asks us to imagine ideal contractors who

> do not know what institutions they are in; their view of the relations of institutions to interests will, thus, be determined only by whatever true facts are presented to them. The contractors only bring the general institution of language with them to the original position, a condition of their rationality; but their ignorance deprives them of knowledge of what specific language they have; rather, it is assumed that the contractors have some universal means of communication.[46]

Richards wants his ideal contractors to hand down the principles of morality from this universal vantage point, the perspective of eternity. And it is precisely their ignorance of what specific language they have, plus reliance on some universal means of communication, that establishes the wanted transcendental standing. Green, too, needs transcendental standing for the original position, for he aims to describe "the conceptual structure of every rational agent." Like Richards, he cannot afford to allow linguistic specificity to infect the contractor's deliberations. If he fails to describe something inherent in the conceptual structure of *every* rational agent, his definition of morality (and the conception of religion he constructs thereupon) cannot perform the hermeneutical wonders Green envisions. But is the notion of a universal means of communication even coherent?

The problem with allowing the contractors to know and use a specific language during their deliberations is that meanings of expressions in this language will already be determined in part by generally accepted and deeply entrenched beliefs. To know and use a language is already to accept a great many beliefs. So if we allow the contractors to use a specific language, we cannot rest content with their agreement as universal. Richards therefore restricts the contractors to deliberation and discourse in some universal language. But what would such a language be like? It would, supposedly, have to be neutral with respect to belief. But if meaning and substance cannot be separated, as both Rawls and Richards have granted,[47] then a *universal language*, a language neutral with respect to belief, would be meaningless. And this would put the contractors at a serious disadvantage, to say the least.

What the contractors are really being asked to do, of course, is to talk the language of rational egoism and moral autonomy. This language already implicitly expresses commitment to a view of human nature's relation to social institutions and a view of the relation between fact and value. Our ideal contractors do not know what institutions they are in, but have they not been shaped by institutions in any event? They do not yet accept moral principles (for that is what they are meeting to agree upon), but are the so-called true facts presented to them completely free of all normative content? If holism is true, it is hard to see how factual and normative content could be so neatly separated. The important point for present purposes is that the language of the original position involves assumptions with which one can disagree — assumptions that may, upon examination, prove to be of relatively recent origin. If so, the original position does not supply transcendental standing in the required sense. Its usefulness as a philosophical and historiographical device is sharply curtailed.

This does not mean that the original position and associated conceptions of morality are useless. If the language of Rawlsian contractors is in fact *our* language, the original position may prove extremely helpful as a device for giving systematic expression to *our* prereflective views about justice and morals. And to show that a Rawlsian analysis of morality gives systematic expression to our prereflective views may be a way to get the upper hand on some versions of utilitarianism — namely, those claiming to offer the best systematization of accepted views — or on those intuitionists who claim that systematization is impossible. But to show this would hardly be to answer either traditionalists or radicals, who place pre-reflective morality under the category of liberal ideology and hope to overturn assumptions built into the language of the original position. Nor would it be to show that the so-called moral point of view is an appropriate *historical* construct for discussing the views of traditionalists and radicals. The contractors may be using *our* language, but it seems that only a historical investigation open to the possibility that this language might not be universally shared can tell us whose language this is.

Consider two concepts of Rawls. The first is that of a Rawls who, persuaded that Quine is right about the inseparability of meaning and substance, plays down the role of definitions in moral philosophy. He strives not for an *analysis,* as a metaethicist might, but rather for a *theory* of justice. His aims are modest. The point of the theory is not to provide transcendental grounding. That could be provided only if the original contractors spoke a universal language. But if Quine is right, no such language could exist. The point of the theory is rather to improve on the theories utilitarians have given and to show, against intuitionists, that a theory of justice is attainable. The theory accepts our own deeply entrenched convictions about tolerance and fairness as moral data to be considered in reflective equilibrium. These data are then systematized and preserved insofar as this is possible, critically revised when over-all coherence requires, and carefully extended by analogical reasoning to areas in which our convictions are less firm.

The second is that of a Rawls who, forgetting his lessons from Quine, attempts to describe our "moral capacity" by articulating a point of view that is part of the conceptual structure of every rational agent — "the perspective of eternity," in a sense peculiar to transcendental philosophy.[48] This Rawls, even after accepting Quine's scruples about meaning and substance, nonetheless needs a meaningful language that is neutral with respect to moral belief. Otherwise, the original position falls short of eternity. He needs, in other words, to separate moral meaning from moral substance. And if the original con tractors are to have access to "morally neutral" facts about society and human nature, he must also separate fact from value, once again violating holistic principles in the theory of meaning. This Rawls, it seems, cannot have everything he wants. Either the Quinean scruples or the transcendental aims must go.

Both Rawlses are Kantians with respect to moral theory; only the latter is Kantian with respect to metaphilosophy. The first Rawls stands within a tradition of moral reflection; the second tries to rise above all tradition. I shall not ask which of these is the "real" Rawls.[49] My point here is simply that Green's Rawls must be the second one. That is, Green *requires* ideal contractors who speak a universal language accessible to *any* rational agent, historical setting and variation in belief notwithstanding. This means that Green cannot be correct if holism is.

As a Kantian and a Rawlsian, Green makes autonomy a mark of the moral. For both Kant and Rawls, one thing morality must remain autonomous *from* is theology. It is interesting that Green, in a book on the relation between religion and morality, has chosen to leave this aspect of his theory implicit. As Rawls points out, his own theory does not strictly entail indifference to religion, but the ideal contractors are not allowed to know, behind the veil of ignorance, what (if any) religious beliefs they do in fact hold.[50] And this makes religious beliefs irrelevant to the choice of social principles. In a discussion of the contractors' agreement to freedom of religion, Richards shows that

> . . . this is made possible by the contractors' ignorance of their religion, which excludes the use of appeals to religious duties to their Catholic or Muslim or Jewish God to override the equal liberty of religious belief. Not knowing which religion, if any, they are, the contractors will not know whether they have access to any source of religious faith; rather, their reasoning in the original position will be based on ordinary principles of empirical inference and induction and the knowledge which such principles yield, not on the special kinds of principles and knowledge which religious faith may involve. Otherwise, the rational choice problem of the original position would be quite insoluble, for the contractors would entertain such irreconcilable kinds of beliefs (based on different religious sources and perceptions) that the unanimity of decision required in the original position would be quite improbable. . . . In general, by depriving the

contractors of knowledge of their specific beliefs in religious duties, this contractual view gives expression to the Kantian, and common Christian, conception that the concept of morality is independent of the concept of God's will; and indeed defines the notion of His goodness.[51]

Our present question is not whether, all things considered, we should stand in the "Christian-Kantian" tradition of moral autonomy, but rather whether morality, thus understood, has *universal* applicability as a historical category. What use will the category have if applied beyond the confines of the tradition from which it has been derived? In particular, how will the category help us describe and understand those who have expressed opposition to that tradition? In a footnote to the passage I have just quoted, Richards refers to Ockham as "a negative example of the Christian conception."[52] But if Ockham (or someone else) is a "negative example," what can Green make of him?

Green seems bound either to treat negative examples as counterevidence to his claim about the "conceptual structure of every rational agent" or to declare all such examples irrational. His conviction that he has given a *transcendental* analysis inclines him toward the latter option. It also drastically limits the value of historical investigation. If the conceptual analysis of morality is deemed transcendental, it is not clear how historical studies could discover something new, call the theory into question, or serve as a test of the method. The value of applying the category to historical cases will simply be that of rendering judgments of rationality from the transcendental position. If Green is in fact rather charitable in rendering his judgments, it is because he systematically excludes an astonishing amount of historical evidence from consideration. The "idea of autonomy," he writes,

> does not necessarily imply (as the term may unfortunately suggest) that the moral law must be acknowledged to be a product of moral reason. It is fully permissible, for example, for an individual to obey the moral law without ever acknowledging that the law itself is a product of reason. And it is even possible for the law's authority to be grounded in beliefs, needs, or desires that have nothing to do with respect for reason. All that is ever required is that whatever reason an individual has for obeying the moral law, and whatever he believes the source of the law's authority to be, these beliefs can never in any way conduce to disobedience to the moral law.[53]

Green is telling us *not* to attend to the reasons actually given by the historical agents themselves as we render our judgments of rationality. We are to listen *only* to their conclusions, judging these in light of Green's a priori constructions.

But if the transcendental argumentation fails, as I have suggested it does, then Green's claim about the conceptual structure of every rational agent becomes an empirical claim to be judged against the historical record. It then becomes crucial to attend with great care to the reasons given by and probably available to the historical agents being studied. Any judgments of rationality will then have to be made relative to available reasons. By assuming at the outset that these reasons *must* be absolutely invariant, Green has insulated himself from the possibility of serious confrontation with the *whole* historical record. He has also insulated his historical subjects from the kind of criticism that takes their own expressions of reasoning seriously.

It is striking to find Green admitting that it is "the common tendency of most" historical religious systems "to provide ultimate reasons for acting" which have "nothing to do with human reason and (are) sometimes even disparaging of reason. . . ."[54] These systems are nevertheless to be deemed rational, according to Green, because they do "motivate compliance with reason's commands." That is, the historical religious systems do tend to include

> . . . a prohibition on killing or inflicting physical injury on other persons; a rule prohibiting various forms of deception and dishonesty; a rule of fidelity requiring the upholding of agreements into which one has freely entered; and a rule of fairness requiring one to do one's part in the maintenance of mutually beneficial cooperative arrangements.[55]

Suppose these rules *are* handed down from a coherent version of the original position. Universal convergence on these conclusions, even if granted as a historical fact, does not secure transcendental status for the original position. The rationality of a conclusion is relative to available reasons, and various sorts of reasons might justify the same conclusions. So if the transcendental argumentation does not work in the first place, judgments about the rationality of conclusions will have to be treated contextually. If some of the same conclusions keep appearing regardless of historical variation in actual reason-giving, there are surely more plausible explanations of this than Green's conviction that, at bottom, all the reasons must be the same.

But the problem does not stop here, for some of the rules handed down from the original position are incompatible with views put forward in the "historical religious systems." It would seem unfair to declare these views irrational without listening to the reasons actually given for them in the religious traditions themselves. Green neglects to point out, for example, that Rawls cites our confidence that religious intolerance is unjust as one of the "provisional fixed points" any theoretical proposal must fit.[56] It is in part because of "our" confidence on this point that Rawls feels justified in keeping his ideal contractors ignorant of their own (quite possibly religiously informed) conceptions of the good. Yet Rawls recognizes that Aquinas did not share in "our" confidence and instead justified the death penalty for heretics by appealing to a religiously grounded conception of the good.[57] Was Aquinas simply irrational? Or did this rational agent's "conceptual structure" supply reasons of a kind at odds with Rawlsian ethical theory? Green's method makes it difficult or impossible for him to consider the second alternative.[58] But what could be a more important question for a student of *religious* ethics to ask?

Green does, of course, follow Kant not only in making morality autonomous from theology but also in taking this understanding of morality as the point of departure for a defense of religion as a "fully rational activity."[59] In this respect he comes much closer to unreconstructed Kantianism than would the vast majority of his fellow neo-Kantians. Allegiance to Kant in this century has usually stopped short of his philosophy of religion. Green both defends the essentials of Kant's philosophy of religion (though without giving Christianity the privileged place Kant gives it) and follows Kant's lead in the interpretation of religious texts.[60] The result, which perhaps should have been called "Religious Studies within the Limits," is meant to displace work in the traditions of positivism, functionalism, Feuerbach, Marx, and Freud. While I find each of Green's major arguments for *religious* reason questionable, it would be beyond the scope of this chapter's concerns to pursue the matter here.

What matters for present purposes is that Green's account of morality gives us a relatively pure example of how transcendental philosophy insulates itself from the historical record and tends to trivialize historical inquiry. It therefore also helps us see more clearly what dangers might be involved in borrowing distinctions from modern philosophy to provide what Little and Twiss call "conceptual and methodological orientation" for the historical study of ethical traditions. If genuinely historical investigation is to teach us what we need to know about morality and its relation to other domains of culture, a philosophy as unhistorical as Kantianism or logical empiricism will have trouble showing us the way. The most useful kind of "methodological orientation" one could give to prospective genealogists of morals would be to highlight the dangers of an occupational disease easily contracted from philosophers — hardening of the categories.

11. On the Morals of Genealogy

Nietzsche once wrote that "Lack of a historical sense is the original error of all philosophers."

> ... they proceed from contemporary man and think they reach their goal through an analysis of this man. Automatically they think of "man" as an eternal verity, as something abiding in the whirlpool, as a sure measure of things. Everything that the philosopher says about man, however, is at the bottom no more than testimony about the man of a very limited period.[1]

A sound warning can be heard through the hyperbole. The genealogist of morals elsewhere mocks those who "wanted to supply a *rational foundation* of morality."

> Morality itself ... was accepted as "given." How remote ... was that task which they considered insignificant and left in dust and must — the task of description — although the subtlest fingers and senses can scarcely be subtle enough for it.[2]

I have no wish to revive the conclusions of Nietzsche's own *Genealogy*, with which I have little sympathy, but I do wish to inquire, as Nietzsche did, into what morals a defensible genealogy of morals might reveal. Whether my own fingers and senses are subtle enough for the task of description this inquiry entails is doubtful. My conclusions will therefore be more tentative than Nietzsche's. But I share his conviction, for reasons I have tried to make clear in the previous chapter, that the ubiquity and constancy of morality cannot be accepted as "given" at the outset. And I harbor the suspicion, for reasons I hope to make clear in this chapter, that much of what we have been told about morality actually applies to a very limited period indeed.

One moral we might draw from a genealogy of morals, then, would be that unhistorical moral philosophy — metaethics, in particular — is incompatible with a plausible reading of the historical record. "The autonomy of morality" has been treated in much recent philosophy as a relatively abstract matter, an issue anyone can care about but only an expert in the "logic" of moral discourse can decide upon. It would be a telling criticism of such philosophy to show that morality emerged as an autonomous sphere only relatively recently, that "the moral point of view" of which we nowadays hear so much is a modern invention. A genealogy of morals need not, however, aim to tell us only what kind of moral philosophy to avoid. It can also seek historical understanding that could actually inform action. If to understand oneself and one's situation is largely a matter of constructing narratives that locate oneself meaningfully *in* one's situation, and our situation is decisively shaped by the emergence of morality as an autonomous sphere, this is something a genealogy of morals should illuminate. It might then have morals for morals, as well as for the practice of moral philosophy.

Such are the explanatory and normative aims in reference to which my descriptive claims can be judged. The point is to explain a feature of our moral situation by narrating its emergence and, by means of this explanation, to improve the prospects of criticism. The descriptive claims that would go into the making of the story must, of course, be held accountable to the historical record. We must not skew the record in hope of satisfying our aims. That would not work, for it is genuine self-understanding we want. But with our aims clearly in view we will at least have criteria of relevance for the descriptions we produce. And if it turns out that the projected story cannot honestly be told, that the autonomy of morals has really been there all along, we can always abandon these aims and return to the old ways of moral philosophy no worse for the effort.

Notice how quickly definitions fall into line once this much has been made clear. In the first place, it matters relatively little how we decide to explicate the term "morality." What matters more is the quality of the story we tell with the words we choose. There is no harm, for example, in giving the term "morality" to the Kantians, using it only to refer to the autonomous (and perhaps quite recent) point of view Hegel dubbed *Moralität*. Defenders of this point of view could then be trusted, within limits, to clarify what "morality," thus defined, would involve. If historical investigation shows that any term used in this sense would have rather limited application — say, to the modern West — we would then have to find some other word to fill out the early parts of the story that needs telling. Hegel's choice was *Sittlichkeit*; we might settle for "ethos." Whatever word we choose, the fitting explication will depend entirely on the history we discover, though it would presumably have to be designed to bring out contrasts with respect to the theme of autonomy. If morality is autonomous, an ethos will be undifferentiated by comparison. Both, of course, would pertain to the appraisal of conduct, character, and community. If such expressions eventually get in our way, we are free to use our explications as rules for elimination, clearing the channels for better conversation. Any words will do, provided the means of elimination are close to hand. Words with intuitive plausibility and a tradition of established usage (like Hegel's) will do best of all. So much for definitions. We can strive for more precision if and when it would repay our efforts. Until then, what Quine calls the maxim of shallow analysis prevails: go no deeper than the purpose at hand requires.

In a discussion of "the idea that the subject matter of Ethics is, so to speak, inherently shifting and unstable because of the phenomenon of social and historical change," and of the charge "that many writers on this subject have taken an excessively static, sometimes even absurdly parochial view of their problems," G. J. Warnock has proposed three "legitimately different lines" one might take in moral philosophy.[3] The first is to define "morality" broadly so as to allow scope for the great "diversity of views as to what is good and bad, right and wrong, in human character and conduct," and to spend one's time charting this diversity in social and historical space. One might, in the second place, undertake a "relatively unhistorical inquiry" by identifying the least common denominator amid all the diversity of morality (broadly defined) and investigating "what might be called the 'logic' of that — the general theory, so to speak, of practical appraisal."[4] Finally:

> "morality" can intelligibly, perhaps usefully, be regarded as a *particular* way, or ways, of looking at issues of character and conduct; these things can be looked at from what is called "the moral point of view" — which is not just *any* point of view the adoption of which issues in practical judgments, but a particular point of view that can be positively identified and described. If so, it is at any rate not obvious that *this* changes. What anthro-

pological evidence, for instance, gives one reason to say, is not this, but rather that, in some societies at some dates, "morality" perhaps is not found at all, or is present only partially, or in some primitive state, or something like that. If appraising character and conduct *morally* is, not just appraising them in any practical way, but in some *particular* way, one might conclude that this does not so much itself change as gradually emerge (and perhaps sometimes disappear again) *in the course of change.*[5]

Warnock himself takes this third line, though, as he puts it, in a relatively timeless way; for his intention is to "characterize, and thereafter critically to consider in various respects, *what* this particular mode of appraisal actually consists in." He seeks an abstract account of the moral point of view, strictly construed, not a historical rendition of its career.

I do not understand Warnock's second possibility — either *how* to pursue the logical study of appraisal as such without studying a highly specific language of appraisal, or the *point* of so doing. Nor do I understand why his third option should be pursued unhistorically. My own proposal, in any event, seems to combine the first and the third. We need some account of what the moral point of view, strictly construed, consists in, but to view it sensitively and critically we shall have to situate it historically. This means that we must consider its place in the history of "morality" in a broad sense of the term. The relevant history might help us grasp why the moral point of view emerged, how its most salient features were shaped by the traditions and problems of the context of emergence, and what alternatives might be open to us. An abstract account alone would not help in these ways. On the other hand, merely to catalogue the facts of ethical diversity without bringing to bear normative and explanatory questions about our own situation seems pointless.

Where should we turn, then, for an account of the point of view we hope to situate historically? My suggestion was that its philosophical defenders can be trusted, within limits, to clarify what the moral point of view — the mind set, as it were, of an autonomous morality — involves. This trust must be limited because we should allow for the possibility that philosophers have confused genuine senses in which modern morality has become autonomous with the notion that (practical) reason can be radically autonomous from tradition. References to "the perspective of eternity" and "the vantage point of noumenal selves" must be greeted with suspicion. But even these phrases can be taken as attempts to explicate a language game and form of life that do exist, and we should be able to learn something about the latter by attending to their philosophical expression. To simplify this discussion and to build on the work of the preceding chapter, let us take Kant and Rawls, respectively, as the most prominent classical and contemporary theorists of the moral point of view. We may legitimately hope that they will also prove the most revealing.

Kant and Rawls both teach, roughly, that the moral point of view is the vantage point of rational individuals under constraints of impartiality. (The real Rawls does not claim to offer a theory of the entirety of morality, so I shall take the liberty of treating his theory of justice as presupposing what commentaries have called a "deeper" theory of morality the inspiration of which is a Kantian view of autonomy.) They assume, with most modern social theory, that we are sensuous beings inclined to act in accordance with our own interests (which may or may not happen to be other-regarding, like altruism or hatred) and that in pursuit of these interests we formulate plans in light of our own conceptions of the good, calculations of utility, and judgments of probability. They also assume, again with much of modern thought, that moral judgment is distinguished by a kind of abstraction from one's own point of view or interests. The prescriptivist theory of universalizability, ideal-observer theories, and utilitarian appeals to the sympathy that would count each rational agent (oneself or another) as one in the calculation of utility can all be read as attempts to explicate or model the kind of abstraction involved. Kant's central model involves his famous distinction between noumenal and phenomenal selfhood. As Wolff puts Kant's view, "Since it is as noumenal agents that we are capable of rational willing, and it is of our phenomenal character that the particularities of our spatio-temporal character can be predicated, we abstract in our role as rational agents from everything that differentiates one of us from another in the field of appearance."[6] Morality is autonomous because it abstracts from all that we are which is particular to us and therefore inessential to our shared essence as rational creatures. Rawls's model is that of the original position, in which the veil of ignorance is meant to deprive the contractors of enough knowledge about themselves to render their judgments impartial without depriving them of so much knowledge that they cannot reach substantive judgments at all.

Rawls's model is revealing mainly because it advances beyond earlier formulations in the Kantian tradition by giving a clearer, more determinate picture of both the "rational individual" and the constraints of impartiality presupposed in modern talk about the moral point of view. Rawls makes clear that the rational individual meeting with his fellows in the original position is not only *self*-interested but also well versed in the language of game-theoretical reasoning. And while Rawls allows the contractors knowledge of basic sociological and psychological facts, the knowledge that their own interests take shape in plans of life, and some "thin" beliefs about "primary goods," he carefully hides their own fully developed conceptions of the good and all knowledge of their own political and religious views behind the veil of ignorance. Intent upon avoiding the vacuity of which Kantian ethical theory has been accused ever since Hegel started his carping, Rawls strives to give the contractors enough information to make the game-theoretical reasoning work without violating our intuitive sense that the process is impartial. There is some question, as I pointed out in chapter 10, whether knowledge of sociology and psychology can be had in the absence of ethical views the contractors are not allowed to have just yet (in that they are meeting to decide which such views to adopt). My interest at the moment is not, however, to show that Rawls's model fails to generate a coherent moral system, but rather to underline his conviction that the autonomy of the moral point of view consists largely in abstraction from one's own conception of the good and one's own (nonliberal) political and religious commitments. For this kind of autonomy is, I think, exactly what makes the moral point of view a distinctively modern phenomenon.

Kant's view that moral thought abstracts from desire and inclination obviously carries on a tradition that reaches at least as far back as St. Paul. But it surely would have seemed odd to St. Paul to hear that he ought to have reached his basic moral judgments from a point of view in which his conception of the good and his religious commitments were systematically excluded from consideration. Yet Rawls helps us see more clearly that this is precisely what the autonomy of morality, as understood in the Kantian tradition, requires. Moral autonomy consists not only in abstraction from *all* desire and inclination but also in the exercise of individual judgment over against traditional authority and in a thoroughgoing subordination of one's own conception of the good, political beliefs, and religious commitments. The autonomy of the person, *qua* rational moral agent, consists both in his independence from traditional authority and in his capacity to take a point of view, in the exercise of his own judgment, that is sharply differentiated from other perspectives he might take — most notably, from that of a religious man convinced he knows what is good for us.

It would have taken a lot of teaching to prepare St. Paul for a place in the original position. He would, in the first instance, have had to learn the language of Pascal's wager and welfare economics — the language, that is, of the new probability presupposed in modern decision theory. This language, according to the doctrine presented in Part I of this book, did not exist before 1660. It is, moreover, a language that replaced, or rather displaced, the language in which probability was what the authorities approved. So on his way to becoming the "rational individual" of the original position, St. Paul would have had to learn one language and forget another. In doing this alone he would already take a major step toward moral autonomy. But, more important, he would still have to learn how to assume the highly differentiated perspective we call the moral point of view, which he could do only by learning to distinguish and then abstract from considerations he never thought to distinguish himself. The distinctions he would have needed for this purpose were not worked out, even implicitly, until the modern era. The perspective taken in the original position is anything but eternal.

Those who have survived the previous chapters will not be surprised to discover that I now wish to connect the emergence of autonomy with the demise of authority in early modern Europe. Kant did not invent the autonomy of morals; he simply tried to understand it. He was handicapped above all by the unhistorical mode of thought he brought to bear on the ethical consciousness of his age. The moral point of view he found implicit in this consciousness was, however, an invention of the sixteenth, seventeenth, and eighteenth centuries, and its purpose was to overcome the crisis of traditional authority and thereby to contain the least attractive effects of religious disagreement. This explains why the autonomy of morals is, even in our own century, closely connected with the Enlightenment's antitraditionalist rhetoric and also why moral and religious points of view had to be distinguished. Any point of view in which religious considerations or conceptions of the good remained dominant was, in the early modern context, incapable of providing a basis for the reasonable and peaceful resolution of social conflict. Incompatible appeals to authority seemed equally reasonable, and therefore equally suspect, as well as thoroughly useless as vehicles of rational persuasion. The resulting dialectical impasse had both intellectual and social consequences. The former were manifested not only in the theological standoff between Protestants and Catholics, but also in the ethical controversies that were rife within the respective traditions. Witness, for example, the many conflicting Protestant attempts to apply scriptural authority to ethical problems, or the disputes among Jesuit casuists (of which Pascal made so much in the *Provincial Letters*) concerning such positions as probabilism. But the social consequences were more telling, for they included the devastation of the religious wars. The moral point of view, I submit, was the product of this period's attempt to circumvent the impasse from which such effects stemmed.

As the most prominent contemporary theorist of this point of view, Rawls is primarily concerned with rights as the possessions of individual subjects, justice as a virtue of the State, and the problem of rationality in social cooperation. All of these topics are modern creations. Far from describing "part of the conceptual structure of every rational agent," Rawlsian ethical theory pertains almost entirely to distinctively modern phenomena. Far from providing the secretly moral basis of the great religious systems, the "original position" is a theoretical reflection of modernity's attempt to *displace* them. I am not suggesting, needless to say, that a person or group of persons *decided* to create something called the autonomy of morals in order to resolve a problem that faced them. I am, however, suggesting that the differentiation of the moral point of view was a result of attempts to nullify the effects of religious disagreement.

The most striking evidence for these claims comes from Quentin Skinner's recent book on *The Foundations of Modern*

Political Thought. The notion of "subjective" right — the sort of right a person can *have* — seems to have originated in the Ockhamist tradition. Whether it goes back to Ockham himself is less clear. It is surely, however, a relatively recent development in the history of thought, a product of the conciliar movement's attempt to limit papal authority with respect to governance of the Church. The Great Schism, the classic ecclesiastical manifestation of the problem of many authorities before the Reformation, gave rise to the conciliar constitutionalism of Jean Gerson and his followers, a general theory of political society applied to the Church as a specific instance. Gerson introduced the notion of subjective rights in order to specify precisely the location of legitimate authority or power within a genuinely political society. His claim was that rulers have duties as trustees of the rights of others but, *qua* rulers, possess no rights of their own. Popes must answer to the higher authority of the General Council, princes to that of representative assemblies. Skinner shows how Gerson's Ockhamistic conciliarism and the related notion of rights were revived by John Mair and his followers in the early sixteenth century.[7] He also shows how the Huguenots, later in that century, drew upon the ideas of conciliarism to "make the epoch-making move from a purely religious theory of resistance, depending on the idea of a covenant to uphold the laws of God, to a genuinely political theory of revolution, based on the idea of a contract which gives rise to a moral right (and not merely a religious duty) to resist . . ."[8]

It is instructive to consider Skinner's analysis of why the Huguenots had good reason to make this "epoch-making move" from a vocabulary of religious duties to one of political rights. Unlike the Calvinists in Scotland and England in the 1550s, who did not appeal to political rights, the Huguenots who had just endured the massacres of 1572 needed to perform "the vital ideological task of appealing not merely to their own followers, but to the broadest possible spectrum of Catholic moderates and malcontents."[9]

> On the one hand, it was essential for them to construct an ideology capable of defending the lawfulness of resisting on grounds of conscience, since they needed to be able to reassure their followers about the legitimacy of engaging in a direct revolutionary confrontation with the established government. On the other hand, it was no less essential to produce a more constitutionalist and less purely sectarian ideology of opposi-

tion, since they obviously needed to broaden the basis of their support if they were to stand any chance of winning what amounted to a pitched battle with the Valois monarchy.[10]

The Huguenots were, like the Jansenists of the 1660s, a beleaguered minority desperately in need of ideological devices capable of persuading others without making appeal to religious conceptions of authority. Religious conceptions of authority, the only available means of legitimating the *religious duty* to resist, were bound to work against the Huguenots. So, also like the Jansenists who invented probable reasoning, they devised tools of legitimation that made religious disagreements inessential, thereby contributing heavily to the secularization of public discourse. Just as the Port-Royal *Logic* helped create a realm of probable reasoning free from religious presuppositions, the French Calvinists of the previous century helped create a point of view from which questions of "rights" and "justice" could be considered without allowing religious commitments to enter in.

The "autonomy" of the moral-political sphere, then, like that of science, was something that had to be carved out by the threatened minorities and weary peacemakers of the sixteenth and seventeenth centuries.[11] Skinner has this to say about the modern concept of the State:

> [T]he acceptance of the modern idea of the State presupposes that political society is held to exist solely for political purposes. The endorsement of this secularised viewpoint remained impossible as long as it was assumed that all temporal rulers had a duty to uphold godly as well as peaceable government. The sixteenth-century reformers were entirely at one with their Catholic adversaries on this point: they all insisted that one of the main aims of government must be to maintain "true religion" and the Church of Christ. As we have seen, this in turn means that the religious upheavals of the Reformation made a paradoxical yet vital contribution to the crystallising of the modern, secularised concept of the State. For as soon as the protagonists of the rival creeds showed that they were willing to fight each other to the death, it began to seem obvious to a number of *politique* theorists that, if there were to be any prospect of achieving civic peace, the powers of the State would have to be divorced from the duty to uphold any particular faith.[12]

The secularized concept of the State and the new concept of distinctively political rights were made for each other. Skin-

ner's book demonstrates that both became central to modern
political thought as a result of attempts to minimize the effects
of religious disagreement. It therefore also places Rawlsian
thought in genealogical perspective, for the concepts Rawls
takes for granted as the appropriate foci of inquiry, the intuitions against which he tests his theory, and the point of
view formally elaborated in his descriptions of the original
position all now appear as the products of highly specific historical conditions and ideological aims. These conditions and
aims, in turn, all relate to a single problem of cooperation.

We should not find it surprising that modern ethical
theorists tend to view morality itself as an institution whose
primary function is to resolve something called "the problem
of cooperation," for the intuitions on which such theorists depend were largely put in place by circumstances that made
cooperation seem more important than other values for which
one could strive. Little and Twiss, while admitting the possibility of exceptions, nonetheless speak of the "general object
of morality" as that of providing "a way of responding to what
we call the 'problem of cooperation' among self-interested,
competing, and conflicting persons and groups."[13] They later
admit that

> . . . particularistic codes exist and are properly spoken of as
> "moral codes." But we do think it can be said that such codes,
> while perfectly comprehensible as instantiations of morality,
> seem to be conceptually odd. For, given our discussion of moral
> legitimacy, it appears that no person can simply be excluded
> from moral consideration. This seems almost analytically true.

They continue:

> This statement appealing to analyticity is not an idle remark
> when one seriously reflects on the point of morality as that of
> countervailing or resolving the problem of cooperation. It is
> clear that a system of action-guides cannot fully achieve this
> end if the scope of these action-guides is confined to restricted
> groups.[14]

It is hard to see how any of the three cases studied in *Comparative Religious Ethics* — Navaho ethnography, Matthew's
Gospel, or the Pali canon — can be viewed as responses to a
general problem of cooperation. The latter two, in particular,
present views of the highest good that seem intended, if anything, to direct attention away from the good of maintaining

society as a system of rules designed to promote the cooperation of "self-interested, competing, and conflicting persons and
groups." The difficulty, I think, is that what seems "almost
analytically true" to Little and Twiss seems that way because
of intuitions originating in the early modern crisis of authority.
Premodern ethical systems are bound to seem paradoxical so
long as these intuitions are themselves treated unhistorically
and uncritically.

Rawls follows the standard pattern when, in the early
pages of *A Theory of Justice*, he defines "society" by reference
to rules that "specify a system of cooperation designed to advance the good of those taking part in it."[15] The passage is an
important one, for it is the priority of the problem of cooperation that leads toward a liberal theory of social life in which
"justice as fairness" plays the central role and in which the
concept of "right" is more basic than that of "good." As Robert
Paul Wolff has pointed out, the "natural inference" to draw
from Rawls's definition of society

> is that the antebellum South, for example, could not be con-
> sidered a *society* unless, at the very least, it could be shown
> that slavery constituted a system of cooperation suited to
> advance the interests of those (including slaves) taking part in
> it, and more strictly, that it was *designed* for that pur-
> pose . . . [16]

Wolff's point is that Rawls's definition makes it difficult to
claim sensibly that there have been *unjust* societies. But the
more telling point would be to say that Rawls's definition
tends to obfuscate the alternative forms of social life against
which liberal society should be judged. For, once the definition
has been assumed, a society like the antebellum South appears
inherently paradoxical — an only partial attainment of its own
essence *as* a society — and therefore *too* easily dismissible.
Because they do not grant the problem of cooperation priority
over other goods a social arrangement might serve, tradition-
alist and radical alternatives to liberalism have been implicitly
ruled out of serious consideration from the start. They are
made to seem hopelessly flawed attempts to be liberal. In this
fashion, Rawls in effect begs the question against his most
interesting opponents.[17]

When the contractors in the original position deliberate on
the selection of social principles, they do so as rational egoists,
though with the decided disadvantage (especially for egoists)

of not knowing *who* they are. The veil of ignorance deprives them, for example, of knowledge of their own religious beliefs and conceptions of the good. Why? Because otherwise unanimous agreement on social principles could not be reached by *rational* means. As Rawls explains, "One excludes the knowledge of those contingencies which sets men at odds and allows them to be guided by their prejudices. In this manner the veil of ignorance is arrived at in a natural way."[18] Rawls here sides with what Gadamer has called the Enlightenment's "prejudice against prejudice." But he does not make clear why religious beliefs and conceptions of the good should be counted as prejudices. He simply asserts that they "cannot be established by modes of reasoning commonly recognized."[19] Now this raises and interesting question. What becomes of Rawls's theory if we grant that what can and cannot be thus "established" changes as the "modes of reasoning commonly recognized" change?

This question reveals once again the historical location of Rawls's theory. For it would seem that Rawls's justification of religious tolerance works only when "modes of reasoning commonly recognized" do not settle questions of religious belief decisively one way or the other. Where religious belief is favored by accepted standards of judgment, Rawlsian arguments can be used to support the persecution of heretics. Where religious belief is undermined by accepted standards of judgment and also, by the same standards, viewed as detrimental to the good, Rawlsian arguments can be used to suppress religion altogether. Everything hangs on whether unanimous agreement can be reached by rational means. Rawls simply assumes that in the sphere of religion rational agreement is impossible. More important, he assumes that conceptions of the good are also insusceptible to the kind of assessment that could lead to rational agreement. In doing so, he either imposes an impossibly high standard in requiring the unanimous assent of *all* rational beings (irrespective of historical setting), a standard which would rule out most of what the contractors are *allowed* to know behind the veil of ignorance, or he begs the question (against those who would make the good prior to the right) by neglecting to argue for and state clearly the standard he is applying. The real contest between Rawlsian liberalism and its most interesting critics relates to whether conceptions of the good incompatible with liberalism can in fact be rationally justified. But on this issue Rawls himself has nothing much to say. What can be granted without hesitation is that liberal principles were the right ones to adopt when competing religious beliefs and divergent conceptions of the good embroiled Europe in the religious wars. Religious beliefs and conceptions of the good were, in that highly particular context, part of a dialectical impasse that made the attainment of rational agreement on a whole range of issues impossible. Whether they remain so is another question — and one well worth asking.

MacIntyre has suggested that "secondary virtues," such as cooperation, fairness, and tolerance, take priority only under certain historical conditions.[20] Rawlsian ethical theory is a good example of how this priority, once achieved, can become forgetful of its origins and accord itself the status of an intuitively obvious truth, one of the "provisional fixed points which we presume any conception of justice must fit." Historical insight is valuable to ethics in part because it helps us remember the origins of our intuitions and gain some critical distance from them. The "provisional fixed points" of modern ethical theory are more provisional and less fixed than we might think.

Rawls and Kant both take pains to stress that the original agreement postulated by social contract theory is purely hypothetical. My investigations suggest, however, that something very much like this agreement was in fact reached — though tacitly, to be sure — by actual historical agents in the early modern period. These agents were not, however, lifting themselves out of a state of nature, but were rather concerned to end a thoroughly social "war of all against all." Their agreement was to grant an important measure of autonomy to the moral-political sphere — specifically, autonomy *from* religious authority.

Our early modern ancestors were right to secularize public discourse in the interest of minimizing the ill effects of religious disagreement. In retrospect, they seem to have had little choice. Nor are we free to evade the conclusions to which the new forms of reasoning led in theology — conclusions that, at least as I have portrayed them in Part II, have left theology unable to step meaningfully again into the public arena. The theology that does step into the public arena pays a price for admission, and this price leaves theology too poor a thing to make much contribution once it has arrived. The theology that thrives in our own day belongs to the solitary genius or the marginal sect. This is a fact of society and history, not a conclusion one would avoid simply by deciding to believe or by crawling into an independent conceptual scheme.[21]

We are not bound, however, to accept our ancestors' interpretation of their accomplishment. They did not, by virtue of criticizing authority and theology, raise themselves above history or make themselves autonomous from tradition. In supposing that they did, they instead shielded their own most significant assumptions from sight and thus made the task of contemporary criticism more difficult. By conflating the moral imperative to contain the effects of religious disagreement with the myth of the completely autonomous man, they made what was in fact a form of self-deception seem the height of virtue. One effect of this self-deception was a highly misleading picture of the past, a picture which obscured from view just those features of the past that might raise doubts about the myth of autonomous man and the limitations of modern morality. Another was the paradoxical idea that the point of view from which we should appraise and select basic social principles is one in which conceptions of the good are in principle accorded the status of prejudices to be ignored.

The myth of autonomous man has taken many different forms in the ethical theory of the modern period. One of these, of course, was the Enlightenment's attempt to place moral knowledge on secure foundations, to restore the confidence of an earlier age that ethical theory belongs to the realm of *scientia*. The most famous expression of this urge was Locke's proclamation

> that, if men would in the same method, and with the same indifferency, search after moral as they do mathematical truths, they would find them [to] have a stronger connexion one with another, and a more necessary consequence from our clear and distinct ideas, and to come nearer perfect demonstration than is commonly imagined.[22]

But the problems of foundationalism proved as intractable in ethical theory as anywhere else, if not more so. For the intuitions from which the reconstruction of moral knowledge was supposed to proceed were far more subject to contention, once the new sciences had taken shape, than the intuitions mathematicians and natural scientists could be thought to share. Foundationalist ethical theory tended initially to reproduce the old division and discord without being able to explain it. The attempt to take all possible sources of conflict out of the foundations by seeking purely factual grounds for moral judgment quickly came to grief in Hume's remarks on "is" and "ought." The difficulty of distinguishing cognitive moral intuitions from the promptings of heartfelt conviction made it hard for intuitionists to hold the line against the theorists of moral sense and, eventually, emotivists and prescriptivists of various stripes. So long as foundationalist assumptions reigned in epistemology, with the help of either Cartesian philosophies of mind or reductionist theories of meaning, moral skepticism was virtually inevitable. Moral discourse seemed to have lost all valid connection with the language of fact. Morality seemed to have become independent from reason itself.

Kantians have always viewed this outcome as a disaster, but their response has been to revise and reinforce, not to reject, the myth of autonomous man. Morality is not independent from reason itself, but this can be shown, according to Kant, only by developing a full-scale critique of reason in its basic employments. Fact and value do fall into separate realms, but only because theoretical and practical reason presuppose distinguishable conceptual schemes. Morality is distinct from the science of nature and more basic than theology. Its principles can therefore be derived neither from a teleological view of human nature like that of Aristotle or Aquinas, nor from appeals to religious authority, even the imperatives of divine command.

Given the historical background sketched thus far, the Kant of Green's universal reason does not appear a very plausible figure, though he may well be (in many respects) the person Kant wanted to be. A more plausible Kant can be found in MacIntyre's ethical historiography.[23] They are very different Kants indeed. Green's Kant merely states clearly and explicitly what all rational creatures have known at some level all along. MacIntyre's Kant, in contrast, is someone who would be unintelligible if uprooted from the historical situation of post-seventeenth-century European culture. This Kant is trying to make sense of morality *after* the rise of Newtonian science and the demise of authority. A teleological view of human nature had once held virtue and happiness together, giving an obvious point to the moral life and blurring the line (from Kant's perspective) between prudential and moral motives. In the absence of this view, virtue and happiness seem unrelated. Striving for happiness could not make one virtuous, though we can *hope* that a virtuous life will someday be crowned with happiness, and we can even speculate that the universe *must* be such that virtue is rewarded. The only good unequivocally worth striving for is that of a good will, a will that acts for the right reasons and therein acts rightly.

What, then, gives the right reasons their legitimacy if not a broader Aristotelian framework? Not divine commands, for they cannot be *known* to derive from a supernatural source. Nor can the authority of a command, from whatever source, be recognized without an independent judgment of its rightness on my part. So the "authority" of moral rules must be independent of tradition and rest within me. Moral rules must be imperatives I address to myself. Whatever authority they possess must derive from the point of view I take when deciding which rules to legislate. But what would make this point of view rational? Theoretical reason is irrelevant. It must be the purely formal characteristics of an imperative, as viewed from a strictly impersonal or universal perspective, that give a moral rule its authority. The principles of justice would be among those which recommend themselves to pure reason in this fashion. They would therefore be such as would be chosen by free and rational men, by persons who can rise above tradition and prejudice to the vantage point of noumenal selves.

This thumbnail reconstruction of Kant's ethical thought can hardly do justice to the subtlety and complexity with which Kant executes his program. But it does have the virtue of *situating* the problems to which Kant responded in a historically intelligible context. Kant's problem would never have occurred to him if an earlier ethos had not collapsed. This ethos was, in point of fact, a shifting mixture of neo-Platonic and Aristotelian conceptions of *telos*, stoic conceptions of natural law, Hebrew appeals to *Torah*, Pauline views of human nature, the life and sayings of Jesus, and probably much more besides. Kant is best viewed, despite all the antitraditionalist rhetoric, as trying to save this traditional ethos by rearranging its various elements into a new pattern fit for duty in late eighteenth-century Europe. He deceived himself in part by misconstruing his task as one of transcendental analysis. When he later turned to history to test his results, the conviction that he *had* given a transcendental analysis fostered hermeneutical principles (of which Green is the most recent defender) that systematically excluded the possibility of a meaningful test.[24] When he looked at the ethical traditions of the West, he saw not his own essential dependence on traditional thought, but only so many historical vehicles of pure rational faith, each to be judged as a more or less successful anticipation of his own conclusions. Nearly complete divergence from these conclusions was not so much evidence of ethical diversity as a sign of the sensuous side of human nature gaining the upper'hand, a symptom of insufficient moral progress.

Kant, I have said, was the great philosopher of differentiation. He did more than anyone else to codify and legitimate a culture of separate compartments. This is a culture in which people are supposed to be essentially alike by virtue of autonomous rational agency — and in that sense homogenous — but also one in which people live their lives by passing through largely distinct cultural provinces: some public, some private, science here, art there, religion, morality, and so on, depending upon the individual. It is natural for us, living in such a culture and in the wake of Kant's accomplishment, to wonder how all of these domains hang together, if at all. We may, even if we reject Kantian hermeneutics as viciously circular, want to ask similar questions of other cultures removed from us in space or time. What, we ask, is the relationship between religion and morality in Nuer society, ancient Judaism, medieval Christianity, or Confucian China? This seems imprecise, so we spend some time sharpening our terms, working out the distinctions until they seem like the well-honed instruments of a real theory. But we ought to be asking whether any such question is likely to be at least slightly misleading. Perhaps the first thing needing to be said about most of these cultures is that they are not differentiated into separate domains. Each has an ethos which must be understood as a whole or not at all.

James Gustafson expresses an entirely justified sense of frustration when he writes that

> The issue is whether, within Jewish and Christian religious communities, morality and religion can be as easily separated as some modern distinctions find possible. . . . I do wish to make the case that discussions of the relation of religion and morality which attend to particular historical religions, those dominant in Western culture, should take into account the theo-

logical premises of those religions, and that if they do, the distinction (not to mention separation) between the two is more difficult to make than appears to be the case in some discussions. Concretely, it is not as easy to distinguish between "religious" and "moral" assertions, obligations, human capacities, and ends, as one might wish for it to be from an interest in logical analysis. In the Western religions, their documents, their histories, and the experiences of their communities, religion and morality are joined together, intertwined, commingled, indeed in some instances and respects even unified. Further, because of this commingling and unification, the concept of morality itself evades the precise definition and usage that philosophers often seek. It is a richer (or perhaps looser), or more complex one in traditional Western religious discourse than it is in some other contexts.[25]

The frustration may be justified, but it is not easy to express without creating an air of paradox. Gustafson seems to presuppose the validity of the distinction he wants to criticize when he speaks of religious and moral elements "commingling." But the paradox can be avoided if we put the point in something like the following terms.

No language can be understood atomistically. It does not follow, however, that the significance of a given collection of expressions in a language depends essentially upon the significance of every other expression in the same language. Any holism that sweeping would fail to recognize very real differences between one language and another. The significance of expressions like "morally right" and "morally blameworthy" in our public discourse depends relatively little, if at all, on the significance of expressions like "God's commands" and "the supernatural end of perfected human nature." The reason is that sentences in which the two sorts of expressions are mixed are no longer deeply entrenched in our discourse or generally accepted by members of our linguistic community. Moral discourse is, for us, at least relatively autonomous from theological discourse. The significance of the latter may depend upon that of the former, but the reverse may not hold. Yet this was not always so. Aquinas's discourse, for example, seems to have been such that expressions we would assign to relatively separate spheres or linguistic strata were commingled in deeply entrenched and generally accepted sentences. His ethos consisted in a complicated network of interdependent beliefs in which elements of various kinds played important, but not "foundational," roles. No such element could have been removed without altering the significance of the whole.

But the significance of the whole is not a matter of two separate domains or sets of meanings being brought together, as if each expression carried with it its own atom of meaning and the whole could be built up by combining these atoms. There are just sentences and their interrelations. The interrelations among *our* sentences are properly described in distinctions between "religious" and "moral" assertions. The interrelations among Aquinas's sentences are not. A theory full of sharp distinctions of this kind would, if applied to Aquinas, be anachronistic, a model of misplaced rigor. The only proper way to proceed is by attending in detail to what Waismann called the "open texture" of the concepts, by *describing* the fuzziness that is there. Our temptation is to think that a clearer picture would be a better one. But this is a case where clarity would be reductive and would therefore reveal less, and that is Gustafson's point.

To understand Aquinas, we must keep all sorts of sentences in view — some expressing commonsensical "intuitions" about the rightness of specific acts, others about the relation between goodness and the natural end of desire, still others in which he narrates the drama of salvation in terms that are both neo-Platonic and Christian. The rightness of an act is related to the divine commands integral to the drama of salvation, but also to the good toward which human beings tend by nature. The God who commands us is the God who created us with his own purposes in view. The world itself is a cosmos, not a universe stretching out toward infinity, but a self-enclosed unity saturated with the intentions of its creator, who went about his work by attending to all the specific details. The structure of human nature conveys a message of creative intent: it tends toward an end which is part of a coherent systems of ends. When God commands me to do something, I have a reservoir of reasons for obeying. I can rest assured that my own real good has been taken into account and that the being to whom I owe obedience is both rational in his requirements of me and loving in his disposition toward me. I need not obey simply because God is powerful. On the other hand, God *is* powerful and worthy of awe and respect for his might. The rightness of an act does not consist in the singular fact that God commanded it, but neither can rightness be fully understood if abstracted from the facts of human nature and its supernatural end.

We could go on and on, translating his sentences into our speech, being careful not to mean too much or too little by what we say. In doing this, we would have to move constantly back and forth, from his actual sentences and their interrelations to ours, trying to describe the similarities and differences. We would do so, of course, in our own language. Our translation would not be a one-to-one mapping of his sentences onto short sentences of our own. Any such mapping would blur important differences. We should have to either aim for a simple mapping and add a lot of commentary, or make the mapping complicated by producing very long sentences on our side, in effect building the commentary into the mapping itself. One function of commentary is to provide enough sentential context for the unfamiliar sentences we map so as to make a grasp of interrelations possible. Another is to ascribe appropriate thoughts (beliefs, intentions, desires, and so on) to authors. Translation is mapping plus commentary.[26] The art of building new sentences of our own onto which foreign sentences can be mapped without making foreigners seem silly is sometimes called hermeneutics.[27] There is no way to make the hermeneutical task simple or unnecessary by getting theoretical distinctions worked out in advance or by adopting a method for reducing a network of sentences to "basic norms." Gustafson is right to insist that "an interest in logical analysis" can lead us astray.

So too can the semantic vocabulary of the analytic tradition, if used without extraordinary care in summarizing our hermeneutical conclusions. MacIntyre has written that "Aquinas' theological ethics is such as to preserve the nontheological meaning of the word *good*."[28] A reductively theological definition of "good" would indeed misrepresent Aquinas's use of the term, and if this is all MacIntyre means to say, there is no problem. We may add that the term is only partly defined by its nontheological uses. If the meaning of the term is determined (still only in part) by *all* the deeply entrenched lawlike sentences in which it appears, and these will include theological sentences making reference to divine commands, it is misleading to say, as MacIntyre does, that "God is good" is for Aquinas a synthetic proposition,[29] as if the meaning of "good" were given exhaustively somewhere else. The contrast between synthetic and analytic propositions is, here as elsewhere, best avoided.

It follows that the contrast MacIntyre develops between Aquinas and Ockham will have to be recast. For on MacIntyre's account, the transition from Aquinas to Ockham is marked by the passage of "God is good" from synthetic to analytic status:

> *Good* is defined in terms of God's commandments: "God is good" becomes analytic, and so does "We ought to do what God commands." The rules which God enjoins upon us can have no further justification in terms of our desires . . . Occam's attempt to base morals upon revelation is the counterpart of his restriction in theology upon what can be known by nature. Philosophical skepticism about some of the arguments of natural theology combines with theological fideism to make grace and revelation the sources for our knowledge of God's will. The oddity of Occam's critical rationalism is that it leaves the divine commandments as arbitrary edicts which demand a nonrational obedience.[30]

The interpretation of Ockham given here is controversial.[31] Let us assume that there was such a thing as Ockhamism, leaving open whether this position began with Ockham himself or with his followers. How shall we describe it? Obviously, "God is good" does not become *true* by definition (in the sense of full-blooded analyticity), since definitions, including Ockhamistic ones, lack the power to make sentences true all by themselves. MacIntyre could not have meant that. His point must be that the meaning of "good" is, in Ockhamistic discourse, diminished so as to be more easily defined in strictly theological terms. A single sentence could thus come closer to exhausting the term's meaning and would, in a weak sense, approach analyticity. Ockhamism is one of those forms of reductionism which reflects, at the level of theory, a real reduction in the meanings of words and sentences. If you start from within the Thomistic web of belief, and proceed to undermine its Aristotelian confidence in the use of human reason as an instrument for discovering the value-laden facts of natural law, but fail to replace what you have thus weakened with something else, you will have greatly diminished the network of "conceptual connections" that donate meaning to moral terms and propositions.

The achievement of the reductive definition would not be cause for rejoicing. For when a term like "good" *can* be thus defined, it has already lost much of its usefulness to thought. It adds nothing. When MacIntyre says that "God is good" becomes analytic in Ockhamism, his entirely legitimate point is that an Ockhamist is not in a position to mean very much when ascribing goodness to God, a fact which will make the theological task hard going and leave ethics without most of its former reasons for obeying the commands that have now become so central. When reductionism in ethics reflects the actual impoverishment of discourse, its proponents are more to be pitied than deplored or refuted.[32]

We now seem to have before us the rudiments of a story of the genesis of our moral situation. We have, first, an ethos, a mature theoretical elaboration of which can be found in the writings of Aquinas. Next, we have evidence of the disintegration of that ethos, in the fact that Ockhamism came to seem plausible as an ethical theory in the eyes of highly intelligent men. We can, further, connect this disintegration to a more sweeping narrative, sketched in the earlier chapters of this book, in which the primary epistemic vocabulary of the culture came increasingly under suspicion during the period from Ockham to Descartes. Ockham's doubts about the scope of *scientia* in a world where God might be freely intervening at any point in the natural course of things foreshadowed the doubts Descartes geared to his demon. If *scientia* seems doubtful, the status of the Thomistic moral science of natural law is bound to seem doubtful as well. Ockhamistic appeals to divine commands are one early sign of the heavy burden that would have to be carried in the early modern period by authority. We have seen that the burden was too heavy to be borne. Given this burden, traditional authority could only collapse. The collapse of traditional authority is the pivot on which our plot turns, the point of dramatic reversal. For arising out of this situation of crisis, we find all of the following: the secularization of public discourse, the differentiation of cultural domains (and of the corresponding spheres of mental life), and the antitraditionalist myth of radically autonomous men.[33] Modern preoccupation with the autonomy of morals becomes intelligible when viewed as one important feature of this dramatic result.

That, in outline, is the genealogy of morals I would propose as an account of the emergence of autonomy. Unfortunately, I lack the space (and no doubt many of the skills, as well) that would be required to fill in the details. Whether further historical inquiry would bear out my proposal remains to be seen. I hope I have at least shown what such inquiry would probably involve. For now, I will content myself with drawing the morals that would follow if my hunches prove right.

First, the expected moral for moral philosophy. If my story is more plausible as history than the kind written under the influence of orthodox moral philosophy, then we have some reason for treating such philosophy with suspicion. The question is whether any philosophy that treats the autonomy of morality as a universal "logical requirement" (Little and Twiss) or as "part of the conceptual structure of every rational agent" (Green) can give a convincing account of its own prehistory. A philosophy that cannot account for itself persuasively in light of the historical record is, other things being equal, inferior to one that can. So if something like my narrative is more plausible than competing accounts, this would tell seriously against orthodox moral philosophy's image of itself as the product of autonomous reason. We cannot turn the case against orthodoxy into a knockdown argument, however. For any a priori account of history can be saved simply by insisting that the reasons ancestors gave in explaining their actions and beliefs were not their *real* reasons, or by accepting the reasons they gave at face value but declaring them irrational. Yet there is surely a point beyond which such tactics seem patently ad hoc — so many attempts to salvage a theory at any cost. A more plausible account of our ancestors would make room for the reasons they actually gave and simultaneously treat these reasons (for the most part) charitably. Such an account becomes possible, I would argue, only when we abandon a priori standing and treat reasons as susceptible to sometimes quite surprising (though by no means limitless) historical variation. Only, in other words, when we move from orthodoxy to historicism.

The first moral puts us in position to draw others, to descend from metaphilosophy to normative ethics. For when we execute the transition to historicism, we come to see orthodoxy not only as a false doctrine of transcendence but also as a symptom of real fragmentation. By placing his predecessor in historical perspective, Hegel was able to view Kant's "transcendence" as another name for alienation, and *Moralität* as the *Sittlichkeit* of another age in ruins. In retracing the movement from Kant to Hegel, we find ourselves arriving once again at conclusions Hegel drew. It is one thing to dismiss Kant's philosophy as unhistorical; it is another to overcome the alienation and fragmentation to which his philosophy gave expression. To reject pure practical reason as an empty abstraction is not yet to lessen our real distance from the tradition in which appeals to authority were central. To show that transcendental philosophy is in many respects parasitic on the tradition it sought to transcend is not yet to make that tradition whole.

The grain of truth in the idea that morality depends upon religion rests in the sound intuition that moral discourse makes considerably less sense to us than it did to Aquinas. The relative poverty of contemporary moral discourse *does* have something to do with the fact that the elements in Thomistic ethics which have since disintegrated have not been replaced by anything equally powerful or coherent. But, perhaps regrettably, these elements *have* disintegrated; Thomistic ethics is not a real option for us as a society. History *has* undermined our ability to settle moral disagreements by appealing to the *telos* of a determinate human nature or the commands of an omniscient and benevolent God. This is why the failure of foundationalist and transcendental philosophy to generate and justify a coherent moral system can only be greeted with sadness. It is also why moral skepticism seems intuitively to have better footing than skepticism about science, despite the ease with which we can show that the problem of "is" and "ought" and the problem of induction arise from precisely the same mistaken assumptions.

Our problem is not that morality is intrinsically noncognitive; nor that the moral point of view is so pure that it has no content; nor that moral judgments are in principle immune to the observational testing we associate with the critical assessment of scientific theories; nor even that moral sentences fail to refer to the kinds of objects one can point at and stub toes on. Aquinas's ethics seems to have been such that its substantive moral judgments *could* be justified in light of the facts of human nature as then best understood. They could also be tested against both the end toward which "perfected" human desire tends and the commands of an omniscient and supremely loving God. Their referential status was no more puzzling than that of a judgment about the quality of doorstops or paperweights would be for us. Our problem is that we have not re-

placed the elements in Aquinas's ethics that have since disintegrated — at least not with anything of equal coherence or
breadth of appeal.

For this reason, Elizabeth Anscombe and Alasdair Mac-
Intyre have been able to write persuasively to the effect that
the distinctively moral "ought" of modern ethical discourse is
best seen as a survival from another age. Our use of this term
has, according to these authors, lost over time its formerly rich
holistic connections with the rest of our language. As Mac-
Intyre has repeatedly announced over the last two decades, our
word "ought" resembles in all important respects the Poly-
nesian word "taboo" and therefore must be taken, in the spirit
of social anthropology, as a residue from an earlier context in
terms of which it once made sense.[34] From MacIntyre's genealogical perspective, the reductionism of an emotivist or prescriptivist account of moral language, like that of an Ockhamist
account, reflects an actual reduction in the intelligibility of
moral judgments — a reduction carried out in historical time
and hardly something one could fight off with an arsenal of
counterexamples. The descriptivist's counterexamples, to
which I referred in passing at the end of chapter 9, show only
that the fragmentation of discourse is not complete, that
among the ruins of the traditional ethos some conceptual formations remain sufficiently protected from the general erosion
to sustain coherent reasoning and foster agreement here and
there. But under the circumstances morality — to a disturbing
though by no means complete extent — *becomes* as a matter
of *fact* what emotivists and prescriptivists take it to be as a
matter of unchanging conceptual truth: a realm in which attitudes can be expressed and the implications of decisions ex-
plored but in which the prospects of rational persuasion are
slim.

We must not overestimate the difficulties or idealize the
past. The upshot of our genealogy of morals is not that moral
skepticism is, even for the time being, justified. Moral knowledge has not lost a foundation. It does not, in any event, need a
foundation. We know a great deal indeed about the rightness
and wrongness of acts, the values worth pursuing in life, and
the virtues worth instilling in children. We know, for example,
that genocide is wrong, that racial supremacy is not a goal to
be encouraged, and that Hitler is not a man to be held up as a
model for imitation. These are extremely important things to

know. Most of the many things we know about morals are both less obvious and less important than these. We also know some things about morals that Aquinas did not. We know, for example, that there are circumstances in which religious differences make secularization of the political sphere necessary. Our problem is that, unlike Aquinas, we lack a confident, widely shared conception of what way of life actually within our reach would really be best for us, as well as any coherent, realistically formulated notion of how to get there from here. This is why so many of our moral disagreements seem intractable, and why we have difficulty giving some kinds of moral endeavor a point without resorting to the wishful thinking of Kant's postulates and Marx's predictions.

If Hegel was right in thinking it impossible to make sense of the moral point of view Kant bequeathed to his twentieth-century followers as anything but a historical residue, where does this leave us? Hegel was saved from the full force of this question by the optimism he expressed in all but his bleakest moods about the prospects for overcoming both social and intellectual fragmentation in nineteenth-century Prussia. He thought he could discern among the ruins of traditional society and thought an emerging *Sittlichkeit*, a form of rational community that would be both the substance of ethical life, by virtue of its network of loyalties and special relations, and the already realized *telos* in which moral endeavor achieved its point. We, however, are the heirs not only of Hegel's critique of Kant, but also of Marx's critique of Hegel. Our question is, essentially, Marx's. How can we make whole what history has put assunder?

Unfortunately, the details of Marx's own "solution" seem increasingly confuted by the course of history subsequent to their invention.[35] Marx was nonetheless right, for all that, to warn against the perils of moralizing in a situation like ours and to insist on the importance of working out a conception of the good that can be both rationally justified and socially achieved. We will not repair the fabric of moral discourse and ethical community simply by moralizing, or by articulating utopian visions, or by acting mindlessly in the pursuit of ends we cannot defend. But we shall surely never learn where we ought to be going or how we ought to get there if we do not learn how we have come to be where we are.

I have tried in these pages not only to underline this need for historical understanding but also, insofar as I am able, to show in what some of this understanding might consist. One task, however, remains. For I promised at the outset to conclude with a relatively straightforward description of the historicism I have espoused throughout. That this historicism is largely ethical in substance and motivation should, by now, be evident. How it relates to its predecessors in the historicist tradition may be less so.

12. Explicating Historicism

Historicism is not what it used to be. Its opponents still worry mainly about difficulties associated with the historicism of the nineteenth century: an overconfident evolutionism, an idealist metaphysics sharply at odds with common sense; and a tendency to collapse, when deprived of evolutionist and idealist underpinnings, into potentially pernicious forms of relativism. But contemporary historicism does not reduce the past to a gradual, progressive curve; it has more to do with empirical approaches to language and sociological conceptions of knowledge than with an idealist philosophy of spirit; and its relativism, properly formulated, is innocuous. Historicists no longer feel the urge to write "history" in capital letters. Indeed, among those I would label historicist are some who prefer to use "historicism" only as a term of abuse for precisely that urge. Such thinkers do not treat ancient events as hints of an original essence, nor do they envision a universal history in which human nature achieves realization. They do not make much of essences or natures at all. They are, moreover, deeply wary of the conceit which would portray the career of a narrow social group, like that of Western intellectuals from Plato to Wittgenstein, as the history of humanity.

Does anything worthy of the title "historicism" survive such severe qualification? I have no stake in saving the term. It is as susceptible to elimination as any other. Nor do I wish to play down the distance we have come since Hegel. Say if you like that "minimal historicism" would fare no better than "minimal foundationalism" as a term of art. The fact remains that a significant tendency in recent thought, represented in figures as apparently diverse in philosophical background as Kuhn and Gadamer, is recognizably Hegelian — both in its refusal to abstract human reasoning from the historical circumstances of human life and in its unwillingness to view culture as a

256

collection of essentially autonomous spheres grounded in universal structures of the human mind. The "new historicism," if I may use the term for ease of reference, continues to rework themes from Hegel's critique of Kant and of the culture for which Kant sought transcendental justification. While historicism has in many respects become less Hegelian, it has thereby become not less but more determined to overcome the unhistorical orientation of foundationalist and transcendental philosophy.

It would be odd if historicism, of all things, were not liable to change over time. There is a clear sense in which historicism has become more historical, and less distinctively philosophical, as it has learned better how to view not only its opponents but also itself as conditioned by historical context. Hegel saw the need to overcome the Enlightenment's overcoming of traditional authority plainly enough. Yet he was not in a position to see the extent to which his own debt to Kantian epistemology and traditional metaphysics would eventually have to be overcome as well. His successors have had an easier time with the metaphysics than with the epistemology. But the chief effect of having overcome the metaphysics first was, as we have seen, conceptual relativism. For an epistemology of scheme and content, if it lacks both Kantian transcendental standing and Hegelian metaphysical backing, suggests a picture of history as a series of perhaps completely discontinuous conceptual schemes, each containing its own standards of judgment, the succession of which can be understood (if at all) only by reference to the more "basic" facts of economic production, social structure, or physiological makeup. Most philosophical thinkers since 1860 have either been so appalled by the implications of this picture as to revive the quest for a perspective beyond history, or so convinced of the quest's impossibility as to adopt the picture and live with whatever consequences followed (toning it down and juicing it up as individual temperament and needs of the moment required). A major aim of the present book has been to make propaganda for the view that there is no such dilemma. Historicism can strengthen its critique of Kantian thought most effectively by becoming less Kantian itself. A historicism without conceptual schemes — without the remnants of Kantian epistemology — would not entail the consequences that make one wish a perspective beyond history were attainable. Transcendental philosophy and conceptual relativism, I argued in chapter 8, are not our only alternatives.

If history is neither the progressive realization of *Geist* nor a succession of discontinuous conceptual schemes, what is it? Perhaps this is a good time to remind ourselves, as Marx put it in *The Eighteenth Brumaire*, that people make their own history, though not under circumstances of their own choosing. The characters in our historical narratives are not finally concepts, like *scientia* and *opinio*, or domains of culture, like morality and religion, or historical forces, like differentiation and secularization. They are people, situated in circumstances that have conceptual as well as other dimensions, struggling to respond to these circumstances with the means at their disposal. Neither character nor circumstance can be understood in isolation. Good history depicts their mutual interaction, showing how they render and determine each other. At its best, it grounds our freedom in the context of problems and choices within which human agency becomes both intelligible and accessible to rational criticism.

As Marx went on to say, historical circumstances do have a certain givenness about them, and this holds for the conceptual dimension of circumstance as much as for any other. If the social and intellectual features of a situation are as interrelated as one might suggest by invoking the Wittgensteinian phrase, "form of life," it should come as no surprise that concepts are as inert — and as plastic — as institutions. Like institutions they shape us, pose problems, determine possibilities — all in ways of which we are normally only partly conscious. They are in this sense autonomous and anonymous, over against us, part of our situation, insusceptible to complete rejection or wholesale replacement. We can pretend, if we like, that we are free to start over again in conceptual circumstances entirely of our own making or that we can purify our thought of all merely contingent considerations so as to achieve a vantage point of neutral universality. But we shall, in that event, be pretending — at no negligible cost to ourselves and each other. For the price would be self-deception, which in turn extracts its price from the sorry consequences of every self-deceiving act.

Situated freedom is a creature of space and time. To locate ourselves in *our* situation, and thereby to make informed moral action possible, is largely to construct the narratives in which the interaction of character and circumstance can be brought to light. Human character, and therefore the capacity to act freely, is shaped not only by its actual past but also by the unending activity of bringing that past to consciousness in narrative. Narrative is thus essential to both the primary formation of character in the education of the young and the continuous re-formation of character in moral discourse and reflection. It matters greatly that we tell stories, that we tell the right stories, and that we tell them well. Bad stories produce bad people — people who cannot act, or who cannot act well, because they lack the virtues of a well-formed character. A person's vices and virtues are largely the vices and virtues of his stories. In neglecting the imperative to narrate well, we impoverish ourselves.

The story of the emergence of modernity is one of incommensurable (and largely irreversible) gains and losses. Like most stories, it would cease to be valuable were it not laden with values. To tell this story, or even some one significant part of it, is to respond more or less sensitively to these values and to stand more or less appropriately *within* the story thus told. Only one-sided, insensitive renditions of the story could issue in stances of self-congratulation or nostalgic longing. Deep ambivalence is, in this case at least, the inevitable consequence of morally balanced depiction. The real struggle is to keep this ambivalence sufficiently close to hope to avoid the immobilizing effects of despair and sufficiently close to sobriety to resist the tempting illusions of utopia.

The continuity of our story is neither that of an unchanging essence nor that of an unfolding idea. But there must be some continuity if there is to be a story at all. I see no way to render Thomistic discourse commensurable with Humean discourse. Yet I also see no way to render the events of the 1660s intelligible without viewing them as integral to a story of human responses to a tradition in crisis. It is paramount to learn how the tradition in question lapsed into incoherence, how competing strategies for recasting the tradition took shape, and how enacted intentions and impinging events turned the tradition around and sent it off in new directions. The fact that major elements in inherited traditions survive any dramatic reversal establishes all the continuity we need. We cannot make sense of the human activity of responding to crisis without recognizing a background of relatively unques-

tioned values, beliefs, and commitments. No part of this background should be deemed, a priori, immune from revision or
rejection. Still, the entire background cannot succumb to doubt
in an instant. To postulate absolutely discontinuous conceptual
schemes is to repeat Descartes's error.

It might be objected, in the spirit of Foucault, that my
Jamesian talk of character and circumstance — indeed, any
mention of story or the continuities of plot — must be viewed
as naive and obsolete in these days of the "new novel" and
"post-structuralist" historiography. I can respond only by saying that I have done my best to free these notions from the
metaphysical and ideological assumptions Foucault and others
find so repugnant. It may have once been necessary to unsettle
essentialist and individualist assumptions precisely by writing
narratives that fail to hang together. But I would hope that we
can now view antinovels and antihistories as a liberating,
though negative, moment which must itself be overcome. We
need no longer write as Artaud, Beckett, Borges, and Robbe-
Grillet have written. It is time to write the narratives they
have made possible, not to repeat what they have already done.
Robbe-Grillet some time ago spoke of the day when antinarratives would become "academic" and young writers would turn
to something else. It may be surprising to hear his actual
counsel:

> Just as we must not assume man's absence on the pretext that
> the traditional character has disappeared, we must not identify
> the search for new narrative structures with an attempt to
> suppress any event, any passion, any adventure. . . . In short,
> it is not the anecdote that is lacking, it is only its character of
> certainty, its tranquility, its innocence.[1]

Antinarratives were always intrinsically parasitic on the forms
against which they rebelled. The current task is how to make
something of these forms in the absence of the essentialist's
all-too-easily-won continuity and the emergent bourgeoisie's
excessively individualist sense of character.

This task, if I am right about the ethical significance of
narrative, is a moral one. When the rebellion against old narratives is mistaken for a positive program, such that all continuity of plot is dogmatically prohibited and the names of
people become no more than "tags for sentences," the moral
capacity to inform action and shape character is lost. For all

its (implicit and explicit) moral fervor, the rebellion then becomes sterile. But if we can learn to be less Kantian, this sterility should come to seem unnecessary. Without the epistemology of scheme and content, we shall no longer feel bound to suppress all continuity by celebrating the differences between one scheme and another. Without the featureless self that twentieth-century thought derived from Kant's moral philosophy, we shall no longer feel inclined to say that character is hardly worth mentioning.

Kant gave us a pure moral will ideally constrained only by the universality of the categorical imperative. Existentialists deleted the categorical imperative, convinced that its putative universality was merely a sign of bad faith, and kept the rest of the picture. Post-structuralists thought existentialists were silly to excite themselves over the pure moral will of a featureless self, and proceeded to drop selves from the picture altogether. This left them with *nothing but* conceptual schemes — and therefore with no means for telling a story. The past became a series of absolute ruptures. Such a past could be edifying only by virtue of teaching us what we are not. But this edification remains useless insofar as we who might make use of it have disappeared. Our own disappearance is the *reductio ad absurdum* of the Kantian premises from which the dialectical progression began. Beyond deconstruction lies a self whose character is not "divorced from the traits that constitute it," whose freedom does not "consist in decisions taken apart from all desires, habits and dispositions,"[2] and whose history is inextricably intertwined with the histories of other selves.

The self of situated freedom is no more free to choose whatever moral principles it pleases than it is to accept whatever scientific theories it wishes were true. Moral and theoretical decision are alike constrained by the values and norms of a living inheritance within which even the changes we call revolutionary leave nearly everything in place. Change the criteria of goodness enough, for either conduct or theories, and you succeed only in changing the subject, not in articulating a *radically* new view on the old subject.[3] The relativist's stress on arbitrary choice derives from the incoherent idea of conceptual possibilities *so* novel that *nothing* could be said in critical assessment of them without begging the question — possibilities we would be free to choose for ourselves if only we had the courage to be.

It will be protested that I have, throughout this book, seriously underestimated the extent and depth of *actual* disagreement. Davidson purports to show that, given his own holistic philosophy of language, there must be limits to the extent and depth of any conceivable disagreement. I have been assuming that Davidson's holistic criticisms of the scheme-content distinction and his attempt to develop these criticisms into an account of the limits of conceptual contrast are both correct. It might be argued, against this assumption, that actual cases of disagreement we could point to show that Davidson must be wrong either in deriving his account of conceptual contrast or in criticizing the distinction between scheme and content itself. This book is long enough as it is, without adding the many pages that would be needed for a complete exposition and defense of Davidson's linguistic theory. I can only ask potential critics to supply *coherent* descriptions of actual disagreements that seem to disprove Davidson's conclusion. I do not know how to supply such descriptions myself. If I did, I would not find Davidson convincing.

The question at issue is not whether especially striking and worrisome cases of disagreement exist, but rather what should be said about such cases when we interpret, explain, and draw morals from them. Is it right to say, for example, that some disagreements are simply incapable of adjudication by rational means? If "rational adjudication" involves a process by means of which neutral rules are brought to bear upon areas of disagreement, then it must surely be granted that rational adjudication will fail whenever the rules we might invoke are themselves in question. Rules neutral with respect to any disagreement whatsoever are wild geese often chased but never found. Rules apparently neutral with respect to some specific disagreement, such as that between two scientists in a Kuhnian revolution, or that between Calvin and Veron over the rule of faith, often seem incapable of rendering a determinate resolution of the matter in dispute. But what moral should we draw from these conclusions? That the decision to take one side or the other in a disagreement beyond "rational adjudication" is arbitrary?

To say that such a decision would be arbitrary is to give far too much weight to the notion of neutral rules. In understanding or judging the rationality of a choice, we need to know *whose* choice we are considering and what the epistemic *situ-*

ation of this choice is. Once the relevant details have been filled in, the sense of arbitrariness will subside. "Neutral" rules distract attention from the very details a situated agent would find most compelling. This does not mean, of course, that the details available to any particular agent will always justify a determinate choice between two competing alternatives. The evidence may be too ambiguous or scanty to tip the scales. Deciding in favor of one option against the competitor would in that event be arbitrary, but only in the (irrelevant) sense that suspension of judgment is the more rational course. Suspension of judgment must be kept in view as one of the alternatives an agent might be obliged to accept, given all the details of the situation of choice.

This relativity of rational choice to actual features of the agent's cognitive context might seem, however, to heighten precisely the fears I am trying to calm. Do not agents raised in different cultures or educated in different research traditions assess competing theories and plans from different perspectives? Can we not then explain important cases of disagreement among such agents by saying that rationality is relative to perspective? In short, is not so-called rational choice utterly *subjective* in the perfectly straightforward and possibly very disturbing sense that even an agent's rationally defensible decisions on theories and plans tell us more about the agent's own perspective than about the objects and values to which he responds?

These questions may seem daunting, but the notion of perspective they employ is too vague as it stands to sustain the implied conclusions for long. We have a right, in the first place, to be suspicious of any metaphor with such close connections to the traditional Platonic imagery of knowledge as vision. If we begin by thinking of knowledge as vision, and it then occurs to us that there are many mental eyes and therefore many angles of vision, we shall certainly soon be worrying about the relativity of knowledge to perspective. The unavailability of a neutral perspective from which all perspectives can be judged will then, most likely, make all claims to knowledge seem inherently subjective and, thus, self-defeating. Knowledge is objective or nothing at all. But it is well worth recalling that all such talk *is* metaphorical, and we should always feel free to ask whether our metaphors are really helping or not. This may be a case where the metaphor is simply a picture that holds us captive — something from which we should seek liberation.

Moreover, the attempt to move beyond the metaphor toward an explicit theory of perspectival relativity seems bound to rely on ideas at least as problematical as those of scheme and content. As Davidson has written, "it is hard to improve intelligibility while retaining the excitement."[4] It is, of course, true that some disagreements can be explained by reference to historical facts about the agents involved — for example, their respective languages, antecedent beliefs, and available reasons. It is also true that even the most rational decisions typically tell us a great deal about those persons who make them. It does not follow, however, that the resulting theories and plans are any less *objective* in the only relevant sense — namely, that they consist in *justified* conclusions *about* the objects and values in question. To create grounds for worry here, we would have to show why some stronger sense of objectivity should be deemed relevant. The difficulty is how to strengthen the notion of objectivity in the required way without immediately sacrificing relevance. Objectivity as "correspondence to uninterpreted reality" may seem a stronger compliment than "justified under the circumstances," but the former (as we have seen) cannot function coherently as a criterion. It is not, therefore, a standard against which our sentences might be judged and found wanting. Without some such standard to invoke, the charge of subjectivity remains empty.

It might nonetheless be suggested that some disagreements are *in principle* incapable of resolution by rational means, whether such means are limited to what we have termed "adjudication" or not. The reasons to which I can appeal in justifying my decisions, and therefore the reasons relevant to anyone's assessment of my rationality in reaching these decisions, are determined by my situation — not only the epoch and culture into which I was born but also various other autobiographical facts that distinguish my reasoning from that of my fellows. The reasons available to you might well differ, given the facts of your situation. You might then reach conclusions which, while justifiable for someone in your situation, could not be so for me in mine. Grant for now that no rules of adjudication, neutral with respect to our differences, can be brought forward to resolve these differences. Even if we can translate each other's sentences, and therefore inevitably share much common ground, should we not say that our disagreements are in principle beyond rational resolution? Would it not follow that two or more incompatible theories or plans could be equally justified, no matter how much evidence we had access to? And would this not mean we lack justification for saying that one person's views are better than another's, provided all persons in question do their best under the conditions within which they find themselves?

These questions lay traps for the unsuspecting. One is the little phrase "in principle." We know of many disagreements that cannot, in point of fact, be resolved by rational means. Many factors — ranging from inner persuasion and nirvanic detachment to stupidity and dementia — can undermine our capacity or will to use the rational means that might, if used well, resolve our disagreements with others. More often we simply lack the time, energy, or occasion to make effective use of these means. Given the number of disagreements any person has with any other and the myriad forces making rational discourse difficult or impossible, it is hardly surprising that some disagreements cannot be resolved reasonably. Even supposing that Hitler was sane and open enough to be at all susceptible to rational persuasion, Churchill would probably have lacked the time and the occasion required to change Hitler's mind by rational means before Nazi theories and plans had taken their deadly toll. Churchill was forced to meet coercion with coercion. But what would it add to say that the disagreements between Hitler and Churchill were *in principle* incapable of rational resolution? The idea seems to be that some disagreements are incapable of rational resolution simply by virtue of their extent, depth, or conceptual structure. Presumably, such disagreements could not be resolved through rational persuasion even by maximally reasonable agents under perfect discursive conditions in an infinite span of time.

Several reminders deserve mention. First, we require some account of how the "extent, depth, or conceptual structure" of a disagreement blocks the possibility of rational resolution. Yet it is by no means clear how such an account can be supplied without resorting to the tactics Davidson diagnoses so tellingly in his criticism of conceptual schemes. So here the argument of chapter 8 applies with full force. Second, we must be careful once again not to confuse the many splendored devices of rational persuasion with the philosophical tradition's procedures of "neutral" adjudication. Even if there are many disputes we could not conceivably resolve by neutral adjudication, these too might count as rationally resolvable "in principle" provided we give the notion of rational persuasion ample scope. This second point leads directly to a third. For if rational persuasion is not conflated with neutral adjudication, then to understand the former we shall have to abandon the transcendental perspective associated with the latter. We must try to think as concretely as possible about rational persuasion, recalling that reason-giving is something *people do*, under historically *specific* circumstances, in conversation with their *contemporaries*. Finally, we should not forget that for as long as anyone can remember people have changed their minds after being given reasons. Scientists switch sides, Californians convert to Buddhism, theologians lose the faith. Why these phenomena should be any less impressive than the phenomena of prolonged disputation, or should be deemed intrinsically nonrational, I do not know.

When we imagine disagreements of the kind that might seem inherently beyond the pale of rational resolution, we tend to leave the people out of the picture. We focus instead on systems of beliefs abstracted from the conditions of human life, and ask which of these systems might be justified. Each system answers in its own terms and in its own favor. Short of Archimedean adjudication, impasse then seems inevitable. Yet no system of beliefs can change its mind; systems have no minds to change. Only people have minds or the flexibility to change them when the circumstances demand. Think of Nuer cosmology and modern liberalism as abstractions in confrontation, and you will have trouble imagining them converging on a common position. Consider this tribesman and that anthropologist as partners in conversation, and you will have no trouble whatsoever. Here is the tribesman acquiring "modern" doubts concerning the status of traditional authority as he learns more about the history of seventeenth-century Europe. There is the anthropologist losing his "liberal" dedication to the value of individual freedom as he learns more about the virtues of tribal cohesion. Both of these changes are in fact highly plausible: many tribesmen have acquired "modern" doubts; many anthropologists have lost their liberalism. Have we any right to conclude that such changes are necessarily nonrational or that, given enough time and energy, such people could not by rational means converge on agreement?

One might answer as follows: "Any reason must be a position within a system of beliefs. Each system has its own reasons, but the space between systems is a vacuum in which no reasons can be found. The transition from one system to the next cannot therefore be reasonable. That is why Kuhn speaks of conversions in his analysis of scientific revolutions. Any choice made between rival systems must be arbitrary."

This answer, with its reification of systems, differs in no significant respect from the appeal to conceptual schemes. Perhaps I can reinforce my rejection of conceptual schemes by questioning standard assumptions about conversion. Kuhn's suggestion that conversions are rife during scientific revolutions was greeted with the horror of those bent on defending the rationality of science, but the reaction presupposed that conversions are inherently nonrational. Conversions in fact have little to do with adjudication. But it is worth recalling that they typically follow crises *within* systems of belief. Internal disintegration, external challenge, and new information can all give us good reason to doubt propositions previously taken for granted and even central to our form of life. If we abandon such propositions and replace them with others, altering our form of life accordingly, it would be fair to say that we have undergone conversion. I conclude that conversions can be reasonable. Suppose my beliefs have fallen into more than the normal degree of disarray. Conversion to a "system" not similarly in crisis may be the most reasonable course open to me under the circumstances. If we can avoid thinking of systems of beliefs as alternative conceptual schemes, we should be able to allow that each moment in a process of conversion might well involve a context of reasons rich enough to justify the decisions then taken.

What makes a revolutionary period seem like a battleground for competing conceptual schemes, of course, is that no one seems able to give conclusive reasons for converting to the new program or standing pat on the old. Both sets of reasons seem equally good, and therefore equally bad, to the dispassionately retrospective eye of the Kuhnian historian. The facts of conversion seem to have more to do with professional standing and social location than with the quality of reasons. Established professors don't convert to the revolution; graduate students and others at the margins of the discipline do. It may seem absurd to hold out, in the face of such facts, for the rationality of conversion.

Keep in mind, however, the circumstances of a scientific revolution. It is intrinsically difficult, for reasons having nothing to do with conceptual schemes, to compare the merits of a long established but increasingly problematical program with a still undeveloped but possibly quite promising alternative. Such programs would be, in an entirely harmless sense, incommensurable. Deciding which program deserves commitment is like deciding whether a massive but slightly diseased oak or a spindly but perfectly healthy sapling is likely to be giving more shade in twenty years' time. If I put my money on the oak, and you put yours on the sapling, we may both have good reasons for our decisions. Two incompatible programs might both be rationally *permissible*. Revolutionary periods are generally such that more than one course is justifiable in this sense. Available reasons, carefully considered, would in such circumstances neither *require* advocacy of one theory nor *prohibit* advocacy of its leading competitors. What separates the various advocates is a temporarily inconclusive epistemic situation, not a rift between conceptual schemes. It even makes sense, when viewed in this light, that the strength or weakness of a scientist's commitment to entrenched models, as determined by purely personal or social factors, can enter crucially into a *reasoned* decision on which theory *he* should support.

Saplings grow. They become mature trees, comparable with other mature trees. Revolutionary programs of research, if carried forward by advocates of any skill and perseverance, eventually display the fruit of success and failure by which we judge them. The ideally successful revolution generates evidence of the kind that gives lingering opponents, as well as graduate-student recruits, good reason for getting in step. Whenever neither of two rival programs of research can explain the common history of their competition to the satisfaction of the other, this is itself an objective indication of weakness in the theories thus far proposed. It remains possible, at least in principle, that one program will improve its theories — and its explanations of the rival's strengths and weaknesses — to the point of converting the reasonable among the holdouts. Another possibility, equally reassuring, is that a third program will arise, displacing the others by the power of its theories and the persuasiveness of its narratives. When such possibilities are realized, holding out for an old theory becomes a sign that reasons have ceased to be the most significant causes at work in determining judgment. If the very best of arguments, put forward in relatively conclusive epistemic circumstances, fails to persuade, this shows only that nonrational factors have gotten the upper hand, not that rational agreement is in principle impossible. Where holding out is still a rationally permissible option, given the availability of reasons and the accessibility of evidence, this shows only that the epistemic circumstances remain inconclusive, not that any theory satisfying its own criteria of excellence is finally as good as any other.

Scientists, it will be said, share an interest in prediction and control, as well as the Popperian values of their academic subculture. This common ground forms the basis of whatever rational agreement they reach. Shared interests and values establish intersubjective criteria for ranking theories and programs in the same domain. The more a theory helps with prediction and control in the long run, the better the theory. The more effectively a program promotes and withstands observational testing of its hypotheses, the better the program. The objectivity of scientific judgment seems, then, to be relative to interests and values. What about the rift between those who accept the interests and values definitive of scientific rationality and those who do not? What claim can scientific standards of judgment possibly make on those whose interests and values belong to traditional society or to modern fideism? Even if the acceptability of theories and programs seems nonarbitrary when scientific interests and values are taken for granted, are not these interests and values themselves ultimately arbitrary in a way that ought to qualify or undermine belief in the objectivity of science — and, for that matter, of *all* thought?

I have already argued, in chapter 10, that explanatory and normative aims figure crucially in the appraisal of descriptive science. Surely such aims are closely related to, and may reasonably be said to reflect, interests and values more or less widely shared. This may seem to commit me to entertaining seriously doubts of the kind just expressed. Notice, however, that these doubts presuppose something suspiciously like foundational status for interests and values. Reasoning relative to interests and values would be arbitrary only if interests and values are immune from critical assessment and possible revision or rejection. Yet I see no reason to suppose that interests and values are immune from criticism. Foundationalism seems reassuring when the proposed foundations are the rationalist's dictates of reason or the empiricist's presentations of sense, infinitely less so when the same role is taken by the existentialist's decisions of principle or the perspectivalist's interests and values. Fortunately, the more worrisome proposals are no more plausible than the others: there are no foundations of either sort for there are no foundations at all.

We have yet to find good reasons for concluding that some disagreements are in principle incapable of rational resolution. If interests and values are as open to criticism as any other element of our inheritance, the fact that they are irreducibly important in the justification of theories and programs does not make such justification "ultimately arbitrary." A disagreement that can be traced to differences in interests and values might well be resolved by means of rational criticism.[5] Whether it will in fact be thus resolved, depends, of course, on many things: the time, energy, intelligence, flexibility, and rhetorical skill of the disputants; the availability of relevant evidence; the presence or absence of conditions conducive to good conversation; the very possibility of having a conversation in the first place; and so on. Now it may be that a disputant's interests and values will bear directly on one or more of these factors, perhaps making the prospects of rational persuasion rather slim indeed. A fundamentalist's or Cartesian's valuation of inner persuasion, for example, can produce a dogmatic inflexibility which reduces the likelihood that conversational persuasion will succeed. A Buddhist's interest in achieving Nirvana can extinguish the motivation to engage in any disputes whatsoever. But in none of these cases would it be right to conclude that rational agreement was in principle out of reach. Fundamentalists, Cartesians, and Buddhists, like the rest of us, *might* be persuaded by rational means despite themselves. Perhaps a century of religious wars will bring home to the fundamentalist why the dogmatic inflexibility of inner persuasion should be overcome. Perhaps the difficulty of distinguishing his "objective certainty" from my "mistakenly heartfelt conviction" will make the Cartesian think twice. Perhaps the Buddhist will overhear Proudfoot on religious experience and find his own interest in Nirvana challenged. I am not claiming that any of these eventualities would necessarily issue in rational persuasion, even under "ideal" discursive conditions, but only that it is not necessarily true that they would not.

One precondition of resolving disagreements rationally is the possibility of bringing the respective parties into actual conversation with each other. We should not be surprised when we have trouble saying what could conceivably settle disagreements between figures separated by several centuries. Aquinas had his reasons, and Hume had others. Their arguments, we are tempted to say, would simply pass each other by. And indeed they would: Aquinas and Hume could never have a conversation in which each learned from the other's reasons. Anyone's dialogue with the dead is onesided in this respect. We can learn from what the dead have left for us, but they shall never learn from us. So when we imagine Aquinas and Hume in heavenly conversation, Aquinas never yields an inch. But under what circumstances in what possible world is the imagined conversation taking place? If we imagine Aquinas transported to the eighteenth century, doing his best to learn new languages and the history of early modern Europe, the prospects of rational agreement immediately improve.

None of this implies that there is no such thing as dialectical impasse. Protestants and Catholics reached dialectical impasse in the sixteenth century, and this was hardly a unique event in the history of the species. Yet if we focus on historically situated people and their attempts to solve problems, instead of on conceptual schemes in static opposition, we should be able to see that impasses can and do get resolved — given enough time, luck, and human ingenuity. To be sure, most of us generally have little interest in, and place little value upon, getting our disagreements with others settled. This is as it should be. There is no harm in disagreement as such. Tolerance is a virtue, diversity a value to be prized.[6] Most disagreements fail to get settled rationally because there is no good reason to settle them. When, however, something of momentous import depends upon our being able to resolve a disagreement, the effects of impasse can be cause for grave concern. Our failure to be rationally persuasive may be the occasion for bearing arms against neighbors or losing all we hold dear. But even when such failure seems total, the problem is not that reason is arbitrary.

Nor is the solution a perspective above history. We should not ask philosophy to perform tasks it cannot perform. Whatever *we* think will, by virtue of the grammar of indexical speech, be *our* thoughts, in *our* culture, *here* and *now*. This idea should be troubling only if we allow ourselves to think uncritically or allow the conceptual resources of our culture to become impoverished — as we do when we pretend to transcend all tradition or neglect the need to narrate our past. The real hope for rational discourse lies in the will to create communities and institutions in which the virtues of good people and good conversation can flourish. Philosophy is no substitute for that, but its value can be measured by the contribution it makes.

Notes

Introduction

1. Ludwig Wittgenstein, *Philosophical Investigations,* trans. G.E.M. Anscombe (New York: Macmillan, 1958), p. 8e.

2. I intend this phrase to be taken in a sense less technical than that preferred by Michel Foucault. Cf. his *The Archaeology of Knowledge,* trans. A. M. Sheridan Smith (New York: Harper & Row, 1972), esp. p. 131.

3. Karl Popper, *The Poverty of Historicism* (Boston: Beacon Press, 1957).

4. See Alasdair MacIntyre, "Epistemological Crises, Dramatic Narrative and the Philosophy of Science," *Monist* 60 (1977): 453-472.

5. I appeal to Quine and Wittgenstein, here and throughout, largely for their symbolic value. Needless to say, I do not accept everything these philosophers have written. That would be impossible, given their obvious differences. Moreover, there is a great deal of Quine's authorship with which I disagree — for example, his doctrine of the double indeterminacy of translation. And Wittgenstein's writings pose infamous problems of interpretation from which I will for the most part stand clear. Nonetheless, Quine and Wittgenstein did more than anyone else to raise doubts about the basic distinctions of analytic philosophy. Quine's "Two Dogmas of Empiricism" and Wittgenstein's *Philosophical Investigations,* both of which appeared in the early 1950s, symbolize the end of the era in which "conceptual analysis" could be taken for granted as a suitable job description for philosophers. Quine made this moral of his work clear by attacking the notion of analysis itself. The corresponding moral of Wittgenstein's work was less clear, in part because Wittgenstein seemed to be *doing* conceptual analysis. But Wittgenstein, like Quine, engendered doubts about the status of the concepts other philosophers thought they were analyzing, and left many readers unsure how anything smaller than a language game could constitute a suitable object of "analysis." The upshot of this was a philosophy in which *no* representations could plausibly be accorded epistemological privilege.

273

For more along these lines, see Rorty's discussion of Quine and Sellars as critics of "privileged representations" in chap. 4 of *Philosophy and the Mirror of Nature* (Princeton: Princeton University Press, 1979).

6. On the role of Russell and Husserl in the professionalization of philosophy, see Richard Rorty, "Professionalized Philosophy and Transcendental Culture," *Georgia Review* 39 (1976): 757-769.

7. Ian Hacking, *Why Does Language Matter to Philosophy?* (Cambridge: Cambridge University Press, 1975).

8. Richard Rorty, "Strawson's Objectivity Argument," *Review of Metaphysics* 24 (1970) : 207-244.

9. I do not mean anything more by the term than this. In particular, I do not mean by "holism" the view that the meaning of an expression depends upon the *entirety* of the theory in which it appears. Nor do I mean to endorse the epistemological corollary of this view — namely, that theories must be tested, confirmed, and disconfirmed as wholes. Such doctrines should be treated only as extreme versions of semantic and epistemological holism, and they do not follow from rejection of the analytic-synthetic distinction. What does follow is that the semantic interpretation and epistemic assessment of a sentence depends upon the other sentences we make it "consort with." For a detailed discussion of these matters, see Clark Glymour, *Theory and Evidence* (Princeton: Princeton University Press, 1980), esp. pp. 145-155. Let "radical holism" stand for the extreme view, and let "thoroughgoing holism" stand for any form of holism, radical or not, which includes both semantic and epistemological theses of a generally contextualist sort.

10. P. F. Strawson, *Individuals* (Garden City, N.Y.: Anchor, 1963), p. xiv.

1. Descartes, the Father

1. Frederick L. Will, *Induction and Justification* (Ithaca, N.Y.: Cornell University Press, 1974).

2. Ibid., pp. 10-11, Will's italics.

3. Harold Bloom, *The Anxiety of Influence* (Oxford: Oxford University Press, 1973), pp. 14, 19-48.

4. Will, p. 185.

5. Ibid., p. 103.

6. Ibid., p. 23.

7. Ibid., pp. 203, 172, 190, 200.

8. William P. Alston, "Has Foundationalism Been Refuted?" *Philosophical Studies* 29 (1976): 287-305.

9. Ibid., p. 287. The first part of this article criticizes Will, the second Lehrer. See Keith Lehrer, *Knowledge* (Oxford: Clarendon

Press, 1974). For Alston's criticisms of Aune, see "Two Types of Foundationalism," *Journal of Philosophy* 73 (1976): 165-185, and "Varieties of Privileged Access," *American Philosophical Quarterly* 8 (1971) : 223-241, esp. 240-241. See also: Alston, "Self-Warrant: A Neglected Form of Privileged Access," *American Philosophical Quarterly* 13 (1976): 257-272, and Bruce Aune, *Knowledge, Mind and Nature* (New York: Random House, 1967).

10. James W. Cornman, "Foundational versus Nonfoundational Theories of Empirical Justification," in *Essays on Knowledge and Justification*, ed. George S. Pappas and Marshall Swain (Ithaca, N.Y.: Cornell University Press, 1978), pp. 229-252. The quoted phrases come from pp. 252 and 229, respectively.

11. Alston, "Has Foundationalism Been Refuted?" p. 291, Alston's italics.

12. Alston, "Self-Warrant," p. 261, Alston's italics.

13. Alston, "Two Types," p. 175, Alston's italics.

14. See Alston's discussion in "Self-Warrant," pp. 266-267.

15. Cf. Cornman, pp. 249-252. See Wilfrid Sellars, *Science, Perception and Reality* (London: Routledge & Kegan Paul, 1963), esp. chap. 5.

16. Alston, "Two Types," p. 170.

17. Alston, "Self-Warrant," p. 258.

18. Ibid., pp. 270-272, and Alston, "Varieties," pp. 236-240.

19. Alston, "Has Foundationalism Been Refuted?" p. 296.

20. Alston, "Self-Warrant," p. 269. Also see Richard Rorty, "Intuition," *The Encyclopedia of Philosophy,* ed. Paul Edwards (New York: Collier-Macmillan, 1967), 4: 205.

21. Willard Van Orman Quine, *Word and Object* (Cambridge, Mass.: The M.I.T. Press, 1960), pp. 258-259.

22. Alston, "Two Types," p. 179.

23. As Alston himself points out in ibid., pp. 181-182.

24. Alston, "Has Foundationalism Been Refuted?" p. 300.

25. Ibid., p. 301.

26. Michael Williams, *Groundless Belief* (New Haven: Yale University Press, 1977), p. 84.

27. Rorty, "Intuition," p. 207.

28. See Williams, pp. 2-3, 22, and passim. Also: Roderick M. Chisholm, *Theory of Knowledge*, 1st ed. (Englewood Cliffs, N.J.: Prentice-Hall, 1966), pp. 24-25, as well as the works by Chisholm cited in Williams.

29. Cf. David Annis, "A Contextualist Theory of Epistemic Justification," *American Philosophical Quarterly* 15 (1978): 213-219.

30. This is the only way to put it. Alston does not, like Cornman, *advocate* minimal foundationalism. He seems to believe, to the contrary, that minimal foundationalism could collapse because of a shortage of immediately justified beliefs to hold up the rest of what

we justifiably believe. It is hard to see, however, why he thinks immediately justified beliefs (in the weak sense) would be in such short supply unless he (wrongly) conflates "being justified in believing something even in the absence of good reasons" with some form of privileged access. See "Two Types," p. 185, and "Has Foundationalism Been Refuted?" pp. 302-303. Note that minimal foundationalism need not restrict the means of justificatory support to deduction or induction by enumeration. See Cornman, p. 252.

31. Bloom, *Anxiety*, pp. 14-15, 49-73.

32. For an example, see the identification of Quine and Sellars as foundationalists in Cornman, pp. 249-252.

33. See Richard Rorty, "Cartesian Epistemology and Changes in Ontology," in *Contemporary American Philosophy*, 2nd series, ed. John E. Smith (New York: Humanities Press, 1970), pp. 273-292.

2. Placing the Father

1. E. Gilson, *Etudes sur le rôle de la pensée médiévale dans la formation du système cartesien* (Paris: J. Vrin, 1951); A. Koyré, *Descartes und die Scholastik* (Bonn: F. Cohen, 1923).

2. Edmund F. Byrne, *Probability and Opinion* (The Hague: Martinus Nijhoff, 1968).

3. Ian Hacking, *The Emergence of Probability* (Cambridge: Cambridge University Press, 1975), chaps. 3-5.

4. See ibid., p. 20.

5. Byrne, p. 64.

6. Ibid., p. 188.

7. Hacking, *Probability*, p. 22.

8. Byrne, chap. 2.

9. This story has been told — with the specific purpose of illuminating Descartes's intellectual context — in Richard H. Popkin, *The History of Scepticism from Erasmus to Descartes* (Assen: Van Gorcum & Co., 1960).

10. Ibid., p. 1, my italics.

11. *Documents of the Christian Church*, ed. Henry Bettenson (Oxford: Oxford University Press, 1963), p. 197.

12. Martin Luther, *Three Treatises* (Philadelphia: Fortress Press, 1960), p. 124.

13. Bettenson, p. 201.

14. See H. A. Oberman, *Forerunners of the Reformation*, trans. Paul L. Nykus (New York: Holt, Rinehart & Winston, 1966), p. 58.

15. See Popkin, pp. 4-6.

16. Bettenson, p. 195.

17. Quoted in Popkin, p. 10.

18. Ibid., pp. 71-72.

19. Paul Feyerabend, "Classical Empiricism" in *The Methodological Heritage of Newton*, ed. Robert E. Butts and John W. Davis (Toronto: University of Toronto Press, 1970), pp. 152-153.

20. René Descartes, *Discourse on the Method*, in *Philosophical Works of Descartes*, trans. E. S. Haldane and G. R. T. Ross, 2 vols. (n.p.: Dover, 1955), 1: 83. Hereafter I shall indicate the title of the work and give the volume- and page- reference to Haldane and Ross directly.

21. Ibid., 1: 86.

22. Ibid.

23. *Rules for the Direction of the Mind*, 1: 4.

24. Ibid.

25. Ibid., 1: 6.

26. Ibid.

27. Ibid.

28. Ibid.

29. *Meditations*, 1: 145.

30. *Rules for the Direction of the Mind*, 1: 3.

31. See Henry G. Van Leeuwen, *The Problem of Certainty in English Thought, 1630-1690* (The Hague: Martinus Nijhoff, 1963), pp. 15-32.

32. Ibid., p. 24.

33. Ibid., pp. 31-32.

34. Ibid., p. 24.

35. Hacking, *Probability*, p. 9.

36. Quoted in ibid., p. 41.

37. Ibid., p. 42.

38. Ibid., p. 44.

39. Ibid., p. 43.

40. I have used the translation of the *Pensées* by A. J. Krailsheimer (London: Penguin, 1966) and the Lafuma numbering of the fragments, which I cite in the text with the symbol "#."

41. Hacking, *Probability*, p. 63.

42. Ibid., p. 64.

43. Ibid., p. 67.

44. Antoine Arnauld, *Oeuvres* (Paris: 1780), vol. 41, *La Logique ou l'Art de penser*. Translations from this work in the text are my own.

45. Hacking, *Probability*, p. 77.

46. Ibid., p. 47.

47. Ibid., p. 81.

3. Displacing the Father

1. Rorty, *Philosophy and the Mirror of Nature*, p. 131.

2. For an introduction to Descartes's mathematical physics and a discussion of his mystical vision, see John Herman Randall, Jr., *The Career of Philosophy*, 2 vols. (New York: Columbia University Press, 1962), 1:371-395.

3. Hacking, *Probability*, p. 46.

4. Quoted in ibid., p. 46.

5. See Van Leeuwen, pp. 106-120 and passim.

6. See Randall, 1: 398.

7. The task has already been carried out expertly by Rorty in *Mirror*, chaps. 1-3.

8. For a statement of this doctrine, see Bloom, *Anxiety*, pp. 94-95. For a criticism, see David C. Hoy, *The Critical Circle* (Berkeley: University of California Press, 1978), chap. 5.

9. Bloom, *Anxiety*, p. 96.

10. Ibid., p. 14. See also pp. 77-92.

11. Ibid., pp. 14-15.

12. Ibid., p. 91.

13. See Rorty, *Mirror*, pp. 9-10.

14. Alasdair MacIntyre, "Epistemological Crises," pp. 457-459.

15. See Bloom, *Anxiety*. p. 64, esp. the passage quoted from Freud.

16. Quoted in Harold Bloom, *Kabbalah and Criticism* (New York: Seabury Press, 1975), pp. 93-94.

17. Bloom, *Anxiety*, p. 15.

18. Ibid., p. 109.

19. Ibid., p. 15.

20. See Stanley Fish, *Self-Consuming Artifacts* (Berkeley: University of California Press, 1972) and chap. 9 below.

21. Nelson Goodman, *Ways of Worldmaking* (Indianapolis, Ind.: Hackett, 1978), p. 20. See also Richard Rorty, "The World Well Lost," *Journal of Philosophy* 69 (1972): 649-665.

22. Bloom, *Anxiety*, pp. 15-16.

23. See Harold Bloom, *A Map of Misreading* (New York: Oxford University Press, 1975), chap. 4.

24. Ibid., p. 101.

25. Bloom, *Anxiety*, p. 122.

26. The reference to a "Paradise within" comes, of course, from *Paradise Lost* (XII). The reference to the Spirit occurs in volume VI of the Yale edition of the *Complete Prose Works of John Milton*, ed. D. M. Wolfe. For a discussion of Milton's attempt to wrestle with the problems of subjectivity posed by his own emphasis on the inner spirit, see Christopher Hill, *Milton and the English Revolution* (London: Faber and Faber, 1977), chaps. 19 and 24.

27. Bloom, *Anxiety*, p. 122.

28. Stanley Cavell, *Must We Mean What We Say?* (Cambridge: Cambridge University Press, 1976), p. xix.

29. Rorty, *Mirror*, pp. 12, 157.

30. Ibid., p. 163.

31. Wilfrid Sellars, *Science, Perception and Reality* (New York: Humanities Press, 1963), p. 170.

32. Feyerabend, "Classical Empiricism," pp. 150-170.

4. Explicating Knowledge

1. Michael Dummett, *Frege: Philosophy of Language* (New York: Harper & Row, 1973), p. 669.

2. Quine, *Word and Object,* pp. 258-259.

3. Ibid., p. 260.

4. Ibid.

5. Ibid., p. 261.

6. Edmund Gettier, "Is Justified True Belief Knowledge?" *Analysis* 23 (1963): 121-123.

7. Williams, *Groundless Belief,* p. 10.

8. Gilbert Harman, *Thought* (Princeton: Princeton University Press, 1973). See chaps. 4-6 for Harman's Quinean critique of analyticity, chaps. 7-12 for his contribution to Gettierology. See also Harman, "Quine on Meaning and Existence, I," *Review of Metaphysics* 21 (1967): 124-151. For part II of this article, see the same journal, 21 (1967): 343-367.

9. Gilbert Harman, "Using Intuitions about Knowledge to Study Reasoning: A Reply to Williams," *Journal of Philosophy* 75 (1978): 438. This article responds to Michael Williams, "Inference, Justification, and the Analysis of Knowledge," *Journal of Philosophy* 75 (1978): 249-263.

10. Harman, "Using Intuitions," p. 433.

11. There is, however, a substantive disagreement between those who prefer a program of naturalization to talk of elimination. See Rorty, *Mirror,* chap. 5. Rorty argues that the naturalizers of epistemology repeat the Lockean confusion between explanation and justification: the latter is a social affair, involving institutions and norms, not a matter of how brains work abstracted from historical context. But my point here is simply that even the naturalizers have, in an important sense, left epistemology behind. What they produce looks like traditional epistemology at times, but only because of what Locke's confusion made *him* say about psychology. The distinctively epistemological part has dropped out.

12. Harman, *Thought,* pp. 18-19.

13. Williams, "Inference," p. 257.

14. As one might expect, social scientists have done a better job pursuing Quine's insights in this area than either Quine himself or other "naturalizers" of epistemology. See in particular the treatment of "intuition" and "self-evidence," as well as the tribute to Quine as the anthropologist's philosopher, in Mary Douglas, *Implicit Mean-*

ings (London: Routledge & Kegan Paul, 1975), chap. 17.

15. Peter Unger, *Ignorance* (Oxford: Clarendon Press, 1975).

16. I shall ignore the (highly questionable) arguments he gives for the further conclusions that no one is ever justified or at all reasonable in anything, including in believing anything. These arguments depend upon the argument I will consider: if the latter does not go through, neither will the former.

17. Oliver Johnson, *Skepticism and Cognitivism* (Berkeley: University of California Press, 1978), pp. 138-148.

18. Ibid., pp. 147-148.

19. Ibid., p. 170.

20. Unger, p. 313.

21. Ibid., p. 5.

22. Ibid., p. 274.

23. Ibid., p. 316.

24. Williams, *Groundless Belief*, p. 4.

25. Ibid., p. 8.

26. Unger, p. 317.

27. Quine, *Word and Object*, p. 264.

28. See Hacking, *Probability*, p. 46, and chap. 3 above.

29. William W. Rozeboom, "Why I Know So Much More than You Do," in *Knowing: Essays in the Analysis of Knowledge,* ed. Michael D. Roth and Leon Galis (New York: Random House, 1970), p. 150.

30. Ibid., p. 151.

31. Harman, "Quine, I," p. 148.

32. David Hume, *A Treatise of Human Nature,* ed. L. A. Selby-Bigge (Oxford: Clarendon Press, 1958), pp. 268-269.

33. See Thomas S. Kuhn, *The Structure of Scientific Revolutions,* 2nd ed. (Chicago: University of Chicago Press, 1970).

34. David Hume, *Dialogues Concerning Natural Religion,* ed. Norman Kemp Smith (Indianapolis: Bobbs-Merrill, 1947), p. 219. See Richard H. Popkin, "David Hume: His Pyrrhonism and his Critique of Pyrrhonism," in *Hume,* ed. V. C. Chappell (London: Macmillan, 1968), pp. 53-98.

35. A. J. Ayer, *Language, Truth and Logic* (New York: Dover, 1952), p. 49.

5. Unfounded Criticism

1. MacIntyre's lectures were published along with Paul Ricoeur's Bampton Lectures of the same year in *The Religious Significance of Atheism* (New York: Columbia University Press, 1969). For "The Fate of Theism," see pp. 3-29.

2. The significance of Hume's arguments, in particular, seems to be underestimated: "Hume could question theism on grounds that,

original in detail though they are, had been available in kind for millenia . . ." (p. 4).

3. MacIntyre, "Fate," pp. 8-9.

4. Mary Douglas, *Purity and Danger* (Middlesex, England: Penquin, 1970), p. 70. See also Douglas, *Natural Symbols* (New York: Vintage, 1973), pp. 60-64, and *Implicit Meanings* (London: Routledge & Kegan Paul, 1975), chaps. 16 and 17.

5. Wayne Proudfoot, "Religious Experience, Emotion, and Belief," *Harvard Theological Review* 70 (1977): 360.

6. Ibid., p. 362.

7. Ibid., p. 361.

8. Ibid., p. 362, Proudfoot's capitalization.

9. For this interpretation of one "strain" in Popper's thought, see Harold I. Brown, *Perception, Theory and Commitment* (Chicago: Precedent Publishing, 1977), chap. 5. The quoted phrase appears on p. 71. I am not maintaining that Brown's interpretation of Popper is correct (or vice versa).

10. MacIntyre, "Fate," p. 10.

11. Karl R. Popper, *The Logic of Scientific Discovery* (New York: Harper & Row, 1968), p. 50. The original German edition appeared in 1934.

12. Ibid., p. 108.

13. Brown, p. 75.

14. Kuhn, p. 146.

15. Alasdair MacIntyre, "Epistemological Crises," p. 468, MacIntyre's italics.

16. Ibid., p. 471.

6. From Mystery to Paradox

1. See, for example, Barry Barnes, "The Comparison of Belief-systems: Anomaly Versus Falsehood," in *Modes of Thought,* ed. Robin Horton and Ruth Finnegan (London: Faber & Faber, 1973), pp. 182-198; and John Skorupski, *Symbol and Theory* (Cambridge: Cambridge University Press, 1976), chaps. 12-13. Also see Robin Horton, "African Traditional Thought and Western Science," in *Rationality,* ed. Bryan R. Wilson (New York: Harper & Row, 1970), pp. 131-171, though Horton's portrait of the scientist in this paper, despite favorable mention of Kuhn, stresses "open-mindedness" in a fashion more Popperian than Kuhnian. For criticisms of Horton, see Barnes, pp. 190-191, and Skorupski, chaps. 12-13, passim.

2. Skorupski, p. 218.

3. Jay F. Rosenberg, *Linguistic Representation* (Boston: D. Reidel, 1974), p. 64.

4. Skorupski, p. 218.

5. Skorupski lists these questions on p. 217.

6. Ibid., p. 216.

7. Alasdair MacIntyre, "Is Understanding Religion Compatible with Believing?" in *Rationality* (see n. 1 above), p. 73.

8. Thomas Aquinas, *Summa Theologiae*, I, 1.2, Blackfriars ed. (Garden City: Doubleday, 1969).

9. Ibid.

10. Ibid., I, 1.8.

11. This helps explain the significance within early and medieval Christianity, of what Jaroslav Pelikan calls "the problem of Patristic consensus," as well as the related problem of heresy. See Pelikan, *The Growth of Medieval Theology (600-1300)* (Chicago: University of Chicago Press, 1978), esp. chaps. 1 and 5.

12. *Summa*, I, 1.8.

13. Ibid., I, 1.5.

14. Ibid., I, 12.13.

15. Ibid. See Victor Preller, *Divine Science and Science of God* (Princeton: Princeton University Press, 1967) for an interpretation of Aquinas that stresses passages like the ones I have cited.

16. *Summa*, I, 1.6.

17. *Philosophical Works of Descartes,* trans. E. S. Haldane and G. R. T. Ross, 2 vols. (n.p.: Dover, 1955), 1: 133.

18. Ibid.

19. Hans Frei, *The Eclipse of Biblical Narrative* (New Haven: Yale University Press, 1974).

20. Ibid., p. 90.

21. Ibid., pp. 4, 42-50.

22. Ibid., pp. 4-5.

23. Ibid., p. 5.

24. Frei writes: "If historical periods may be said to have a single chronological and geographical starting point, modern theology began in England at the turn from the seventeenth to the eighteenth century" (p. 51). There is more than a grain of truth in this remark, but we must beware of treating seventeenth- and eighteenth-century Britain in isolation from Continental developments (especially in France). G. R. Cragg writes that "Intellectual history can seldom be confined within national frontiers, but in this case the nature of the subject makes the limitation possible. . . ." See his *Reason and Authority in the Eighteenth Century* (Cambridge: Cambridge University Press, 1964), p. viii. What makes this odd is that France was not thus slighted by the great thinkers of seventeenth- and eighteenth-century Britain, most notably Locke and Hume. The former relied heavily upon the Port-Royal *Logic*, Descartes, and Gassendi (see John W. Yolton, *The Locke Reader* [Cambridge: Cambridge University Press, 1977] , "Introduction," esp. p. 3). The latter's connections with France are well known and equally important.

25. See Van Leeuwen, pp. 32-48.

26. For a discussion of Wilkins's relation to Chillingworth and Tillotson, see Van Leeuwen, pp. 50-71.

27. Hacking, *The Emergence of Probability* pp. 82-83.

28. Quoted in ibid., p. 83.

29. Ibid., p. 83.

30. See James Collins, *The Emergence of Philosophy of Religion* (New Haven: Yale University Press, 1967), p. 19.

31. For an introduction to the relevant literature on this topic, see Cragg, esp. chaps. 1-3.

32. I have been aided greatly in formulating my remarks about Locke by J. Richard Ciccotelli's as yet unpublished critique of Paul Helm's article, "Locke on Faith and Knowledge," *Philosophical Quarterly* 23 (1973): 52-66. For an account of Locke's variations on themes from Chillingworth, see Van Leeuwen, chap. 5. The decisive passages in Locke come from the correspondence with Stillingfleet and from *An Essay Concerning Human Understanding* (New York: Dover, 1959), vol. II, book IV.

33. Frei, *Eclipse*, pp. 52-53.

34. Bishop Atterbury raises this question early in the debate. As Cragg summarizes Atterbury's charge, "Those who rejected so much could hardly retain the bare essentials of the Christian faith, and, having gone so far, they would find that the logical outcome of their arguments would be stark unbelief" (p. 90). For Atterbury, of course, this charge amounts to a *reductio ad absurdum*. Hume will later embrace the skeptical conclusion as anything but absurd.

35. For an account of Hume's essay that minimizes its originality and establishes its connection with latitudinarian and deistic controversies, see Robert M. Burns, "David Hume and Miracles in Historical Perspective" (Ph.D. dissertation, Princeton, 1971). Burns's work is a needed corrective to the common (but undefended) assumption that "Of Miracles" represents an entirely novel development. Burns shows, I think, that Peter Annett anticipates Hume's central argument at least a year before *An Enquiry Concerning Human Understanding*, of which "Of Miracles" is the tenth section, appears in 1748. Burns makes similar claims for William Wollaston, but I find these less convincing. Burns also makes a good example of the position against which I shall soon argue — namely, that which takes Hume's critique of religion as a consequence of his empiricist epistemology, and, hence, as the bad fruit of a bad vine. There are several other points on which Burns and I differ, but we all owe him gratitude for restoring the British debate on miracles to view.

36. See, for example, Collins, pp. 64-65.

37. *Enquiry*, section X, par. 36. I shall cite Eric Steinberg's 1977 edition (Indianapolis: Hackett) of the 1977 version of the *Enquiry*, published posthumously with Hume's final revisions.

38. Ibid., par. 8.
39. Ibid., par. 9.
40. Ibid., par. 12.
41. Ibid., par. 12
42. Ibid., par. 40.
43. Ibid., par. 41.
44. I have used the Norman Kemp Smith edition (Indianapolis: Bobbs-Merrill, 1947). See parts II-VII.
45. Ibid., parts X and XI.
46. *Enquiry*, sec. XII, par. 34.
47. What makes this comparison especially interesting, of course, is that both Aquinas and Hume are famous for heightened states of emotional arousal but gave to these experiences sharply divergent interpretations. (I do not mean to suggest that they had the *same* experience but interpreted it differently, for this phrasing seems to presuppose the scheme-content distinction I will be attacking in chap. 8. Whether the experiences were the same or different strikes me as precisely the kind of unanswerable question we ought to dismiss as *Sprachstreit*.)
48. MacIntyre, "Is Understanding Compatible?" p. 72.
49. Ibid., p. 73.

7. Paradox Lost, Paradox Regained

1. Cavell, 1976, p. xxii.
2. Richard Rorty, "Dewey's Metaphysics," in *New Studies in the Philosophy of John Dewey*, ed. Steven M. Cahn (Hanover, N. H.: University Press of New England, 1977), pp. 68-69.
3. Gellner, *Legitimation of Belief* (Cambridge: Cambridge University Press, 1974), p. 185.
4. See Richard Rorty, "Keeping Philosophy Pure," *Yale Review* 75 (1976): 336-356.
5. On Kant and disenchantment, see Gellner, *Legitimation*, pp. 184-191.
6. Friedrich Schleiermacher, *On Religion: Speeches to Its Cultured Despisers*, trans. John Oman (New York: Harper & Row, 1958), p. 36.
7. Ibid.
8. Ibid., pp. 37-38.
9. See Gordon E. Michalson, Jr., *The Historical Dimensions of a Rational Faith* (Washington, D.C.: University Press of America, 1977).
10. For an extended discussion of Schleiermacher's role in the history of these developments and for a criticism of his epistemological failings, see the forthcoming book by Wayne Proudfoot, entitled "Religious Experience." My own discussion of Schleierma-

cher's difficulties owes much to my good fortune in having the opportunity to read Proudfoot's work in progress.

11. *Hegels theologische Jugendschriften,* ed. Herman Nohl (Tübingen: J.C.B. Mohr, 1907), p. 61. See Stephen Crites, *In the Twilight of Christendom* (Chambersburg, Pa.: American Academy of Religion, 1972) for an illuminating discussion of Hegel on folk religion and Christianity. Crites discusses the passage just cited on pp. 37-38.

12. See Crites, pp. 41-57.

13. Emil L. Fackenheim, *The Religious Dimension in Hegel's Thought* (Bloomington: Indiana University Press, 1967), p. 323, without Fackenheim's italics. See also Karl Löwith, *From Hegel to Nietzsche,* trans. David E. Green (Garden City, N.Y.: Anchor, 1967), and the chapter on Hegel in Karl Barth, *Protestant Thought: From Rousseau to Ritschl* (New York: Simon and Schuster, 1969).

14. Fackenheim, p. 233.

15. Ibid., pp. 234-235.

16. James A. Massey, "The Hegelians, the Pietists, and the Nature of Religion," *Journal of Religion* 58 (1978) : 108-129.

17. Albrecht Ritchl, *Geschichte des Pietismus,* 3 vols. (Bonn: Adolph Marcus, 1880-1886).

18. Karl Barth, "On Systematic Theology," *Scottish Journal of Theology* 14 (1961): 225.

19. Hume, *Enquiry,* sec. X, par. 41.

20. Søren Kierkegaard, *Concluding Unscientific Postscript,* trans. D. F. Swenson and Walter Lowrie (Princeton: Princeton University Press, 1941), p. 199.

21. Ibid., pp. 324-325.

22. Søren Kierkegaard, *On Authority and Revelation,* trans. Walter Lowrie (Princeton: Princeton University Press, 1955), p. 165.

23. Karl Barth, *Church Dogmatics* II, 1 (Edinburgh: T. & T. Clark, 1957): 636.

24. As Hans Frei has shown in "Niebuhr's Theological Background," in *Faith and Ethics,* ed. Paul Ramsey (New York: Harper & Row, 1957), pp. 40-53. See Karl Barth, *Anselm: Fides Quaerens Intellectum,* trans. I. W. Robertson (New York: World, 1960).

25. Frei, "Niebuhr's Background," p. 46.

26. Ibid., p. 51.

27. Hans Frei, from an unpublished review of Eberhard Busch's biography of Barth, pp. 12-13 of typescript.

28. Ibid., p. 15.

29. Ibid., p. 16.

30. MacIntyre, "Fate," pp. 25-26.

31. Alasdair MacIntyre, "Can Medicine Dispense with a Theological Perspective on Human Nature?" in *Knowledge, Value and Belief,* ed. H. Tristam Engelhardt, Jr., and Daniel Callahan (Hastings-on-Hudson, N.Y.: The Hastings Center Institute of Society, Ethics

and the Life Sciences, 1977), p. 36.

32. Cf. Thomas Luckman, *The Invisible Religion* (New York: Macmillan, 1967).

33. MacIntyre, "Fate," p. 24.

34. Ibid.

35. See, for example, Van A. Harvey, *The Historian and the Believer* (New York: Macmillan, 1966); "The Pathos of Liberal Theology," *Journal of Religion* 56 (1976) : 382-391; and his review of Anders Nygren's *Meaning and Method* in *Religious Studies Review* 1 (1975): 13-19.

36. Harvey argues that Barth himself vacillated on how revelation is related to history. See *The Historian and the Believer*, chap. 5.

8. Explicating Rationality

1. Skorupski, p. 204.

2. Steven Lukes, *Essays in Social Theory* (London: Macmillan, 1977), chaps. 6-8. Chap. 6, "Some Problems about Rationality" (pp. 121-137), appeared originally in the *European Journal of Sociology* and was included in *Rationality*, ed. Bryan R. Wilson. Chap. 7, "On the Social Determination of Truth" (pp. 138-153), first appeared in *Modes of Thought*, ed. R. Horton and R. Finnegan. Chap. 8, "Relativism: Cognitive and Moral" (pp. 154-176), was originally published in the *Proceedings of the Aristotelian Society*.

3. Ibid., p. 158.

4. Ibid., pp. 141-142. The quotations, of course, are from Kuhn's *The Structure of Scientific Revolutions*.

5. Ibid., pp. 142-143.

6. Rorty, "The World Well Lost," p. 663.

7. D. C. Makinson, "The Paradox of the Preface," *Analysis* 25 (1964) : 205-207.

8. As Keith Lehrer implies in his *Knowledge* (Oxford: Clarendon Press, 1974), p. 203.

9. See Ian Hacking, "The Theory of Probable Inference: Neyman, Peirce and Braithwaite," in *Science, Belief and Behavior*, ed. D. H. Mellor (Cambridge: Cambridge University Press, 1980), p. 153.

10. Nicholas Rescher and Robert Brandom, *The Logic of Inconsistency* (Oxford: Basil Blackwell, 1980). For a treatment of the so-called Preface Paradox discussed by Makinson and Lehrer, see pp. 47-49.

11. P. F. Strawson, *Introduction to Logical Theory* (London: Methuen, 1952) and Steven Toulmin, *The Uses of Argument* (Cambridge: Cambridge University Press, 1958).

12. Harman, *Thought*, p. 162.

13. Ibid., pp. 161-162.

14. Frederick L. Will, *Induction and Justification* (Ithaca, N.Y.: Cornell University Press, 1974), pp. 244-245.

15. Harman, "Quine on Meaning and Existence, I," pp. 132-133.

16. Ibid., p. 133.

17. See Quine's discussion of deviant logics in his *Philosophy of Logic* (Englewood Cliffs, N.J.: Prentice-Hall, 1970), pp. 80-94.

18. Lukes, p. 144.

19. Donald Davidson, "On the Very Idea of a Conceptual Scheme," *Proceedings and Addresses of the American Philosophical Association* 47 (1973-1974) : 5-20.

20. Ibid., p. 20.

21. Actually, despite his explicitly stated conclusions, Lukes sometimes seems content with this more modest finding. At one point, for example, he entertains the possibility of a deviant logic and concludes only that "certain limited logical divergences . . . cannot go too far without incomprehensibility setting in" (p. 158). Unfortunately, he returns in the next paragraph to his claims about universal criteria. Elsewhere, he speaks without qualification of the "essentially provisional nature of all cognitive judgments" (p. 153), but he nowhere draws the appropriate moral with respect to his own stand on fundamental criteria.

22. Rorty, *Philosophy and the Mirror of Nature*, p. 316. Rorty's book also includes a defense of Davidson against the charge of "verificationism" (pp. 299-311).

23. For an interpretation of Kuhn along these lines, see ibid., pp. 322-333. For an example of Kuhn's remarks on truth, see *Structure*, p. 206. For MacIntyre's worries, see "Epistemological Crises," pp. 469-470.

24. Davidson, p. 17. For more along these lines, see Rorty, "The World Well Lost," pp. 649-655; and Harold Brown, *Perception, Theory and Commitment*, pp. 153-155.

25. Larry Laudan, *Progress and Its Problems* (Berkeley: University of California Press, 1977), p. 123.

26. For a discussion of "available" reasons, see Gilbert Harman, *The Nature of Morality* (New York: Oxford University Press, 1977), pp. 125-126, 128-131.

27. Thomas S. Kuhn, *The Essential Tension* (Chicago: University of Chicago Press, 1977), p. xii.

28. Harman, *The Nature of Morality*, p. 131. Harman goes on to say that "We must therefore assume that our reasoning works in the same way the other person's reasoning works." But this is misleading, for the "sameness" involved is surely a matter of degree. If two people — say, Aquinas and Hume — possess different epistemic principles as well as different beliefs about the world, their reasoning would in an important sense work differently. But, if Davidson is right, there always will be enough in common between

two language-users to permit Harman's appeal to the sympathetic imagination.

29. See Preller, passim.

30. MacIntyre, "Is Understanding Compatible?" p. 76.

31. Whether any well-known, living author (such as the real Peter Winch or D. Z. Phillips) should be interpreted as a fideist is a question I shall leave open.

32. Alasdair MacIntyre, *Against the Self-Images of the Age* (Notre Dame, Ind.: University of Notre Dame Press, rpt. 1978), p. 257.

33. See, for example, David Bloor, *Knowledge and Social Imagery* (London: Routledge & Kegan Paul, 1976), chap. 1.

34. See, in particular, Max Weber, *Economy and Society*, ed. Guenther Roth and Claus Wittich (Berkeley: University of California Press, 1978), vol. 1, part 1, chap. 3. I shall return to legitimation as treated in the Weberian tradition in chap. 10 below.

35. Quentin Skinner has documented this transition in *The Foundations of Modern Political Thought*, 2 vols. (Cambridge: Cambridge University Press, 1978), 2: 189-358. For more on Skinner and his topic, see chap. 11 below.

9. Beyond Metaethics

1. William K. Frankena, "Is Morality Logically Dependent on Religion?" in *Religion and Morality*, ed. Gene Outka and John P. Reeder, Jr. (Garden City, N.Y.: Anchor, 1973), pp. 295-317.

2. See Fish, *Self-Consuming Artifacts*, chap. 2.

3. Ibid., p. 91.

4. Ibid.

5. Frankena, "Is Morality," p. 295.

6. Ibid., pp. 295-296.

7. Ibid., pp. 296-297.

8. "We cannot verify moral choices. They may be vindicated, but not validated. It was David Hume who set out this elementary point in its enduring form for British and American thinking. Believers or unbelievers (theologically speaking), we are all bound to acknowledge that we simply cannot climb across the gap from descriptive to prescriptive propositions; from 'is' statements to 'ought' statements. We have to make jumps, faith leaps. They are not steps in logic or even in common sense." Joseph Fletcher, *Situation Ethics* (Philadelphia: Westminster Press, 1966), p. 49, the same page cited by Frankena.

9. Frankena, "Is Morality," p. 298.

10. Ibid., p. 313.

11. Ibid., p. 303.

12. William K. Frankena, *Ethics*, 2nd ed. (Englewood Cliffs, N.J.: Prentice-Hall, 1973), p. 101.

13. Frankena, "Is Morality," p. 315.

14. John Stuart Mill, *Utilitarianism*, ed. Oskar Piest (New York: Bobbs-Merrill, 1957), p. 7, quoted in ibid., p. 315. See also *Ethics*, p. 107, and *Perspectives on Morality: Essays by William K. Frankena*, ed. K.E. Goodpaster (Notre Dame, Ind.: University of Notre Dame Press, 1976), pp. 95, 139.

15. Frankena, "Is Morality," p. 316.

16. Ibid., pp. 316-317.

17. Fish, p. 101.

18. Ibid., p. 124.

19. Frankena, *Perspectives*, p. 108.

20. Quoted in ibid., p. 110.

21. Ibid.

22. For another statement of this and related points, see my "Metaethics and the Death of Meaning: Adams and the Case of the Tantalizing Closing," *Journal of Religious Ethics* 6/1 (1978): 1-18.

23. Frankena, *Perspectives*, p. 145. Cf. *Ethics*, pp. 110-114.

24. Philosophers who oppose Kantians on other matters often side with them on this one. See, for example, MacIntyre's discussion in "Atheism and Morals," the second of his Bampton Lectures printed in *The Religious Significance of Atheism*, pp. 31-55.

25. See Glenn Graber, "In Defense of a Divine Command Theory of Ethics," *Journal of the American Academy of Religion* 43 (1975) : 62-69.

26. See ibid.; and Glenn Graber, "A Critical Bibliography of Recent Discussions of Religious Ethics by Philosophers," *Journal of Religious Ethics* 2 (1974) : 53-80; and Robert Merrihew Adams, "A Modified Divine Command Theory of Ethical Wrongness," in *Religion and Morality*, ed. Outka and Reeder, pp. 318-347. For a discussion of Adams, see my "Metaethics and the Death of Meaning," cited above. For a further development of Adams's theory and a response to my criticisms, see his "Divine Command Metaethics Modified Again," *Journal of Religious Ethics* 7 (1979) : 66-79.

27. See Richard Rorty, "Verification and Transcendental Arguments," *Nous* 5 (1971) : 3-14, and "Transcendental Arguments, Self-Reference and Pragmatism," in *Transcendental Arguments and Science*, ed. Peter Bieri, Rolf Horstmann, and Lorenz Kruger (Dordrecht: Reidel, 1979), pp. 77-103.

28. Philippa Foot, "Goodness and Choice," in *The Is/Ought Question*, ed. W. D. Hudson (London: Macmillan, 1969), pp. 214-227, esp. p. 216.

29. The classics of prescriptivism are R. M. Hare, *The Language of Morals* (Oxford: Oxford University Press, 1952) and *Freedom and Reason* (Oxford: Oxford University Press, 1963).

30. For related arguments, see "Metaethics and the Death of Meaning," pp. 13-15.

10. Toward a Genealogy of Morals

1. David Little and Sumner B. Twiss, *Comparative Religious Ethics: A New Method* (San Francisco: Harper & Row, 1978); Ronald M. Green, *Religious Reason: The Rational and Moral Basis of Religious Belief* (New York: Oxford University Press, 1978).

2. David Little, *Religion, Order and Law* (New York: Harper Torchbooks, 1969).

3. Paul Feyerabend, *Against Method* (London: NLB, 1975); Hans-Georg Gadamer, *Truth and Method,* trans. William Glen-Doepel (London: Sheed and Ward, 1979).

4. Willard V. O. Quine, "Two Dogmas of Empiricism," *Philosophical Review* 40 (1951) : 20-43.

5. Little and Twiss, p. 8.

6. Carl Hempel, *Fundamentals of Concept Formation in Empirical Science* (Chicago: University of Chicago Press, 1952).

7. Little and Twiss, p. 12.

8. Hempel, *Fundamentals*, p. 80.

9. Ibid., pp. 10-11.

10. Ibid., p. 12.

11. Little and Twiss, p. 4.

12. MacIntyre, *A Short History of Ethics* (New York: Macmillan, 1966), pp. 3-4.

13. Carl Hempel, "On the 'Standard Conception' of Scientific Theories," in *Analyses of Theories and Methods of Physics and Psychology*, ed. Michael Radner and Stephen Winokur (Minneapolis: University of Minnesota Press, 1970), p. 163.

14. See chap. 9 above. In fairness to Little and Twiss, I should point out that one sentence in their concluding chapter hints at a more complicated view of the relation between description and explanation than the one they present elsewhere in the book: "In addition, insofar as the reconstruction of the logical relations or the internal structure of culture values amounts to an explanation, we do explain the data" (p. 253). David Little has suggested in conversation that this sentence can be interpreted as falling within the tradition sometimes called "intellectualism." See Skorupski, *Symbol and Theory* for a discussion of intellectualism as a program of research. Since it remains unclear what or how much Little and Twiss want to make of this hint, I have taken their other comments on explanation at face value. But it would be interesting to see the hint elaborated, especially in light of what Little and Twiss inherit from Weber.

15. Little and Twiss, p. 69.

16. Herbert Feigl, "Validation and Vindication: An Analysis of the Nature and Limits of Ethical Arguments," in *Readings in Ethical Theory*, ed. Wilfrid Sellars and John Hospers (New York: Appleton-Century-Crofts, 1952), pp. 667-680.

17. See Hans Reichenbach, *Experience and Prediction* (Chicago: University of Chicago Press, 1938); Reichenbach, *The Theory of Probability* (Berkeley: University of California Press, 1949); Herbert Feigl, "De Principiis Non Disputandum . . . ?," in *Philosophical Analysis*, ed. Max Black (Ithaca, N.Y.: Cornell University Press, 1950), pp. 119-156.

18. Quine, "Two Dogmas," p. 43.

19. Sellars, *Science, Perception and Reality*, p. 355.

20. See chap. 8 above. See also Harman, *Thought*, pp. 155-172.

21. Little and Twiss, pp. 29, 97-98.

22. Ibid., p. 102.

23. Ibid., p. 103.

24. J. B. Schneewind, "Moral Knowledge and Moral Principles," in *Knowledge and Necessity*, ed. G. N. A. Vesey (London: Macmillan, 1970), p. 254.

25. Little and Twiss, p. 109. See John Ladd, *The Structure of a Moral Code* (Cambridge: Harvard University Press, 1957), pp. 152-162.

26. Little and Twiss, pp. 109-111.

27. Ibid., p. 120.

28. Ladd, p. 447.

29. See Harman, *Thought*, p. 162.

30. See Kuhn, *The Structure of Scientific Revolutions*.

31. Hans Frei, *The Identity of Jesus Christ* (Philadelphia: Fortress Press, 1975).

32. Richard Rorty, "Professionalized Philosophy and Transcendentalist Culture," *The Georgia Review* 30 (1976) : 757-769; Bruce Kuklick, *The Rise of American Philosophy* (New Haven: Yale University Press, 1977), p. 566.

33. Rorty, "Professionalized Philosophy," p. 766.

34. In an article entitled, "Theology Confronts Technology and the Life Sciences," *Commonweal* (16 June 1978), James M. Gustafson has posed the problem by suggesting that a "religious ethicist" may just be "a former theologian who does not have the professional credentials of a moral philosopher" (p. 386). "It is the 'religious ethicists' who have most to be anxious about, in my judgment. They will either have to become moral philosophers with a special interest in 'religious' texts and arguments, or become theologians: Christian theologians, or natural theologians, or 'religious dimensions' theologians. Only indifference to what they are writing, or exceeding patience with inexcusable ambiguity, can account for the tolerance they have enjoyed" (p. 392). I am suggesting that *Comparative*

Religious Ethics, if I may borrow a Durkheimian turn of phrase, *is really about* the professional dilemma Gustafson poses.

35. See Thomas E. Willey, *Back to Kant: The Revival of Kantianism in German Social and Historical Thought,* 1860-1914 (Detroit: Wayne State University Press, 1978), esp. chaps. 6 and 7.

36. This paragraph draws on Richard Rorty, "The World Well Lost," pp. 649-665.

37. Green, p. 7: "My purpose is . . . to determine whether a method of understanding religion helps illuminate these traditions in a new way." Cf. Little and Twiss, pp. 251-255.

38. Green, p. 5.

39. Ibid.

40. John Rawls, *A Theory of Justice* (Cambridge: The Belknap Press of Harvard University Press, 1971). Green also cites Bernard Gert, *The Moral Rules* (New York: Harper & Row, 1970) and David A. J. Richards, *A Theory of Reasons for Action* (Oxford: Clarendon Press, 1971) as important contributions to Kantian ethical theory.

41. Green, pp. 5-6.

42. Ibid., p. 4.

43. Ibid., p. 18.

44. Ibid., p. 19.

45. Ibid., p. 21.

46. Richards, p. 86.

47. See Rawls, pp. xi, 55, 111, 130, 150, 201, 578-579; Richards, p. xiv.

48. See Rawls, pp. 46-47, 587, for Rawls's use of the quoted phrases.

49. Note that Rawls backs off from the *claim* that his theory describes part of the conceptual structure of every rational agent, though he seems to think it might (p. 50). On the other hand, note Rawls's suggestions "that we think of the original position as the point of of view from which noumenal selves see the world" (p. 255).

50. Ibid., pp. 214, 206.

51. Richards, pp. 123-124.

52. Ibid., p. 318.

53. Green, p. 111. Nothing could be further from Wittgenstein's view of the matter: "In considering a different system of ethics there may be a strong temptation to think that what seems to *us* to express the justification of an action must be what really justifies it there, whereas the real reasons are the reasons that are given." As quoted in R. W. Beardsmore, *Moral Reasoning* (New York: Schocken Books, 1969), p. viii.

54. Green, p. 112.

55. Ibid., p. 22.

56. Rawls, pp. 19-20.

57. Ibid., p. 215.

58. Cf. Robert Paul Wolff, *Understanding Rawls* (Princeton:

Princeton University Press, 1977), p. 75; Gerald Dworkin, "Non-Neutral Principles," in *Reading Rawls*, ed. Norman Daniels (New York: Basic Books, 1975), pp. 137-140.

59. Green, p. 4.

60. Robert Merrihew Adams has argued persuasively that Green unwittingly diverges from Kant in at least one important respect besides the one noted here. See his review of *Religious Reason* in *Religious Studies Review* 6/3 (1980) : 183-188.

11. On the Morals of Genealogy

1. Friedrich Nietzsche, *Human, All-Too-Human*, trans. Walter Kaufmann, in *The Portable Nietzsche* (New York: Viking, 1968), p. 51.

2. Friedrich Nietzsche, *Beyond Good and Evil*, trans. Walter Kaufmann (New York: Vintage, 1966) p. 97.

3. G. J. Warnock, *The Object of Morality* (London: Methuen, 1971), pp. 2, 8.

4. Ibid., p. 9.

5. Ibid., p. 10.

6. Wolff, p. 114. My debt to Wolff's book extends well beyond this single passage.

7. Quentin Skinner, *The Foundations of Modern Political Thought*, 2 vols. (Cambridge: Cambridge University Press, 1978), 2: 113-123.

8. Ibid., 2: 335.

9. Ibid., 2: 322.

10. Ibid., 2: 310.

11. Cf. Rorty, *Mirror*, p. 330.

12. Skinner, 2: 352.

13. Little and Twiss, pp. 26-27.

14. Ibid., p. 45.

15. Rawls, p. 4.

16. Wolff, p. 78.

17. For a useful corrective to Rawls's massive *petitio*, see the "Epilogue" to Brian Barry's critique of Rawls in *The Liberal Theory of Justice* (Oxford: Oxford University Press, 1973). For an indication of how much can be learned about the weaknesses of liberalism by taking seriously, instead of rendering invisible, the critique of liberalism implicit in the ideology of the antebellum South, see Eugene Genovese, *The World the Slaveholders Made* (New York: Vintage, 1971), esp. pp. 165-195, 235-244.

18. Rawls, p. 19.

19. Rawls, p. 215.

20. Alasdair MacIntyre, *Secularization and Moral Change* (London: Oxford University Press, 1967), pp. 48-49.

21. I should perhaps add that the most serious attempts to bring theology into the public arena now seem to be taking one or the other of two forms: either a philosophical defense of theology in terms of the categories of *scientia* (e.g, demonstration and necessity), as opposed to the concepts that cluster around the new probability; or a revolutionary program intended to transform radically the forms of life and discursive practices that pushed theology from the center in the first place. The former is essentially an academic enterprise and can be seen in the work of such figures as Alvin Plantinga and certain followers of Whitehead. The latter, while not essentially academic, does have numerous academic manifestations, as in the work of Jürgen Moltman, Johannes Metz, and James Cone. Nothing I have said in this book rules out the possibility that efforts like these will someday emerge victorious. The odds, however, seem slight. The philosophical theologians will have all the traditional difficulties of *scientia* to deal with — difficulties which such recent inventions as Kripkean necessity and Whiteheadian metaphysics seem unable to surmount. The religious revolutionaries, even if they manage to achieve their social hopes without becoming indistinguishable from Marxists, will have the problems of sixteenth-century Europe to face all over again — as the recent history of Iran makes so painfully evident.

22. John Locke, *Essay concerning Human Understanding*, 2 vols. (New York: Dover, 1959), 2: 211.

23. See, for example, MacIntyre, *Short History*, pp. 190-198, 267: *Against the Self-Images of the Age*, p. 85; and *After Virtue* (Notre Dame, Ind.: University of Notre Dame Press, 1981).

24. Mike Michalson made this criticism of Kant's *Religion* in a paper delivered to the American Academy of Religion in 1978.

25. James M. Gustafson, "Religion and Morality from the Perspective of Theology," in *Religion and Morality*, ed. Gene Outka and John P. Reeder, Jr. (Garden City: Anchor, 1973), pp. 129-130. Cf. MacIntyre, "Atheism and Morals," pp. 49-50.

26. In chap. 8 above, I held, with Lukes and Davidson, that untranslatable languages — that is, languages which could not *in principle* be translated into our own — are fictitious entities. I did not mean to suggest that all languages can be translated into our own by way of a one-to-one mapping of short sentences onto short sentences *sans* commentary. On my account, translation always involves commentary, at least implicitly. Sometimes translation is difficult, mappings are clumsy, and commentaries require volume upon volume of contextual detail, but this does not show that translation is impossible in a sense relevant to conceptual relativism. Anyone who feels the need to insist, in the name of common sense, that translation is sometimes impossible in principle is probably assuming a notion of translation much less complicated than the one in use here.

27. See Richard Rorty, *Philosophy and the Mirror of Nature* (Princeton: Princeton University Press, 1979), chap. 7, for a related use of "hermeneutics."

28. MacIntyre, *Short History*, p. 118.

29. Ibid., p. 119.

30. Ibid.

31. See David Clark, "Voluntarism and Rationalism in the Ethics of Ockham," *Franciscan Studies* 31 (1971) : 72-87; Kevin McDonnell, "Does William of Ockham Have a Theory of Natural Law?" *Franciscan Studies* 34 (1974) : 383-392; and Linwood Urban, "William of Ockham's Theological Ethics," *Franciscan Studies* 33 (1973) : 310-350.

32. In a brief discussion of G. E. Moore's thesis that "good" is indefinable, Richard Rorty argues convincingly that "In its homely and shopworn sense, the reason why 'good' is indefinable is not that we might be altogether wrong about what good men or good apples are, but simply that *no* interesting descriptive term has any interesting necessary and sufficient conditions" (*Mirror*, p. 307). A corollary would be the view, suggested here, that when a term like "good" is discovered to have interesting necessary and sufficient conditions — as in Ockhamism — it ceases to be an interesting descriptive term.

33. It was, of course, men, and not other members of the species, who were both the creators and the primary subjects of this myth. The myth of radically autonomous women came later.

34. See, for example, *Short History*, p. 86; *Against*, pp. 165-172. See also G. E. M. Anscombe, "Modern Moral Philosophy," *Philosophy* 33 (1958) : 1-19. My debt to these writings is considerable.

35. For a penetrating discussion of the strengths and weaknesses of the Marxian tradition, see John Dunn, *Western Political Theory in the Face of the Future* (Cambridge: Cambridge University Press, 1979), chap. 4.

12. Explicating Historicism

1. Alain Robbe-Grillet, *For a New Novel*, trans. Richard Howard (New York: Grove Press, 1965), p. 33.

2. Donald Davidson, "On the Very Idea of a Conceptual Scheme," *Proceedings and Addresses of the American Philosophical Association* 47 (1973-1974) : 7. My views on this and related matters have been shaped by Stanley Hauerwas, *Character and the Christian Life* (San Antonio, Tex.: Trinity University Press, 1975), and Iris Murdoch, *The Sovereignty of Good* (London: Routledge & Kegan Paul, 1970).

3. See R. W. Beardsmore, *Moral Reasoning* (New York: Schocken Books, 1969), p. 35: ". . .[A]lthough it is not possible to exclude *a priori* any feature of an object as a possible criterion of its goodness,

we *can* say that if anything is to count as a criterion, then it must in principle be possible to see some relationship between it and the other things which count as criteria of goodness." See also Rorty, *Mirror*, pp. 306-311.

4. Davidson, "On the Very Idea," p. 5.

5. For persuasive arguments in support of this conclusion, see Renford Bambrough, *Moral Scepticism and Moral Knowledge* (London: Routledge & Kegan Paul, 1979).

6. Note well that I write "tolerance," not "pure tolerance," and "diversity," not "pluralism."

Index